MOVIE WARS

How Hollywood and the Media Conspire to Limit What Films We Can See

Jonathan Rosenbaum

ⓐ cappella

Library of Congress Cataloging-in-Publication Data

Rosenbaum, Jonathan.
  Movie wars : how Hollywood and the media conspire to limit what films we can see / by Jonathan Rosenbaum.
    p. cm.
    Includes index (p. 227).
    ISBN 1-55652-406-4
    1. Motion pictures—United States.   I. Title.
PN 1993.5.U65 R575 2000
791.43'0973—dc21

00-038407

©2000 by Jonathan Rosenbaum
All rights reserved
First edition
Published by A Cappella Books,
An imprint of Chicago Review Press, Incorporated
814 North Franklin Street
Chicago, Illinois 60610
ISBN 1-55652-406-4

Printed in the United States of America

5 4 3 2 1

Contents

Acknowledgments   v

Introduction: Is the Producer Always Right?   1

Chapter One: Is the Cinema Really Dead?   19

Chapter Two: Some Vagaries of Distribution and Exhibition   39

Chapter Three: Some Vagaries of Promotion and Criticism   49

Chapter Four: At War with Cultural Violence: The Critical
    Reception of *Small Soldiers*   63

Chapter Five: Communications Problems and Canons   79

Chapter Six: The AFI's Contribution to Movie Hell: or, How
    I Learned to Stop Worrying and Love American Movies   91

Chapter Seven: Isolationism as a Control System   107

Chapter Eight: Multinational Pest Control: Does American
    Cinema Still Exist?   129

Chapter Nine: Trafficking in Movies (Festival-Hopping
    in the Nineties)   143

Chapter Ten: Orson Welles as Ideological Challenge   175

Conclusion: The Audience Is Sometimes Right   197

Index   227

Acknowledgments

Although some of them are already thanked separately in the text, a good many friends, colleagues, and acquaintances have assisted me in all sorts of ways, and deserve my gratitude for their thoughtfulness and support: Patrick Arden, Raymond Bellour, Catherine Benamou, Nicole Brenez, Meredith Brody, Cecilia Burokas, Pat Dowell, Roger Ebert, David Ehrenstein, Vanalyne Green, Shigehiko Hasumi, Alexander Horwath, Kent Jones, Dave Kehr, Chika Kinoshita, Stuart Klawans, Kitry Kraus, Bill Krohn, Adrian Martin, Patrick McGavin, Jean-Luc Mengus, Marco Müller, Daniel Neppl, Susan Ohmer, Ray Pride, Mehrnaz Saeed-Vafa, Barry Schein, Hans Schmid, Joel Shepard, Yuval Taylor, Alison True, Peter von Bagh, Alan Williams, and Michael Witt.

Introduction
Is the Producer Always Right?

> To refer to a producer's oeuvre is, at least to me, as ignorant as to refer to the oeuvre of a stockbroker.
> —David Mamet

There are a lot of complaints these days about the declining quality of movie fare, and the worsening taste of the public is typically asked to shoulder a good part of the blame.

Other causes are cited as well. The collapse of the old studio system meant the loss of studio heads who lent their distinctive stamp to each of their pictures—often vulgar and overblown, to be sure, but also personal and engaged—to be replaced largely by cost accountants and corporate executives with little flair, imagination, or passion. The exponential growth of video has made home viewing more popular than theatrical moviegoing and has therefore helped to diminish everyone's sense of what a movie is, so that the size and definition of the image, a clear sense of its borders, the quality and direction of light, and the notions of film as community event, theatrical experience, or "something special," have all suffered terrible losses. More simply and immediately, there's the preference for loud explosions and frenetic comic-book action over drama and character, escalating violence over tenderness, torrents of profanity over well-crafted dialogue.

But most of the blame falls on the overall coarsening of the audience. According to conventional wisdom, most movies are targeted to the teen and preteen market; the decreased literacy of the filmgoing public rules out most subtitled movies; and there is an overall dumbing down of

1

American movies, with a notable increase in anti-intellectualism, according to essayist Phillip Lopate, who cites *Pulp Fiction, Ed Wood, Natural Born Killers, Bullets over Broadway,* and *Barton Fink,*[1] edgy American independent fare. Many industry commentators are quick to add that as the public grows increasingly apathetic, apolitical, jaded, and cynical, movies designed for their delectation would naturally follow suit.

Let's concede that there's *some* measure of truth in all these assertions—as there is in most assertions, at least if one bothers to look for it. But focusing on the last statement for a moment, might not the industry commentators have their cause and effect reversed? Couldn't the movies, rather than their designated spectators, be spearheading as well as defining this decline—or don't they need to share at least part of the responsibility for this overall dumbing down? Given the uncritical promotion of the major studio releases, one might even posit that the press, in order to justify its own priorities, maintains a vested interest in viewing the audience as brain-dead. After all, if it showered most of its free publicity on more thoughtful and interesting movies, it would run the risk of being branded elitist. How much easier it becomes to wallow in the slime if you and your editor or producer are persuaded that it's the audience's natural habitat—that the audience, not the press working in collaboration with the studios' massive publicity departments, calls all the shots.

Furthermore, or so the producers tell us, the highly sophisticated forms of market research and testing that shape major releases at every stage in their development, from initial treatments to previews to final ads, scientifically prove that the studios are correct in their low estimation of the public taste. This is clearly the surest indication of what the audience actually wants, so how can the producers be faulted for catering to their preferences?

I suggest that this line of reasoning is even more stupid, self-serving, and self-deluded than the worst of these movies, deriving from a set of interlocking rationalizations that extend all the way from studio heads to reviewers. Since the majority of movies made according to these "sci-

---

[1] This was in a 1996 essay ("The Last Taboo: The Dumbing Down of American Movies," reprinted in Lopate's *Totally Tenderly Tragically,* New York: Anchor Books, 1998, pp. 259–279). For more recent examples, consider *There's Something About Mary, Happiness,* and *Life Is Beautiful.*

entific" principles bomb, it wouldn't even be worth considering if it didn't provide one of the essential rationales for making so many bad movies, as well as one of the most dubious recipes for moviemaking and profit making alike.

As a bracing rejoinder to this set of assumptions, try the following on for size:

> It seems legitimate to wonder how men of the perspicacity which has distinguished some of the best work in market research could have failed to realize from the beginning that most of their research practices were not adaptable to the cultural field. The very attempt to adapt them to that field was virtually certain to cause damage.
>
> Obviously, the premise of a stable audience with reasonably permanent and objectively verifiable needs simply does not hold in the cultural field. Transplanted from economics, this premise becomes an obvious interference with the free play of human intelligence. To say that men would always need warm clothing in cold weather obviously was a statement of fact; but to say that men would always need soap operas in America was just as obviously a plain insult. Yet the pollsters, straightfaced and single-minded, proceeded to ram their hypothesis down the public's throat; the public, unaware of what was happening, had barely time to gag.
>
> What was this hypothesis and how did it affect the public's mental health? Adapted from mercantile economics to a field where mercantilism does not apply, the theory assumed a shallow, slothful, and unchangeable crowd, forever doomed to frustration and thus forever dependent on the wish fulfillment of certain minimum needs—sex, glamor, adventure, wealth, power, and the rest of them. The whole range of subtleties which make up the pattern of civilized behavior was not only rejected as being beyond the grasp of the audience—it was dismissed as irrelevant to their real desires.

Ernest Borneman's commonsense dismissal of the basic assumptions of the American film industry in "The Public Opinion Myth" appeared in the July 1947 issue of *Harper's* magazine.[2] But give or take

---

[2] I'm indebted to film scholar Susan Ohmer for alerting me to this article and sending me a copy of it.

Ernest Borneman was a German psychotherapist (1915–1995) who was also a novelist, playwright, cameraman, film director, screenwriter, writer for TV and radio, prolific journalist, and jazz musician. Borneman worked for Orson Welles in the late forties and early fifties by scripting an adaptation of Homer's *The Odyssey—*

a couple of sexist coinages that are standard for that period, I don't see how it could be improved much today. Whether it can be absorbed and heeded is of course another matter, but if it could be, a revolution every bit as far-reaching as feminism would take place. Why it should be heeded—and what might start to happen if even a few of its simple observations were put into practice—is the subject of this book.

Why it's unlikely to be heeded is simply a matter of economics: even by 1947, the industry founded on the public opinion myth was already too vast and too solidly in place to contemplate the prospect of dismantling it. If one compares it to this country's military-industrial complex—which was getting established over the same period, justified by fears of the encroaching Communist menace—one might just as well hypothesize that once those fears had finally evaporated or died of old age, the massive military budget that had consumed so many of this country's resources might be redirected to peacetime uses. The fact that it hasn't been and won't be seems every bit as unalterable as the public opinion myth, regardless of whether either rationale can be defended, because too many vested interests are committed to keeping these systems in place.

These interests are bolstered by a series of countermyths—chiefly the preservation and protection of "the free world" to justify the military-industrial complex, and "giving the public what it wants" to justify what might be called the media-industrial complex. And in the spirit of Noam Chomsky interrogating and critiquing just what we mean—and what we often don't mean—when we speak of "the free world," I'd like to talk about precisely what we mean and don't mean when we speak of "giving the public what it wants" in relation to movies.

---

eventually realized in altered and uncredited form by producers Carlo Ponti and Dino De Laurentis, actor Kirk Douglas, and director Mario Camerini as *Ulysses* (1955)—and by writing several scripts for the radio series *The Adventures of Harry Lime*; he was also apparently responsible for Welles's discovery of Eartha Kitt. Borneman's fascinating and multifaceted career—which began in the United Kingdom with studies in social anthropology and archeology and ended in Austria with studies in sexuality and child psychology—clearly merits further research; for most of the information in this footnote, I am grateful to Welles scholars Hans Schmid, who interviewed Borneman shortly before his death, and James Naremore, who lent me his copy of Borneman's first novel, *The Face on the Cutting-Room Floor* (1937), a mystery credited pseudonymously to Cameron McCabe that includes a detailed account of Borneman's career in its afterword (New York: Penguin Books, 1986).

Though the implication of this introduction's title is that the audience is sometimes right, I'm not really in a position to declare whether the audience is right or wrong about anything. Properly speaking, the audience is so many things, all of them overlapping and most of them scarcely known, that assigning it a label in advance effectively means ruling it out of discussion — which market research usually does. So my challenge is offered in a spirit of Hegelian antithesis to a thesis (the audience is to blame) that has riddled the film world to disastrous effect for much too long; hopefully, out of the synthesis might grow a more measured approach to something that no one — least of all market researchers — knows much about. And one extra advantage of my antithesis is that it opens up possibilities about what movies and audiences might be; the prevailing thesis can only close them down by ratifying policies that have already turned most of our movie culture to mush.

* * *

I strongly suspect that any studio publicist or production executive who read Borneman's article today would maintain that movie market research was still in its infancy in 1947, that the nature of both the audience and the film industry has radically changed since then, and that even if Borneman's argument once had some validity, it can no longer be applied to the contemporary realities of developing, making, testing, revising, publicizing, distributing, and exhibiting movies. Not only has the market research industry become more sophisticated, but the audience has undergone profound changes, temperamentally as well as demographically: it's more demanding about some things (such as the quality of special effects) and less demanding about others (such as plots that make sense); it's much younger; moreover, the video revolution has transformed everything having to do with movies. Today's markets are defined differently because people attend movies as special events rather than as an everyday activity, the older segments of the audience tend to stay at home, and so on.

All these things are certainly true, but I can't see how they alter the basic thrust of Borneman's charge. Then and now, the operations of the media-industrial complex have been predicated on certain highly questionable assumptions about the audience, and charting box-office grosses to "prove" those assumptions is merely indulging in a self-serving form of circular reasoning. The bottom line is always the same: the audience is ultimately to blame for what it winds up seeing. We are told that this is the downside of democracy—we can't always expect to like what the mass public endorses—a sentiment that can only provoke me into citing Borneman again:

> Does the whole process of audience testing . . . really qualify as a democratic process? Does it not resemble an election in which only one candidate has ever been introduced to the electorate? Have we ever been given a freely available standard of comparison between the pollsters' "control card" and its best alternative? If the difference between any two alternatives is so negligible as to defeat judgment, have we, the public, truly returned a valid opinion? And, finally, have the pollsters ever provided us with the aesthetic training which would have enabled us to make a reasonable decision?

Let's translate these skeptical questions into a few practical applications pertaining to the nineties. The December 17, 1993 *Wall Street Journal* carried a story headlined, "Film Flam Movie-Research Kingpin Is Accused by Former Employees of Selling Manipulated Data." The story reported that about two dozen former employees of National Research Group, Inc., which handled most Hollywood test marketing, stated that their data were sometimes doctored to conform to what their paying clients asked for. These former employees ranged "from hourly workers to senior officials" and mostly included people who had left the company voluntarily. All the examples given in the story (e.g., *L.A. Story; The Godfather, Part III; Teen Wolf*) involved boosting a movie's score, but one could easily surmise that the reverse could have happened on occasion when the studio for one reason or other wanted a movie to fail—which actually happens more often than most moviegoers realize. Before dumping Peter Bogdanovich's *The Thing Called Love*, for instance—a film about country-western music hopefuls in Nashville, all of them played by nonmusicians such as River Phoenix, Samantha Mathis, and Sandra Bullock—Paramount test-marketed it by showing it to country-western music fans, a move that seems about as logical as previewing *One Flew over the Cuckoo's Nest* in a mental institution. This may not constitute "doctoring" test results in the usual sense, but it certainly sounds a lot like predetermining the outcome.

As a result of this *Wall Street Journal* story, National Research Group, Inc. lost most or all of its Hollywood clients, and I've been told that its successors have proceeded more cautiously. One might think that such a revelation would cast doubts among reviewers and other industry commentators on an already highly dubious practice, but no such reflection or soul-searching ever took place. The industry needs its self-fulfilling prophecies too badly to tolerate skeptics, and, as I hope to show in this book, most film reviewers are hardly independent of either studio interests or their alibis.

Writer-director James L. Brooks, who received most of his training in TV sitcoms, is a talented filmmaker who believes so religiously in test marketing that he seems fully willing to compromise his own work to the point of unintelligibility in order to conform to its supposedly exacting standards. This curious devotion to the mythology of market research as an exact science was demonstrated most cripplingly in the fate of his 1993 musical about contemporary Hollywood filmmaking, appropriately named *I'll Do Anything*. This movie was eventually released in 1994 as a nonmusical after a series of test screenings gradually persuaded Brooks to remove all of the movie's musical numbers. As a reductio ad absurdum of the perils of test marketing, *I'll Do Anything* should be seen by everyone in its musical *and* nonmusical versions, but of course it won't be, because seeing how much better it was before all the meddling took place exposes the patent absurdity of the process.

So I'm afraid you'll have to take my word for it: having had the opportunity to see *I'll Do Anything* as a musical, I can report that it was immeasurably better in that form—eccentric and adventurous, to be sure, but also dramatically and emotionally coherent.[3] The fact that the

---

[3] Albert Brooks—one of the movie's costars, and a good friend of James Brooks—agrees with me. He said to Gavin Smith in *Film Comment* (July-August 1999), "I wish you could have seen the musical [version]. That was the greatest thing in the world, and it broke my heart that the movie came out like it did. The irony of that movie is, the very thing it was about was what it succumbed to. I mean, here's a movie whose whole being is about testing and succumbing to the testing, and that's exactly what happened to Jim [Brooks]. I understand why, but the ambition was so great, if he had stuck to it, in my opinion, it certainly wouldn't have done any worse, and in the long run it would have been a really important movie."

movie bombed at the box office as a nonmusical doesn't of course mean that it would have scored commercially in its original form, but considering that it had an artistic logic and integrity, surely it had a chance of finding an audience if the studio had known how to market it. (Ironically, part of the movie's plot is directly concerned with test marketing.) By the same token, it seems impossible to imagine how the release version could have found an audience under any circumstances because its emotional and dramatic raison d'être had been removed; following the biblical injunction, "And if thy right eye offend thee, pluck it out," Brooks wound up eliminating so much of his original conception that what remained was meaningless.

If test marketing was used exclusively to determine how certain pictures could best be marketed and advertised, I would be inclined to consider it defensible on those grounds; clearly studios have to determine what segments of the audience a movie is most likely to appeal to, and to represent that movie in advertising according to their discoveries. In some cases, I might even defend the use of preview screenings to determine whether certain pictures could turn a profit and therefore whether they should be released. And I would agree that some directors, especially directors of comedy, can benefit from previewing their rough cuts to see when and how they get laughs before making their final cuts.

But using test marketing to impose last-minute changes on movies seems much harder to justify, especially because it assumes that an audience is qualified to make decisions of this kind. Of course we wouldn't dream of policing the writing of novels or the composing of symphonies in this fashion. And if knowledge and expertise are necessary to arrive at intelligent decisions, it's hard to defend the idea of spectators without these qualifications determining the shape and effect of theatrical features.

Test marketing assumes that an audience confronted with something new will arrive at a permanent verdict immediately after seeing it. But our experience of movies—apart from the most routine fare—seldom works that way. Our expectations play a considerable role in determining our first reactions, and once we get past them all sorts of delayed responses become possible; a day or a week or a month later, what initially made us querulous might win us over completely. The film industry factors out responses of this kind—responses that suggest we're capable of learning and growing—thus denying our capacity to change before we can catch our breaths. Determining that a film's success or failure has to register instantaneously, the studio then becomes locked into a treadmill of other assumptions that degrade the audience even further.

Let's consider another contemporary application of Borneman's remarks. The mantra that Americans hate subtitles—periodically brought forth to explain why so few foreign-language films are distributed in the United States—conveniently neglects such facts as (a) most Americans have never even seen a subtitled foreign-language film, and (b) few if any spectators have complained about the extensive use of subtitles in *Dances with Wolves* or *Schindler's List*, or stayed away from either of these movies as a consequence. It's difficult to understand how Americans can hate something they've never experienced—or have experienced only in a situation when they didn't consider it a problem. A more accurate mantra might be, "Americans hate subtitles—except when they don't." Similarly, if one bears in mind both the crippling refusal of most producers to invest in black-and-white pictures and the extensive use of black-and-white videos on MTV, one might hazard the statement, "Teenagers hate to watch anything in black-and-white—except when they don't." In other words, the audience is always to blame, except for when it no longer makes any sense to blame them, at which point the operative premises are forgotten. The alternate possibility, which I explore in this book, is that we aren't seeing certain things because the decision makers are narrow-minded simpletons who want to cover their own asses—interested only in short-term investments and armed mainly with various forms of pseudoscience—and it becomes the standard business of the press, critics included, to ratify these practices while ignoring all other options.

It might of course be countered that *Dances with Wolves*, *Schindler's List*, and most black-and-white music videos that American audiences see are American products, so that audiences are really objecting to (a) foreign-language films from other countries and (b) black-and-white features. But who says they're objecting, and what do these alleged objections actually mean? Black-and-white features started to become almost impossible to finance once TV pollsters concluded that teenagers tend to shift channels whenever they chance upon one. Even though a significant number of the few recent black-and-white American movies actually turn a profit—*Pi* is one example—film labs rarely manufacture black-and-white film stock any longer, and those that do charge more for it than for color stock. If this represents democracy in action, then film audiences of the thirties, forties, fifties, and sixties who had a choice about whether to see movies in color or in black-and-white were more democratically empowered than audiences are today. But this has nothing to do with democracy and a great deal to do with ill-conceived, short-range business investments. In a witty and clarifying essay about movie colorization, Stuart Klawans provides an interesting complement to some of Borneman's observations made almost half a century earlier:

> It is certainly possible, though more difficult to prove than the executives claim, that people prefer to watch television in color. The issue, though, is not the public's taste. It's the way some executives, those with enough power to dominate their markets, decide in advance what people want, then justify their decision by noting that people have indeed bought the only available products. With entertainment, moreover, as with drugs, the product eventually creates a demand for itself. The public may be expected to want colorization once the marketers have habituated them to it.[4]

Distinguishing between culture, education, and advertising has never been more problematic. When Disney holds all-day "seminars" about Native American culture and animation techniques for grade school children in shopping malls as part of its campaign to promote *Pocahontas*, the point at which advertising ends and education begins (or vice versa) is difficult to pinpoint. And when teachers welcome such assistance, how far are we from the prospect of Disney being asked to take over public education? Similarly, when university film professors—who have already agreed, in most cases for budgetary reasons, to show videos instead of actual prints—restrict the films they show to English-language works because "that's what the students want," they're capitulating to the same process.

---

[4] "Rose-Tinted Spectacles," in *Seeing Through Movies*, edited by Mark Crispin Miller, New York: Pantheon Books, 1990, p. 156.

But, as Borneman rightly asks, how can the public know what it wants if it doesn't know its choices? If someone dying of thirst is offered a choice between liquid soap and shoe polish, can the selection honestly be equated with what he or she "wants"? Babies don't like to be toilet trained either. And the studios not only treat the audience like babies, but also never even consider toilet training.

Getting used to subtitles takes time and experience, and if the larger distributors were thinking more in terms of long-term investments, showing more subtitled pictures wouldn't seem nearly as risky. But as long as business thinking remains short-term, it's much easier to justify one's business decisions tautologically and blame the audience. It calls to mind the joke about the Florida orange juice stand that offers "all the orange juice you can drink for a dollar," only to inform its customers after they've consumed a single thimble-sized glass of juice, "That's all the orange juice you can drink for a dollar." From a certain point of view, orange juice and cinema vendors have every right to adopt this policy if they conclude that their customers are too stupid to know they're being fleeced. But can we celebrate such a policy as consumers if all the cinema we can see for seven or eight or nine dollars is radically restricted to what other people want us to see, not what we want to see? This glib acceptance of the vendors' position is part and parcel of the isolationism that has crippled this country culturally over the past few decades, and whether this isolationism is as necessary to our souls and our economy as our tastemakers like to pretend is a question that can't be raised often enough.

The MPAA is another way the industry and its propaganda machine routinely mask their operations. The usual deference with which the media regards this organization hardly qualifies as a critically weighted assessment; though critics grumble about some of its judgments, they regard it more as a fact of life than a lobby with special interests. ("I stopped taking the Motion Picture Association of America Rating Board seriously," wrote Anthony Lane in the April 5, 1999 issue of *The New Yorker*, "when it demanded the removal, from a trailer for *Six Degrees of Separation*, of a glimpse of the naked Adam on the ceiling of the Sistine Chapel"; but such curt dismissals are few and far between.) In fact, the way most people defer to the movie ratings system implies that it's an impartial means of conveying information about the violence, sexual content, and language of specific movies and about their suitability to separate age groups as a result. Though I doubt that many would regard the MPAA as a government-run organization, the authority of its judgments is often given the sort of sanction accorded to the Food and Drug Administration, which we mentally translate into an official stamp. That the MPAA is in fact operated and regulated by the film industry is less often acknowledged; though it's not exactly a secret, the implications of this control are seldom explored in depth. So the MPAA's lenient treatment of studio releases and severe treatment of independent releases—a double standard that is taken for granted by industry insiders—is unlikely to be noted by moviegoers, many of whom, thanks to careful industry training fostered by name-brand associations, already share the same prejudicial bias.

The obfuscation goes further if one considers the deceptiveness of some of the brand names themselves. We all know that a Disney movie is wholesome and a Quentin Tarantino movie is funky, right? Wrong, because all of Tarantino's movies to date have been released by Miramax, a company that belongs to Disney. "Disney" includes Touchstone, Hollywood, and Miramax, which allows it to work both sides of the street—deceptively maintaining all the brand-name associations of Disney on the one hand, and, on the other, obscuring its seedier enterprises under different logos. And when it comes to Tarantino, other ideological con games can be perpetrated as extensions of this cosmetic camouflage. It's easier to call Tarantino an independent filmmaker if he makes his movies for a supposedly independent company like Miramax; and it's perfectly true that Miramax operates in relative independence from its parent company, Disney. But just because Tarantino is answerable to Harvey Weinstein at Miramax rather than to a suit at Disney doesn't mean that he has autonomy.

My idea of an independent filmmaker is someone who has final control over his or her work, and Tarantino has never enjoyed this freedom. Jim Jarmusch and Rob Tregenza, who have final cut on all their own features and even own all their negatives, obviously qualify, but in recent years it has been Tarantino and not either of them who has been celebrated as an American independent—a gross misconception that will continue to prevail as long as the studio's shell-game persists.

Let's consider another consequence of the studio propaganda machine. A widespread controversy surrounding the 1999 Academy Awards—only marginally apparent in the broadcast of the ceremony itself, but the focus of a great deal of debate in the media over the preceding weeks—was the granting and presentation of a Lifetime Achievement Award to Elia Kazan. The issue at stake was not whether his work as a film director warranted such an honor, although one could certainly question the usual privileging of such features as *Gentleman's Agreement*, *On the Waterfront*, and *Splendor in the Grass* as his major achievements over *Panic in the Streets*, *Baby Doll*, and *Wild River*. The issue, rather, was whether Kazan, having named many of his former colleagues for the House Un-American Activities Committee, should have been forgiven. Admittedly, a good many other prominent people in the film industry ratted on their coworkers in order to protect and sometimes boost their own careers. But Kazan was in a strong enough position at the time to have defied this committee without taking the same sort of risks as such fellow directors as John Berry, Jules Dassin, Cy Endfield, Joseph Losey, and Abraham Polonsky, all of whom refused to give names and had to suffer for the remainder of their careers as a consequence. (The first four of these, in fact, continued to work only by becoming European expatriates; and in the cases of Endfield and Losey, due to threats from the American projectionists' union, they initially were able to work abroad only secretly, assigning part of their salaries to others who agreed to serve as "fronts.") Moreover, Kazan went much further than those directors who eventually buckled under pressure, such as Edward Dymtryk and Robert Rossen, by offering scant resistance to HUAC; he even took out an ad in *The New York Times* defending his own behavior and never subsequently apologized or expressed any serious misgivings. According to this argument, Kazan was not only cooperative with the Hollywood blacklist, he was complicitous, and he was rewarded for his behavior with a lucrative studio contract. For many if not all members of the Hollywood left, honoring such an individual even four decades later was an unconscionable act—perhaps even comparable to Ronald Reagan's notorious Bitburg speech that forgave the atrocities of Nazi soldiers.

I could agree with many of the people who protested the award, especially those whose lives had been damaged by the blacklist. But I continue to find inexplicable why Kazan was judged so harshly when the perpetrators of the blacklist—the studio heads who refused to hire black-listed individuals—got off with a clean bill of health. Even if all these moguls are dead, the industry often granted them accolades and tributes when they were still alive, and to the best of my knowledge, not a word of protest was heard against their honors because of their behavior during the blacklist. These moguls, after all, were less the facilitators or the patsies of the blacklist than they were the blacklisters themselves. Moreover, most of them were Jewish, and one of the few who wasn't, Darryl F. Zanuck, was an avowed liberal. As Neal Gabler's book *An Empire of Their Own: How the Jews Invented Hollywood* demonstrates, these moguls' creation of the American Dream through their studio pictures was largely an act of ethnic disavowal, which makes their collective behavior even more odious. (According to Gabler, Hollywood's dream image of the Good Life grew out of the attempts of Adolph Zukor, Carl Laemmle, Louis B. Mayer, the Warner brothers, and Harry Cohn to escape from their European Jewish roots. Because a good many of the blacklist victims were also Jewish, their scapegoating by the studios functioned, in Gabler's analysis, as a kind of Jewish anti-Semitism—Jews throwing other Jews to the wolves as an unconscious act of self-protection.)

So even the protest against Kazan's honor implicitly kowtowed to industry priorities, allowing the major culprits of the blacklist to go unchallenged. It was entirely in keeping with Richard Dreyfuss's presentation of an Irving Thalberg Award to Steven Spielberg at an Oscar ceremony in the early eighties, when Dreyfuss praised Thalberg's "courage" in defying Erich von Stroheim—that is, his courage in slashing Stroheim's two greatest films, *Foolish Wives* and *Greed,* to pieces and making sure that all the deleted material was destroyed afterward. The odds of the Academy of Motion Picture Arts and Sciences ever applauding the courage of a Stroheim, by contrast, are about as remote as their ever bestowing similar honors on the courage of blacklisted workers who refused to cave in under industry pressures.

* * *

Against the claims of our cultural commissars that they're merely giving the public "what they want," let's consider why newspapers, magazines, and entertainment news on television list the ten top-grossing movies every week, often with the grosses listed alongside them. It's a fashion supposedly dictated by public interest, yet for roughly the first eight decades of this century, there was little evidence that such interest existed, even in embryo. If a newspaper in the thirties, forties, fifties, sixties, or even seventies had started to list the ten top grossers every week, its readers would have supposed that the editor had rocks in his head. So why, then, did the readers of the eighties suddenly start to become interested in facts and figures that formerly had captured the interest only of people working in the industry? Why, after all, should anyone care how much money a particular picture makes? Wouldn't we find it peculiar if newspapers routinely listed the ten top-selling soft drinks or fast-food outlets or cars every week, complete with a rundown of the gross figures taken in by each product?

The simple reason is that this interest was cultivated, like so much else in this culture that goes under the guise of spontaneous combustion. If it hadn't been promoted in the first place by publications such as *Premiere,* it probably wouldn't have caught on in other media venues. And if it was possible for a magazine like *Premiere* to promote such an interest, why wouldn't it be possible for *Premiere* or another magazine to cultivate an interest in foreign language films?

If this hypothesis sounds far-fetched, consider the career of one of the inventors of public relations, Edward L. Bernays, an American nephew of Sigmund Freud. The same man who convinced the American people, at the behest of the American Tobacco Company, that women smoking in public was an act of female liberation, previously used the same promotional techniques to successfully sell first the Russian Ballet and then Enrico Caruso to a recalcitrant American public. Larry Tye, in his recent biography *The Father of Spin: Edward L. Bernays and The Birth of Public Relations,* charts the applications of Bernays's techniques still further: "The selling of America on the Persian Gulf War was a public relations triumph . . . crafted by one of America's biggest public relations firms, Hill and Knowlton, in a campaign bought and paid for by rich Kuwaitis who were Saddam [Hussein]'s archenemies." [5] One of my main points in the chapters that follow is

---

[5] New York: Crown, 1998, Preface, p. vii.

that there are much better movies for us to see than the Persian Gulf War, if only we can discover how to find them.

* * *

In the summer of 1998, after striking a deal with Blockbuster Video, CBS, TNT, Turner Classic Movies, and the home-video divisions of thirteen film studios, the American Film Institute made a last-ditch effort to raise some money to replace its shrinking state grants. It created a ludicrous list of the "One Hundred Greatest American Movies"—a short-sighted hit parade of recent box office champs and forgettable Oscar winners larded with a few familiar classics. (For a further discussion of this list, as well as an alternative selection, see Chapter Five.) The public outcry was immediate and palpable, but this was far from the first time that marketers and publicists supplanted the roles of historians and critics. If the press hadn't already been nodding at the switch, such an unwitting insult to the intelligence of the public might not have ever been conceived—much less delivered in the form of a summerlong media blitz—because the credibility of such ventures has always depended on the willingness of the press to grant them space and respect. As I hope to demonstrate, the press's abnegation of any commitment to the public beyond a servicing of privileged business interests has allowed such crass undertakings to dominate what remains of American film culture.

On the other hand, the AFI had also been given a clean playing field by most of film academia, which has avoided promulgating overt film canons since the early eighties. How this curious turn of events came about is one of the issues I'll be discussing in Chapter Four, but for the moment, without proposing any conspiracy theories, I'd like to suggest that the passive behavior of this country's critical community inside both academia and the mainstream press has paved the way for an unblocked proliferation of marketing schemes by an industry that knows only what it has to sell—not why it's worth selling or why anything else might be worth selling in its place. Significantly, while a good version of *The Birth of a Nation*—the only silent film on the list apart from Charlie Chaplin—is available on video from a company called Kino, the AFI chose to "recommend" (i.e., advertise) an abominable, much reduced rerelease version offered by one of the thirteen studios.

* * *

To pursue my argument in this book, I've loosely organized my discussion around a few overlapping topics and examples selected to illustrate as well as debunk some of the fallacies that currently govern what passes for film culture in this country: the matching notions that the audience is to blame for what it sees and that producers and studio heads are relatively blameless (which I've already begun to address in this introduction); the myth that declares that the cinema is over (which paradoxically winds up endorsing and perpetuating the status quo); two chapters on the vagaries of distribution, exhibition, promotion, and criticism; a discussion of the contrasting American critical receptions of *Small Soldiers* and *Saving Private Ryan*; "Communications Problems and Canons" (which addresses both the issue of information flow and the frequent failure of academic film study to engage meaningfully with American film culture as a whole); the assumptions and implications underlying the American Film Institute's unspeakable list of the "hundred greatest American movies"; American isolationism as a form of economic and cultural control; and then a discussion of the ways in which an American national cinema may no longer exist (with *Starship Troopers* used as an example of where some of the problems lie). The last three chapters seek to develop and illustrate many of the concerns that have already been voiced in the book: the first of these focuses on some of the film festivals I've attended in recent years; the second discusses the much misunderstood career of Orson Welles, who, as an exemplary figure, continues to pose ideological challenges to the film industry; and I conclude with a summary of my arguments in the form of a self-dialogue that explains why I think the audience is closer to being right than most industry "experts" admit.

Above all, I'm interested in isolating those elements in contemporary American film culture that alienate us from its possibilities. If my purpose in zeroing in on these misunderstandings is polemical, hence "negative," this is simply because they block us all from enjoying the kind of positive experiences at the movies that are still theoretically available to us—if only we know where to look and how to find them.

Chapter One
Is the Cinema Really Dead?

[The] early nineties have not been as encouraging as the early seventies. . . . It is not as easy now to believe in the medium's vitality or its readiness for great challenges. So many of the noble figures of film history are dead now, and who can be confident that they are being replaced? . . . . The author sees fewer films now. He would as soon go for a walk, look at paintings, or take in a ball game. [1994]

It has become harder, this past year, to go back in the dark with hope or purpose. The place where "magic" is supposed to occur has seemed a lifeless pit of torn velour, garish anonymity, and floors sticky from spilled sodas. Forlornness hangs in the air like damp; things are so desolate, you could set today's version of *Waiting for Godot* in the stale, archaic sadness of a movie theater. . . .This is not just a lamentation that movies are in a very bad state. Rather, I feel the medium has sunk beyond anything we dreamed of, leaving us stranded, a race of dreamers. . . . [1996]

I still look at movies the same way today that I did [at the time of the New Wave], but I know it's not the same world, exactly. Even if we enter the theater the same way, we don't go out the same way. [Question: How is it different?] Less hope . . . . [1996]

Cinema's hundred years seem to have the shape of a life cycle: an inevitable birth, the steady accumulation of glories, and the onset in the last decade of an ignominious, irreversible decline. This doesn't mean that there won't be any more new films that one can admire. But such films won't simply be exceptions; that's true of great achievements in any art. They have to be heroic violations of the norms and practices which now govern moviemaking everywhere in the capitalist and would-be

19

capitalist world—which is to say, everywhere. And ordinary films, films made purely for entertainment (that is, commercial) purposes, will continue to be astonishingly witless; already the vast majority fail resoundingly to appeal to their cynically targeted audiences. While the point of a great film is now, more than ever, to be a one-of-a-kind achievement, the commercial cinema has settled for a policy of bloated, derivative filmmaking, a brazen combinatory or recombinatory art, in the hopes of reproducing past success. Every film that hopes to reach the largest possible audience is designed as some kind of remake. Cinema, once heralded as *the* art of the twentieth century, seems now, as the century closes numerically, to be a decadent art. [1997]

It is perhaps too late to lament the disappearance of the foreign film from a major place in our culture. After many depressing conversations, I have found that younger moviegoers, reared on little but American movies, imagine that mourners for the foreign cinema are talking about some fool's paradise of zinc counters and cappuccino, a pretentious refuge for bearded losers and solemn girls in black. "Cinéastes"—isn't that what they used to call them? It is worse than useless to tell such moviegoers that Bergman and Kurosawa, Antonioni and Fellini, Godard and Truffaut—to name just the most obvious figures—defined our moods in late adolescence, enlarged our sense of romance and freedom and passionate melancholy as well as the expressive possibilities of movies, and that their influence was so pervasive that *Bonnie and Clyde* as well as the careers of Woody Allen, Paul Mazursky, Robert Altman, and a host of other American directors would not have been possible without them. . . . One must quickly add that the current French, Italian, German, and Japanese cinemas are but a remnant of their former selves, and that the new movies from China, Russia, Finland, and Iran, however fascinating, cannot replace the old masterworks in excitement and glamour. "Where are the great foreign films now?" a friend asks, by which he means that he refuses to feel guilty about not going when there are no masterpieces to see. He has a point, but even when a good French movie opens here (like Claude Chabrol's *La Cérémonie*, in 1996), it's hard to scare up much of an audience for it. [1998]

One could cite other recent texts voicing the same sentiments, but these five representative samples—drawn from four highly respected writers whom I'd prefer not to identify right away—should suffice. I won't identify them just yet because I'm interested primarily in what they're saying, not who they are. Their striking similarity in tone and position tempts one to conclude that they all swim in the same water, which further suggests that they must be right to some extent.

But are they? Or, more to the point, *can* they be right? The first quotation laments our lack of confidence that "the noble figures of film history . . . are being replaced" and the fifth is equally morose: "the new movies from China, Russia, Finland, and Iran, however fascinating, cannot replace the old masterworks in excitement and glamour." But if I complained that no messiah has come along in two thousand years to replace Jesus, that we haven't yet found adequate substitutes for Brueghel or Shakespeare, that no novelists have come along lately to fill the gaps left by Proust and Faulkner, and that no jazz musician since the fifties has displayed the genius of Charlie Parker, would I be saying versions of the same thing, or something different? A replacement implies a duplication, or at least an equivalent, rather than something new. Furthermore, since Jesus, Brueghel, Shakespeare, Proust, Faulkner, and Parker may not have been adequately appreciated in their own times, anyone who came along to "replace" them probably wouldn't be adequately appreciated either.

Maybe the first and fifth quotations are implying that, rather than insufficiently recognized "noble masters" or "masterworks," we lack masters and masterworks period—and that, unlike most of our historical predecessors, we're fully capable of rooting them out and recognizing their merits. But how do we root them out? Only a tiny fraction of finished films actually arrive in theaters, and if we're talking about foreign-language films in this country, we're talking about less than one percent of what gets shown commercially; very few critics nowadays—including the four represented above—are likely to see all of these. If the handful of foreign films that open here, the elite less-than-one-percent, were the absolute best that's being made— which automatically assumes that "the best" equals the most commercial—then we might have the basis for making such a generalization. But what evidence supports that belief beyond wishful thinking? Are we confident, for starters, that distributors see all the possible candidates? And that they have such impeccable taste that they would recognize the best films as a simple matter of course? Or that the best films, even if they saw them and recognized their merits, are invariably commercial propositions worth investing in?

Still, it's the usual role of critics—bolstered by such adages as "Cream rises to the top" (even if it takes a few centuries for someone like Jesus)—to make such pronouncements. To put it bluntly, we more or less have to make such sweeping generalizations from time to time if we expect to be listened to. To some degree, we all have to assume that we have some idea of the value of what's being produced in a given art form, even if we prove to be wrong in the long run, because to assume otherwise is to abnegate all responsibility about such matters.

But once critics make such judgments, they owe it to their audiences to convey how they arrived at them. So unless foreign film distributors in the United States are all-seeing, all-knowing, preternaturally gifted guides in determining what's best in world cinema—not only in the present, but also in the indefinite future—there must be other sources for these conclusions about the state of world cinema. Maybe these critics attend certain foreign film festivals where they can view wider samples (although these, too, are highly restricted in relation to the sheer volume of the films that get made), and maybe they read critics in other countries in order to get some estimation of what others think about what's important—although, in point of fact, two of the four writers cited above rarely attend foreign festivals, and if they read foreign critics, there's scant evidence of it in their work. Maybe they read what some of their local colleagues write about such festivals, and arrive at certain conclusions on the basis of whether or not they agree with the overall drift of their colleagues' opinions. Or maybe they're simply pretending to possess a certain expertise on matters that they know little or nothing about.

My quarrel here is with texts and positions, not individuals, and I hasten to add that I would never lodge an accusation of posturing against Susan Sontag, the author of the fourth quotation (drawn from her article "A Century of Cinema")—a world traveler fluent in several languages who attends many film festivals abroad. Though she doesn't regard herself as a film critic, she has done enough legwork to qualify her to judge the current state of world cinema, and even though I don't agree with many of her conclusions, I don't consider her presumptuous in making them. The third quotation, which is more about the climate of moviegoing than the state of the art per se, comes from Jean-Luc Godard's press conference at the Toronto Film Festival in 1996, and I've included it here only because Godard's own pronouncements about the death of cinema over the last several years have probably influenced other commentators—perhaps Sontag most of all. But when David Thomson, the author of the first two quotations, and David Denby, the author of the fifth, make comparable claims about the contemporary state of the art, I'm less inclined to take them seriously, because I see a good deal more than they do and seldom feel that they're attentive to anything more than what's currently available, commercial, and fashionable (a very thin slice of the pie)—thereby leaving out most of what keeps the art of world cinema, including American cinema, alive.[1]

If Thomson and Denby suddenly changed their minds and decided that exciting and important things were happening in the cinemas of Iran and Taiwan, they would probably no longer be publishing in the same magazines, because mainstream publications aren't interested in such subjects, even as theoretical possibilities. They're interested almost exclusively in commerce and fashion, not in art when it comes to film, and for this reason alone declarations about the death of cinema as an art form from the likes of Denby, Thomson, and even Sontag can easily be translated into expedient defenses of these magazines' own positions as commercial vendors. Such declarations even become godsends to editors who are tired of feeling challenged by the number of things going on in world cinema that they choose to ignore. (Although, as I'll show a little later, even Sontag's more nuanced and informed articulation of the death-of-cinema position had to be significantly modified before it could appear in a mainstream American publication.) Paradoxically, they also want to promote—and to benefit from the promotion of—new commercial films as art objects, because unless one decides that art and entertainment are incompatible, new works of entertainment have to be praised as works of art if they're going to be taken seriously.

So the ideal film columnist in a magazine like *Esquire* would write alternate columns declaring the death of cinema as an art form and the rebirth of cinema as an art form every time a "special" mainstream

---

[1] The second quotation is the beginning and end of Thomson's first movie column for *Esquire*, "Who Killed the Movies?," published in December 1996, and the fifth comes from the middle of Denby's article "The Moviegoers" published in the April 6, 1998 issue of *The New Yorker*. The first quotation comes from Thomson's introduction to the third edition of *A Biographical Dictionary of Film*, and helps to explain why this 1994 volume contains no entry about any filmmakers from Iran and Taiwan, nor any about Chantal Akerman, Atom Egoyan, Jon Jost, Emir Kusturica, Kira Muratova, Mark Rappaport, Raul Ruiz, Aleksandr Sokurov, or Béla Tarr—among many others.

property comes along. Thomson filled that bill perfectly during his extended stint at that magazine. He boldly inaugurated his column by declaring that movies were at an end, then promptly resurrected them in his second column in order to praise *L.A. Confidential*, something he would do again for *The Truman Show*. In a comparable spirit, Denby, who didn't share Thomson's enthusiasm for *The Truman Show*, seemed to base much of his own despair about the future of film as an art form on the "difficulty [of *L.A. Confidential*] in finding a large theater audience"—"a matter of much chagrin to me and a number of other movie critics I've spoken to." I don't happen to share Thomson and Denby's enthusiasm for or even their interest in that particular film, but even if I did, I doubt that I could rest my conclusions about the survival of cinema as an art form on either the existence or the commercial success of one particular movie. I'm pretty sure that they don't either, but it's part of the peculiar hysteria produced in mainstream pop culture to foster such temporary impressions. And one of the natural consequences of such a stance is that Denby, like Thomson and some of his other colleagues, seesaws regularly between announcing the death of cinema and hyping a certain number of current releases. One feels at times that he and his colleagues are merely trying to do what's expected of them, and contradictions of this kind are virtually inscribed in the editorial dynamics at their publications.

Indeed, a good deal of journalism is devoted to creating feeding frenzies that are subsequently forgotten, usually in order to make room for new ones. It's a syndrome I'm susceptible to as well, for the pressure on consumer-oriented reviewing is always to make the products of a particular week or month seem important regardless of whether they are or not; after all, to treat a movie as unimportant is often tantamount to telling a reader to stop reading. But when another week or month rolls around and it becomes necessary to treat another movie or set of movies as important, the reviewer and reader both have to experience temporary amnesia in order to keep the process going.

* * *

Tweaking the doomsday positions of Sontag, Thomson, Denby (in earlier pieces), and others in the April 1997 issue of *Vanity Fair*, James Wolcott countered their gloomy claims about the state of cinema with a list of twenty-odd recent favorites, not one of which was in any language other than English. *L.A. Confidential,* which hadn't yet been released, didn't make it onto his hit parade, but his common ground with Thomson and Denby, when it comes to nonmainstream world cinema, is more significant than any polemical differences. In fact, Wolcott's deepest scorn was reserved for those "sullen *Village Voice* reviewers" who "praise movies so obscure that simply getting to the theater counts as a quest for the authentic." One of them, he pointed out, had the nerve to write hyperbolically about a recent Godard video—something that Wolcott presumably couldn't be bothered to see himself.

In other words, American film reviewers are expected to dispense a certain comfort to moviegoers by assuring them that what's available at their local multiplex or video store is all that's worth seeing. If these reviewers happen upon films that aren't available at those outlets, they won't be able to run reviews of them in mainstream publications; so unless they want to feel frustrated about their jobs, they accept the choices made by large distributors on their behalf. Assigning central importance to someone like Godard in these circumstances can only sound irritating and elitist, and it's important to underline that there's nothing new about this bias; in mainstream terms, Godard has remained a marginal spokesman since the sixties, even if many of his critical and cinematic ideas have periodically entered the mainstream in simplified or garbled form.

Writing in *New York* magazine in 1980, Dan Yakir noted that Godard "had become a cultural nonperson," and blithely added that "It's possible that Godard was not even surprised" after Jean-Paul Belmondo—Godard's star in *Breathless* (1959) and *Pierrot le fou* (1965)—recently asked him, "Can you still direct?" The fact that Godard had directed over half a dozen released features and two extended French TV series during the seventies—a corpus of work with the collective running time of almost two days—obviously didn't count in this reckoning either for Belmondo or Yakir because none of the Hollywood studios were distributing this work. In other words, out of sight, out of mind—and anything not for immediate sale is out of sight. (As I'll show later, the same skewered reasoning has given Orson Welles a mainstream profile of artistic inactivity over the last quarter-century of his life, while he was working on literally dozens of projects.)

One of the most sophisticated American film critics I know refused to see Béla Tarr's seven-hour *Sátántangó* at the Toronto Film Festival because he knew that if he really liked it he would feel frustrated about not being able to write about it: "I'd rather see four terrible films," he bluntly informed me. An equally sophisticated colleague of his made it to the first couple of hours of *Sátántangó,* which he liked, but then had to leave in order to attend the screening of something else he liked less that he knew his editor expected him to review. Although the prospect of a seven-hour film seems daunting—even if it's shown with two intermissions, as *Sátántangó* usually is, in accordance with the filmmaker's wishes—when I selected the film as a "critic's choice" for the Chicago International Film Festival, it drew nearly a full house at a commercial cinema, and there were very few walkouts. By contrast, the press screening in Toronto attracted only a handful of reviewers; most of the others logically concluded that such an experience, no matter how rewarding, would only interfere with their jobs.

Anomalies of this kind are both frequent and on the rise nowadays, especially at film festivals, and they point to a contradiction that is even more damaging than coupling end-of-cinema pronouncements with the hawking of new commercial products: the assumption that audiences, unlike sophisticated critics, are intolerant of films that demand some thought or patience. In my experience almost the reverse is true, and part of the reason for the critics' intolerance is the intolerance of most of their editors. This is what makes the death-of-cinema racket so attractive to certain critics as well as editors; if you decide in advance that something like *Sátántangó* has to be a waste of time—unlike the usual trash that gets reviewed—you're bound to experience a certain relief.

* * *

Susan Sontag's essay "A Century of Cinema"—a generational lament whose validity for me both rests on and is partially thrown into doubt by its generational stance—has by now appeared in many languages around the world as well as in many different English-language publications, including the *The New York Times Magazine* (February 25, 1996), the "movie issue" of *Parnassus: Poetry in Review* (volume 22, nos.

1 & 2, 1997), *The Guardian,* and at least two book-length collections of essays. I've noted many interesting variations in this piece as it's appeared in various settings, and assume that some of these represent subsequent revisions or afterthoughts on Sontag's part. But the most striking differences appear between the first version published in America — in *The New York Times Magazine,* with the strikingly different title "The Decay of Cinema" — and all the others, and I assume that these, including the title, stem from editorial interventions, or at the very least collaborations between Sontag and her editor or editors at the *Times.* These differences reveal a great deal about mainstream positions on the movies in general and the cinema-is-dead postulate in particular, especially as these positions become translated into editorial decisions. They expose an ideology of avoidance that I consider central to the habits of mainstream publications I have already been discussing.

Missing from the *Times* version were almost all of Sontag's references to such filmmakers as Theodor Angelopoulos, Shohei Imamura, Miklós Jancsó, Alexander Kluge, Nanni Moretti, Nagisa Oshima, Edgar Reitz, Aleksandr Sokurov, Hans-Jürgen Syberberg, Andrei Tarkovsky, Béla Tarr, and Krzysztof Zanussi, as well as the titles of some of their films — a virtual honor role of contemporary filmmakers whom Sontag regards as important. (In one of the later incarnations of her essay, Abbas Kiarostami's *Through the Olive Trees* was added to her list of "wonderful films [that] are still being made.") Although it appears that Sontag's article was cut for length so that it could fit into a two-page spread, it hardly seems accidental that most of these dozen figures hadn't curried much favor in recent years with either *Times* reviewers or U.S. distributors, and consequently couldn't be counted on as familiar names to *Times* readers. Perhaps for the same reason, the *Times* version contained one sentence that can't be found in any of the other versions: "In this country, the lowering of expectations for quality and the inflation of expectations for profit have made it virtually impossible for artistically ambitious American directors, like Francis Ford Coppola and Paul Schrader, to work at their best level."

In other words, even in an article decrying Hollywood's ruinous effect on world cinema, Hollywood directors had to be given more attention — and overseas directors less — when the piece was published in the *Times.* (Perhaps for the same reason, the names of many great non-American filmmakers of the past—including Jean Cocteau, Rainer Werner Fassbinder, Akira Kurosawa, Kenji Mizoguchi, Yasujiro Ozu, Marcel Pagnol, and Pier Paolo Pasolini—were excluded from the *Times* version of Sontag's article as well.)

It reminds me of Marshall McLuhan's account in his Introduction to *Understanding Media* of the "consternation of one of the editors of this book. He noted in dismay that 'seventy-five percent of your material is new. A successful book cannot venture to be more than ten percent new.'" By the same standard, any article about world cinema that appears in the *Times*—even, and perhaps especially, a death-of-cinema article—can't present too much new information, including unfamiliar names and film titles. That's apparently why the frustrations and disappointments of Coppola and Schrader become ipso facto more germane to the *Times'* interests than the acknowledged achievements of twenty others. Unless there's a new commercial picture around to hawk, evidence of the death of world cinema is mainly what the *Times* considers fit to print; evidence of its past and present life only gets in the way of its everyday operations.

* * *

As I've already suggested, the cinema-is-dead position can at least partially be traced back to various pronouncements by Jean-Luc Godard, as well as certain assumptions embedded in much of his recent work. It should be stressed that Godard's version of this position is a highly personal and idiosyncratic one. As the English Godard scholar Michael Witt has argued, in a conference article[2] that part of this chapter is indebted to, Godard has increasingly identified the cinema with his own life and body on the one hand and with the twentieth century on the other.

Godard's recently completed eight-part video series *Histoire(s) du cinéma*, which was in the works for almost a decade, is centrally con-

---

[2] "The Death(s) of Cinema According to Godard," delivered at *Screen* Conference, Glasgow, Scotland, July 3, 1998, and published in *Screen*, vol. 40, no. 3, Autumn 1999, pp. 331–346.

cerned with the history of the twentieth century as perceived through cinema, and, conversely, with the history of cinema as perceived through the twentieth century—and both these histories are viewed as stories that are essentially over. As Witt points out, Godard's association of both these histories with his own autobiography can be traced back to a more general impulse to "give cinema a body": using the figure of Fritz Lang to embody classical cinema in *Contempt* (1963) and then filming a dialogue with Lang for French television shortly afterward entitled "The Dinosaur and the Baby"; more recently, using the figure of the American-born European actor Eddie Constantine, the star of Godard's 1965 *Alphaville,* to embody cinema shortly before his death in Godard's film *Germany Year 90 Nine Zero* (1991). Witt also recalls that Godard inserted himself in the same metaphor as early as *Band of Outsiders* (1964) by assigning himself the opening credit "Jean-Luc Cinema Godard," and he cites many other, more recent instances of Godard "[giving] cinema a human form and life cycle" in this fashion: "If Godard, in a gesture as self-promotional and narcissistic as it is . . . has repeatedly suggested that the cinema is likely to die more or less when he does (!), then he has, for a good ten or fifteen years, exploited his own body and its physical aging as illustrative and exemplary of the winding down of cinema as an art form."

One has to discriminate, of course, between the critical wisdom of Godard's position and its artistic utility in his work. Just as we can distinguish the relative foolishness of Leo Tolstoy's populist theory of history in *War and Peace* from the richness of the fictional world that it helps to make possible, it doesn't help us very much to dismiss Godard's solipsism if we fail to note some of the positive consequences it has on his art. In his interviews, moreover, Godard tends to be much less monolithic about his apocalyptic theory; when I said to him in Toronto in 1996 that one of the implications of *Histoire(s) du cinéma* seemed to be that the cinema was over, he was quick to add, "The cinema we knew. We also say that of painting."[3]

---

[3] See "Godard in the 90s: An Interview, Argument, and Scrapbook," *Film Comment,* September-October 1998.

Unfortunately, there are no such demurrals or positive consequences when Denby, Sontag, or Thomson offer equally autobiographical and self-regarding but less nuanced versions of the same position—especially because they, unlike Godard, are speaking in
mainstream forums where the implications of their remarks coincide
rather neatly in certain particulars with corporate interests and don't
fuel any artistic projects of comparable weight. And when mainstream
commentators like Wolcott come along to challenge their doom and
gloom, the counterevidence remains strictly sui generis and astutely
dry-cleaned to remove any contaminating foreign influences, giving
further credence to the premise that the choices made on our behalf
by studios, publicists, distributors, and exhibitors are our only real
possibilities.

* * *

Let me propose a pedagogical exercise: first reread the extended quotation from David Denby in *The New Yorker,* the fifth and longest of
the death-of-cinema pronouncements cited at the beginning of this
chapter, and then look up Denby's dismissive review of *Taste of
Cherry*—the first film of Iranian filmmaker Abbas Kiarostami that he
bothered to see—which appeared in *New York* magazine the same day.
In the latter, you find him writing, "I can't help thinking that the com-
parisons [of Kiarostami] to De Sica and Satyajit Ray and other masters
betray a degree of critical desperation. Is this movie rich enough—does
it show the many-sided vitality of the great movies of the past—to warrant the extravagant praise? Or are critics, depressed by the obvious aesthetic poverty of the world cinema, arguing themselves into it, placing
their bets on Kiarostami because they have no other cards to play? . . .
This is a movie of great interest—an original work—but it lacks the
courage, the surprise, the ravenous hunger for life, of a serious work of
movie art." To contextualize Denby's latter statement, two recent and
unproblematically "serious" works of movie art by his lights, presumably displaying courage, surprise, and a ravenous hunger for life, are
Pulp Fiction and *L.A. Confidential.* (Personally, I would argue that
both movies display at best a ravenous hunger for media that constitutes
most of their surprise as well as their "courage.")

My pedagogical exercise contains a third step: to look up the original New York reviews of films by Antonioni, Bergman, Fellini, Godard, Kurosawa, and Truffaut—the directors who, according to Denby's *New Yorker* article, "defined our moods in late adolescence, [and] enlarged our sense of romance and freedom and passionate melancholy as well as the expressive possibilities of movies"—when they opened in the sixties. I'll wager that most of them resemble Denby's review of *Taste of Cherry*, showing just as much skepticism and just as little enthusiasm. How could it be otherwise, when "new" masterpieces are obliged by definition to evoke and even conform to old ones? If you're looking for a "remnant" of former French cinema in, say, *Irma Vep*—a film that Denby incidentally likes because for him it exposes the bankruptcy of contemporary French cinema—then the very idea of a French film addressing the nineties rather than the sixties is ruled out-of-order. So it's only logical that Kiarostami, who was already making films throughout the seventies without Denby's interest or awareness, has to be measured against a sixties reading of De Sica or Satyajit Ray rather than against a nineties reading of anything. (We have to bear in mind that during Denby's alleged Golden Age, films from Iran, China, Taiwan, Africa, and most of the remainder of the so-called Third World weren't even being seen in the West, much less considered, and what we were seeing from Japan, Russia, eastern Europe, and Latin America was extremely limited.) The fact that I happen to find Kiarostami a great deal more interesting and important than either De Sica or Ray is virtually beside the point. Denby, who isn't remotely interested in catching up on any of the two decades of Kiarostami's work that preceded *Taste of Cherry*, is asking for a time-tested and culturally authenticated master to be made apparent on the basis of a single feature. And if the cultural authorities who deemed De Sica and Ray masters didn't familiarize themselves with Kiarostami's earlier work, presumably it must be Kiarostami who's to blame.

When Denby complains that "it's hard to scare up much of an audience for" *La Cérémonie* in 1996, the implication is that New York audiences in the sixties were storming the art theaters to see *L'avventura*, *Shoot the Piano Player*, *Shame*, *Fellini Satyricon*, *High and Low*, and *La Chinoise*, which clearly wasn't the case. Most of them were flops with limited support from mainstream critics, and if Denby was bucking the establishment back then and deciding for himself that they were major "mood-defining experiences," it would be interesting to learn more of the circumstances of such encounters. Speaking for myself, I took a bus all the way from New York to Philadelphia on March 23, 1968, when I was twenty-five, to see *La Chinoise* at a film club screening two weeks prior to its New York opening, when it ran for just a single week. Part of the reason why I went to such lengths was that Godard was scheduled to appear with the film in Philadelphia; in fact he never turned up, but I never regretted making the trip as a consequence. In fact, when I boarded the bus I discovered that a cinephile friend from college was making the same trip for the same reason. When we boarded the bus back to New York a few hours later, he bought a copy of the Sunday *New York Times* to bring with us, and I'll never forget finding there a lengthy irate letter to the editor written by me a few weeks earlier, defending Godard's films against charges of arbitrariness and lack of structure as propounded by the late Eugene Archer (incidentally the major mentor of Andrew Sarris, and ironically one of the first American champions of *la politique des auteurs*, which subsequently became mutated through Sarris's efforts into what became known as "the auteur theory"). "[Godard's] most recent films," I concluded in my letter, "are simultaneously investigations into and lessons about how to see, hear and understand our everyday existence. Regardless of how one ultimately judges them, it is irresponsible to call them frivolous; far more frivolous is the critical intelligence which refuses to grapple with them."

It's also worth adding that during the week's run of *La Chinoise* that started at New York's Kips Bay Theater on April 3, my friends and I went to see it more than once. Some of these friends were attending Columbia University at the time, and when the campus was taken over by students a short time later, I couldn't help but think that Godard's film had inspired and influenced their militancy. Maybe part of this was wishful thinking, but maybe not: word of mouth traveled more quickly in those days — faster than *The New York Times*, faster even than television — because there was less media to compete with. Not that the media didn't exist, but it was believed in much less by people of my and Denby's generation; all one had to do was read — or, on television, see — the reports of the demonstrations we participated in, against the

Vietnam war and on behalf of civil rights, in order to understand that the truth of what happened was available only from fellow demonstrators and other members of the counterculture, not from the "official" channels. And the same thing was true when it came to finding out about movies: the David Denbys and the Eugene Archers of the sixties were not the authorities one had to turn to.

Admittedly, by waxing nostalgically as well as egotistically about such a period, I'm potentially fostering the same argument of generational entitlement and narcissistic authority that Denby, Sontag, and Thomson set forth. But my argument differs from theirs in my conviction that the legacy of the sixties is not quite as dead as they—and Godard, for that matter—assume. And to account for this conviction, I paradoxically need to cite a film that's even more forgotten today than *La Chinoise: Far from Vietnam*—a collectively made piece of French agitprop about the war that was concurrently waged by the United States in southeast Asia.

The directors involved in this episodic feature were Godard, Joris Ivens, William Klein, Claude Lelouch, Alain Resnais, and Agnes Varda, and the editing was carried out collectively in Paris under the supervision of Chris Marker.[4] The film premiered at the New York Film Festival in 1967, which was where I first saw it; I recall the controversial press screening, punctuated by much booing as well as applause. It carried an enormous emotional value for me at the time, in spite of the unequalness of its parts, because of its strong feeling of interconnection—the conviction that you could still say something important about an American war in Vietnam when your base of operations happened to be France. Around this period I had already become acquainted with the work of five of the seven filmmakers who contributed to this feature—Godard, Resnais, Lelouch, Marker, and Varda, but not yet with Ivens or Klein. Yet it was probably Klein who affected me the most when he focused on how an American Quaker,

---

[4] Anecdotal and historical aside: when I met Marker for the first time at the Festival of the Midnight Sun in Finland in June 1998, he recalled that the protracted editing of *Far from Vietnam*—which took so long because it was carried out collectively—was carried out at Antégor, the same Paris editing studio where Orson Welles put together *F for Fake* a few years later.

Norman Morrison, following the example of several South Vietnamese Buddhist monks, protested the war by burning himself alive in Washington, D.C.

Like many, perhaps most Americans at the time, I already knew who Morrison was and what he had done, but all I had heard about his act from friends and colleagues was that he was a madman whose suicide had accomplished nothing. What Klein, an American expatriate in Paris, had shown me was that what Morrison had done meant a great deal, not only to his own family, but also to the North Vietnamese, who had even named a street after him. These were simple facts, but nothing I had come across in American journalism at the time had made them available. Consequently, the importance of this information—like the importance of all the new films that mattered most to me in the mid-sixties—wasn't part of the media as I understood it then, but part of something else. It was like receiving a letter from friend who lived far away but knew exactly what I was thinking. That's still what matters most to me in movies, and the major legacy of the sixties for me is the certainty that there are still friends of this kind scattered across the globe, regardless of the state of our postal delivery.

It's the state of our postal delivery, cinematically speaking, that most of the remainder of this book will be concerned with. The insistence that there's no longer a great deal of mail worth delivering or receiving apart from the bills and advertising fliers that we can already count on is for me the bottom line of all the end-of-cinema manifestos, and the reason why these arguments need to be interrogated so closely.

* * *

Perhaps the most categorical of all these doomsday manifestos is the one voiced by Gilbert Adair in the Preface to his recent British collection *Surfing the Zeitgeist*—that all contemporary art without exception is in a state of precipitous decline. Decrying "the persistent and concerted stroking of our national ego, as though it went without saying that ours was one of the Golden Ages of artistic endeavour," Adair provides the following counterblast:

> Briefly, about that Golden Age. The louder the hyperbole, the more vociferous the self-trumpeting, the harder it becomes to credit that any-

one is truly taken in (even among the trumpeters themselves—Salman Rushdie, for one). I offer no counterargument here, as it would be a waste of both time and space, the naming of names being all that is really needed. So, to cast the net no further back than to the last of the genuine cultural Golden Ages, the first fifty years of this century, I name: Picasso, Mondrian, Matisse, Kandinsky, Stravinsky, Debussy, Bartok, Schoenberg, Proust, Joyce, Kafka, Mann, Rilke, Yeats, Brecht, Pirandello, Genet, Chaplin, Ozu, Dreyer, Vigo. I could go on, as I am sure the reader could (for there are innumerable more where these came from), but it would be as pointless an exercise as would be pitiful any attempt to match such names from the past with those of supposedly comparable creators from the present. Only an idiot or an opportunist or a congenital optimist would dare to suggest that ours is anything but a period of profound cultural mediocrity and stagnation. That is neither an insight nor an idea but an inescapable fact.[5]

Unlike the hand-wringing of Denby, Thomson, Sontag, and even Godard, this uncharacteristically links what's happening in film to what's happening in the other arts, something that Sontag herself did cogently and innovatively in the sixties. It's certainly enough to give one pause, because Adair's honor roll of twenty-one names from the first half of the twentieth century does seem hard to top.

Yet if we consider only the four filmmakers who conclude that list, something crucial becomes immediately apparent. Apart from Chaplin, recognized throughout most of the century as a major artist—discounting that period near midcentury when he was hounded out of this country and denied reentry because of his leftist sympathies, his sexual behavior, and the bad impression left by *Monsieur Verdoux,* one of his greatest films—the other three filmmakers remain esoteric at best to most American moviegoers, and their greatness was far from recognized even among many specialists until well after their deaths.

Let's take them in order. Although Yasujiro Ozu (1903–1963) was celebrated in Japan throughout much of his career, he remained unknown in the West (apart from Japanese movie houses on the West Coast and in Hawaii) until *Tokyo Story* (1953), which surfaced in the United States at the University of California film festival in 1956. Even after that, screenings of his work in the West were so rare and sporadic

---

[5] London: Faber and Faber, 1997, pp. ix–x.

that when the first Ozu retrospective at the Cinémathèque Française—much of which I attended—played in 1972, it was the first prolonged exposure to his work that most Parisian cinephiles had, and most American film buffs had to wait much longer. Even today, though all of his surviving features are available on video in Japan, only half a dozen of these are available in the United States, and this doesn't include any of his silent films[6]—a rich and strikingly different part of his oeuvre comprising thirteen surviving features made between 1929 and 1935 (as well as a short documentary and twenty-odd more films that are either lost or survive only in fragments). Even in Japan, it would be a gross exaggeration to say that his surviving work is known in any detail; when I participated in an Ozu symposium in Tokyo in late 1998, many of the film scholars I met there had not seen several of his key pictures, including most of the silent ones.

Carl Dreyer (1889–1968), born in Sweden and raised in Denmark, is even less well known in the United States than Ozu. From the sound period onward, all of Dreyer's features were commercial flops practically everywhere they showed, and I think it would be fair to call him the artist in Adair's list of twenty-one whose works have been hardest to access, with the possible exception of Pirandello. Some of his masterpieces are completely out of reach (apart from unsubtitled prints at New York's Anthology Film Archives), and others have been available only in abysmal prints that barely hint at their richness. One of the greatest, *Day of Wrath* (1943), is a film I only started to appreciate in any detail after I was able to see a new print in Paris in the late eighties; prior to that, neither the sound nor the image was adequately discernible in the battered 16-millimeter prints I had seen, and since then—until Home Vision Cinema recently brought out a gorgeous video version—the only way I was able to return to it in a watchable form was on a French video, playable only on a tristandard VCR (which is itself a pretty scarce item in this country). Happily, Home Vision Cinema has also just brought out comparably exquisite video versions of Dreyer's two final features, *Ordet* (1955) and *Gertrud* (1964), so thirty-two years after his death, his late work is finally becoming avail-

[6] Happily, as this book went to press, *I Was Born, But . . .* , perhaps the greatest of Ozu's silent features, was released by New Yorker Films.

able in some form—though I can't vouch for how widely available these videos are. (Over the past couple of decades, whenever I've been asked to pick my "all-time" favorite film, my usual response depends almost entirely on which of these three Dreyer masterpieces I've seen last.) And when it comes to silent masterpieces like *The Parson's Widow* (1920) and *Mikael* (1924), the chances of encountering them in *any* form nowadays are pretty slim. Fortunately, *Master of the House* (1925), *The Passion of Joan of Arc* (1928), and *Vampyr* (1932) are somewhat easier to come by, at least on video, and the restored, original version of the second has also surfaced recently on film and video alike. Whether or not this will lead to a belated recognition of Dreyer's genius in some quarters depends almost entirely on the word getting out.

Jean Vigo (1905–1934) only lived long enough to make four films, and only one of these (the 1934 *L'Atalante*) is long enough to qualify as a feature; fortunately, a restoration of that film in the early nineties received enough play to make this work more available in recent years than anything by Ozu or Dreyer. But his equally great *Zéro de conduite* (*Zéro for Conduct*, 1933) probably remains known today chiefly by film students. And prior to the restoration of *L'Atalante*, the story of the reception of his work is mainly a protracted nightmare: most of it was banned, mangled beyond recognition, and/or marginalized while he was alive, then buried for years afterward. The original U.S. premiere of both *Zéro de conduite* and *L'Atalante* wasn't until 1947.

What's the point of rehashing all these hard-luck stories? Simply to point out that if the major works of three of the four names cited so confidently by Adair remained inaccessible for decades, and remain so to most people today, what about the major works of filmmakers who have emerged during the second half of the twentieth century, some of whom Adair might not have encountered or even heard of yet? Or better yet, if we accept his hypothesis that world art has been in overall decline for the past half century—based on the premise that, unlike our predecessors, we're fully in a position to know what's around—when are most people going to get a proper opportunity to see all of the great films made during the previous fifty years, even just those on his admittedly abbreviated short list?

I'm reminded of the pipe dream of the late Carlos Clarens, a Cuban-born film buff and critic who spent most of his adult years in Paris and

New York—perhaps the two cities in the world where one can see the greatest number of important films, new as well as old. Carlos used to fantasize that one year the studios would fail to release a single new movie and would instead be forced to revive all the unseen and unseeable glories they had locked up in their vaults. Similarly, if the decline in world cinema is as serious as Denby, Thomson, Sontag, Adair, and others insist it is, then we could still catch up on all the wonders that they and we have missed—and revive the great works that never fully made the rounds.

Chapter Two
Some Vagaries of Distribution and Exhibition

How often are aesthetic agendas determined by business agendas? This question is not raised often enough.

Terminology plays an important role here. For example, once upon a time, previews of new releases were called "sneak previews" because the titles of these pictures weren't announced in advance. Most industry people continue to use the term, despite the fact that the titles are announced and even advertised, so that the original meaning gets obfuscated: the only thing "sneaky" is the fact that they're called "sneak previews."

This is a relatively trivial example of how terminology alienates us from what goes on in the world of movies. A more significant example is how we use an extremely loaded term like "independent." An independent filmmaker traditionally meant a filmmaker who worked independently, free from the pressures of the major studios. If you believe what the media say about independent films, then the mecca for independent filmmaking would be the Sundance Film Festival, an event where independent films and filmmakers congregate annually. But the festival was started by a prominent movie star, Robert Redford, and has been dominated for years by studio producers, studio-owned distributors, and agents with strong ties to the studios. For independent filmmakers to "succeed" at Sundance almost invariably means selling their films to studios—which means in most cases losing control, including final cut. Ergo, to succeed at the mecca for independent filmmaking is to lose one's independence. It's as simple as that, but you rarely if ever find an acknowledgment of this in the media celebrations of Sundance (many of which take place in *The New York Times,* which for years has been one of Sundance's corporate sponsors). Instead you hear about the prize catches of "independent" companies like Miramax (a company owned by Disney) and October (a company that until recently was owned by Universal): Quentin Tarantino or Kevin Smith, for example.

* * *

When it comes to the role of business in shaping cinephilia, criticism is often simply in denial. How much do commentators on the French love of American cinema after the war factor in the crucial part played by the Marshall Plan in making sure that this American cinema was available in profusion in France, and not necessarily because everyone wanted it? When dealing with new versions of movies labeled "restorations" and/or "director's cuts," how often do critics bother to ascertain the accuracy of these claims? (Sometimes a "restoration" means simply striking a new print, and sometimes—as in the case of the new version of Orson Welles's *Othello,* discussed in Chapter Nine—it means effacing and altering the original. No less often, reinserting material that a director deliberately omitted yields what many publicists call a "director's cut.") And when it comes to film cults, how often is it acknowledged that their existence depends on a system of independent exhibition that is practically extinct nowadays?

To understand a few basic facts about both cult films and art films in the United States, it is helpful to sketch in a little bit of economic history. In 1938, the U.S. government filed an antitrust action against Paramount Pictures, objecting to the monopolies of movie theaters held by the studios; by the end of 1946, a court judgment enjoined not only Paramount, but also Loew's, RKO, Warner Bros, and 20th Century-Fox from acquiring additional theaters and engaging in other anti-competitive practices prohibited by the Sherman Antitrust Act, such as blind bidding, forced rentals, and refusing to rent certain films to certain exhibitors. This had many consequences, the most important of which was a substantial reduction in the control of the Hollywood studios over what moviegoers saw in theaters. Paramount, which controlled the largest of all the studio-run theater chains, had nearly fifteen hundred theaters operating in the late forties. In 1953, their theaters were purchased by American Broadcasting Companies, Inc.—ABC television and radio—but because of all the sales of theaters required by the government decree, this chain was reduced to a little over five hundred theaters by 1957. By the late fifties and early sixties, the more equitable and open market for movie exhibition created by these rulings led to more independent theaters, including art houses that specialized in foreign films and, by the early seventies, midnight movies. These flourished on the basis of films being rented for a flat fee rather than on a percentage basis, granting a lot of creative freedom to individual exhibitors and programmers.

After the studios were forced to sell off most of their theaters, they used five methods of licensing or distributing movies: competitive bidding, competitive negotiations, non-competitive negotiations (limited to areas with only one exhibitor), tracking (an exclusive arrangement worked out informally between a distributor and a particular exhibitor), and splitting (an agreement among exhibitors about who would negotiate initially for a given film: after distributors sent out competitive bid letters, only the designated exhibitors would bid on the film, the others awaiting their turns). The latter two methods were the ones most commonly used in the fifties, sixties, and seventies; although they were challenged on occasion, the courts found them to be an efficient means of preventing the wealthiest exhibitors from cornering the market.

In April 1977, the Justice Department reversed its thirty-year position and declared splitting to be an illegal form of rigging the licensing of pictures. The federal court in Virginia where the Justice Department brought suit, however, decided that if distributors acquiesced in splitting arrangements then they weren't illegal. In the early eighties, the Justice Department again challenged splitting, this time among the four largest exhibitors in Milwaukee, and on this occasion splitting was declared illegal, a position affirmed by the federal appeals court in Chicago in 1985.

Over the next couple of years, the Justice Department imposed heavy fines on several exhibitors nationwide for splitting, a move that put studios in a better economic position to handle exhibition. Then, in 1988, Warner Brothers petitioned the federal district court in New York for an order modifying its antitrust decree, allowing Warners to

join forces with Paramount in taking ownership of Cinamerica Theaters—a chain encompassing over a hundred movie houses, including
the Mann chain—and after a year-long review the Justice Department,
under the Reagan administration, allowed them to go ahead. When the
federal appeals court in New York affirmed this decision and made it
even more conclusive by being nonrestrictive, the argument they used
was that allowing the studios to compete with distributors—many of
which came into existence thanks to the economic boom of the eighties—was only fair, because the studios had been under the thumb of
the courts and the distributors weren't.[1]

My own cinephilia arose from the fact that I grew up in a family in
Alabama that ran a chain of movie theaters. Curiously, however, I was
the only member of my family who qualified fully as a cinephile, then
or now. My grandfather, who started the business, enjoyed movies but
was no aficionado, and my father, who worked for him, was usually far
from passionate about seeing them; he preferred to read books. My
three brothers went to movies more often than most of their friends, but
more out of habit than out of any sense of vocation.

My grandfather had partners in Tennessee who owned other theaters, and in the late forties the government, as a test case, sued him
and his partners for holding a monopoly of theaters in that part of the
South. As a consequence the partnership had to be dissolved, and my
grandfather's chain became reluctantly independent in 1956; it
remained so until these theaters were sold in 1960. (By that time, I
should add, my cinephilia was fully formed, and I had already left
Alabama to attend school in the North.) During those last four years,
these theaters probably showed more foreign-language pictures than
they ever had before.

This is because during the same period, art cinemas, a particular
example of independent exhibition, were springing up all across America. This movement was spearheaded by the enormous success of two
Roberto Rossellini films in 1946, *Open City* and *Paisa*, each of which

---

[1] For all the information in this section, as well as some later facts about current control of exhibition, I'm deeply indebted to Chicago lawyer and film buff
Daniel Neppl, who generously gave me a crash course in the subject.

grossed close to a million dollars in the states—an enormous sum in those days. By the time my family's business became Rosenbaum Theaters, there were hundreds of such art theaters in America, and by the late sixties—when the French New Wave and the popularity of other European directors like Michelangelo Antonioni, Ingmar Bergman, Bernardo Bertolucci, Federico Fellini, Miklós Jancsó, and Andrzej Wajda was already in full flower—there were over a thousand. (Although this seems to contradict my assertion in the previous chapter that many films by these directors flopped, the expectations of small businesses versus those of the large studios and corporations accounts for this discrepancy. By analogy, I've often marveled at the relative capacity of French publishers to print limited edition publications of a thousand copies or less and deem their efforts completely successful if these editions sell out.)

Films showing at these independent theaters were usually rented for a flat fee—unlike big Hollywood films, which were booked on a percentage basis, with the distributors collecting a particular fraction of the ticket prices. Many of these theaters eventually became repertory and revival houses, and during the seventies, they began to show midnight movies such as *Night of the Living Dead*, *The Rocky Horror Picture Show*, and *Eraserhead*—a form of exhibition that became possible only because the theaters were independent.

Within such a setup, it was even possible to experiment and develop certain tastes that otherwise might have never prospered. In the book *Midnight Movies* (Harper & Row, 1983; second edition, Da Capo, 1991) that I coauthored with J. Hoberman, there is a detailed account of how former distributor Ben Barenholtz kept *Eraserhead* playing in theaters at midnight for week after week and month after month before the film finally found its audience, thereby launching the career of David Lynch. There were only twenty-five people in the theater on opening night in New York's Cinema Village in 1977, twenty-four the second night, but Barenholtz persisted and kept the film running for almost a year. A year later, Barenholtz opened it again in New York at the Waverly, where it more than doubled its first run—playing ninety-nine weekends through mid-September 1981, a run that ended only when the theater closed to build a second screen. According to Lynch himself, there was never a single point when the film simply "took off":

"It was a very gradual incline." But it proved that persistence of this kind—which is possible only in independent theaters, at least according to the way most chains are run—can eventually reap spectacular dividends, especially when it comes to creating and developing new markets. And nurturing offbeat films remained possible even for certain movies that didn't play at midnight. In the early eighties, when enough independent theaters were still around, Dan Talbot of New Yorker Films was able to work comparable wonders with the art-house releases of Wayne Wang's *Chan Is Missing* and Louis Malle, Wallace Shawn, and André Gregory's *My Dinner with André*—keeping both films playing in theaters week after week until they eventually attracted sizable audiences.

In spite of the gradual erosion of this practice, for reasons that I'll get to shortly, there are still occasional films that manage to find their audiences over a period of weeks rather than simply over a matter of days. According to Ted Hope, cochairman of the independent production company Good Machine, Mike Leigh's *Life Is Sweet*, released in 1990, did its best business during the eighth week of its run. Whether it had a ninth week isn't something I've gotten around to researching, but independent producer Christine Vachon, the source of this quote, adds, "Less than a decade later, a movie would never get to its eighth week unless it was doing gangbusters." She cites in particular Todd Haynes's first-rate *Safe*, which she produced: "By the time people were starting to talk about the film, it was gone from the theaters."[2]

It was the proliferation of independent theaters in the fifties, sixties, and seventies that made the eventual success of an *Eraserhead* and a *Life Is Sweet* possible. In the eighties, however, the Justice Department under the Reagan and Bush administrations began to stop enforcing the antitrust laws in the manner described earlier; in Washington, D.C., I'm told, the antitrust division, which still exists as a ghost of its former self, is jokingly referred to as the "trust division." As the market for independent theaters began to shrink accordingly, the alternative venues represented by foreign films and midnight movies became increasingly specialized and rarified, apart from the few foreign pic-

---

[2] *Shooting to Kill*, London: Bloomsbury/New York: Avon Books, 1998, p. 315.

tures that studio-owned distributors such as Miramax decided to put their weight behind. Meanwhile, the growth of the so-called "infotainment" industry over the same period—devoted to granting free publicity in all the media to studio product and practically nothing to anything else—has made the survival of independent movies and theaters even more precarious than it used to be. Finally, the recent decimation of the National Endowment of the Arts—which funds not only independent filmmaking, but nontheatrical distribution and exhibition—has more or less delivered the coup de grâce to practically everything except what the studios decide to shove our way. (*The Blair Witch Project*, boosted by alternative methods of advertising, might be termed the exception that proves the rule—a rare instance of a public demand forcing exhibitors to go along with it. One can only hope that other exceptions may also challenge the rules.) Even before this decimation, the U.S. government gave fewer and smaller grants to artists than almost any other industrialized country in the world; the annual grants given to military marching bands were bigger than all its arts grants combined.

While researching this chapter, I spoke with Chicago movie theater consultant Barry Schein and a representative of the National Association of Theater Owners (or NATO) in California, asking each of them how many independent movie theaters currently existed in the United States, and the difference between their responses was instructive. Shein told me that the fifty most powerful and successful American movie exhibitors had 47.2 percent of the locations and 76.5 percent of the screens, which breaks down to an average of 7.09 screens per location. The other exhibitors had 52.8 percent of the locations and 23.9 percent of the screens, which breaks down to an average of 1.5 screens per location. He added that in January 1999—we were speaking the following July—there were 7,811 movie theaters in the United States with 34,186 screens, and that each year there was roughly a 1.14 percent decrease in theaters and a 6 to 8 percent increase in screens.

But when I asked the NATO representative, whom I spoke to the same day, how many U.S. theaters were independent, he replied that he couldn't answer that question because the term meant so many different things to different people that it was effectively meaningless. Personally, I don't see how "independent theater" could ever be meaningless, because the differences between an art theater showing independent features and a mall theater showing studio product are apparent to everyone. No matter how one defines "independent," at least in relative terms there are fewer independent movie houses today than there were even before 1948. Today the major markets in American film exhibition are controlled and owned mainly by the Paramount-Warners partnership, Sony (which owns Columbia/Tri-Star and Loews), Matsushita (the parent of Universal, which owns half of Cineplex Odeon), United Artists Theatre Circuit, American Multi-Cinema, General Cinema, Carmike, Cinemark, and National Amusements—in most cases, major corporations. In 1997, Sony merged with Cineplex Odeon, and although they were legally required to divest certain theaters, they still continue to rule most of the Chicago film scene monopolistically, without challenge from the Justice Department. On the other hand, even the handful of independent theaters that have managed to survive in the nineties are hampered by having to play ball with the studios to get some of the pictures they need to show in order to survive. In order to play a *Pulp Fiction*, for instance, they typically might have to show several other pictures handled by the same distributor. (Guess which one.) And to make matters still worse, the question of what is and what isn't an independent feature has been thoroughly muddled by the media, by the distributors, and by the Sundance Film Festival, all these institutions often working in cozy tandem.

Now that truly independent features are becoming as much of an endangered species as independent theaters—a situation that so far seems only marginally improved by the runaway success of *The Blair Witch Project*—the game essentially belongs to movies that can prove their box-office mettle the same weekend that they open, whether these are independent or studio efforts, and in order to score in those terms, millions of dollars usually—if not invariably—have to be spent. What effect does this pressure wind up having on most of the movies we hear about? See the next chapter.

* * *

Writing around the time of the release of *Star Wars, Episode I—The Phantom Menace*, I've encountered more acknowledgment than usual in the press that the will of the audience and the success of a movie at the box office aren't necessarily interchangeable. J. Hoberman's review in the *Village Voice*, for example, spells out some of the reasons why:

> However anticlimactic, *The Phantom Menace* is not only critic-proof but audience-resistant as well. The movie has already made its money back ten times over through Pepsi's just launched merchandising blitz alone, and thanks to Lucas's pressure on theatrical exhibitors to guarantee lengthy exclusive runs (and the decision by rival distributors to cede him the rest of the spring), it would take the consumer equivalent of the Russian Revolution to keep *The Phantom Menace* from ruling the box office for weeks.[3]

What's new about *The Phantom Menace* is not so much the business methodology as the size of the apparent discrepancy this creates between what an audience wants and what it gets. Back in the mid-seventies, when I was working as assistant editor on *Monthly Film Bulletin* at the British Film Institute in London, I can recall seeing and reviewing one of the worst big-budget messes I've ever encountered in a lifetime of moviegoing—a caper movie about liquor smugglers in 1930 dodging the U.S. Coast Guard in San Diego and living it up in Tijuana. Here's an excerpt from my review to give you some idea of what was involved:

> With an outsized budget estimated variously at $12,600,000 (*Variety*) and £10,000,000 (*Daily Mirror*), three box-office favorites [Gene Hackman, Liza Minnelli, Burt Reynolds], and a script deliberately written, according to co-author Gloria Katz, as "the most commercial thing we could think up," *Lucky Lady* is both conspicuously overproduced and undernourished. The presence of Stanley Donen [as director] seems to count for little in a project that might more logically have been entrusted to a computer. All it has to express, quite simply, are its deliberations: to combine as many saleable features as can be packed on a screen within the space of two hours. A little of everything is thus tossed into the mixture; and a great deal of nothing emerges out of the isolation and autonomy of the assorted elements. For *Cabaret*-like nostalgia, [cinematographer] Geoffrey Unsworth creates a hazy milk-of-magnesia look with a dull sheen that obscures the details of the expensive sets and sea battles, both of which

---

[3] "All Droid Up," *Village Voice*, May 19–25, 1999.

seem to derive from other models. As the leading lady, Liza Minnelli is dressed in a fright wig worthy of a nightmare dreamed by Robert Aldrich, given two unmemorable songs to sing, and encouraged or allowed to deliver each comic line (sample: "It's so quiet you can hear a fish fart") as if she were explaining it to a child of four, crushing gags like so many acorns in her wake. . . . It is harder to guess at a strategy behind the tinny soundtrack—where all the voices seem to occupy the same disembodied plane—unless one cites a box-office precedent like *Deep Throat* or *The Night Porter*. . . . If, however, [the film] had concluded with the entire fleet of battling ships and all the characters consumed by one enormous tidal wave, thereby assimilating the disaster film and the science fiction epic into its strategies, it might have broadened its horizons far enough to encompass a few moments of old-fashioned entertainment.[4]

Nearly a quarter of a century has passed since then, and I have yet to encounter a single individual anywhere in my travels who admits to finding *Lucky Lady* halfway bearable, much less enjoyable. Yet only a year after its release, in *Variety*'s annual list of the "two hundred top moneymaking films of all time" (i.e., in movie-industry hyperbole, up until early 1977), it wound up in the one hundred and thirty-ninth place, having somehow grossed $12,107,000 in rentals—or about half a million less than its cost.

A veritable miracle, one might say. How could this have happened? It was easy. Given the stars and budget, Twentieth Century-Fox demanded in advance that *Lucky Lady* be kept in theaters for extended runs if those theaters wanted to book it at all—a bargaining chip quite similar to George Lucas's demand to exhibitors wanting to show *The Phantom Menace*, incidentally handled by the same studio. This meant that for long periods of time, in small towns across America, *Lucky Lady* was often the only movie playing, even if every one in town who'd already seen it hated it. So if you wanted to see a movie—any movie, for any reason—you saw *Lucky Lady*, regardless of what your friends said. It's a bit like the orange juice and liquid soap jokes cited in the introduction: for years after its release, Fox executives could confidently claim that *Lucky Lady* was exactly what the American public wanted, because that's what they went to, in droves.

---

[4] *Monthly Film Bulletin*, February 1976, vol. 43, no. 505, p. 31.

Chapter Three
Some Vagaries of Promotion and Criticism

A much more common and systematic method of obfuscating business practices in the film industry, especially in blurring the lines between journalism and publicity, is the movie junket. Here's how it generally works: a studio at its own expense flies a number of journalists either to a location where a movie is being shot or to a large city where it is being previewed, puts the journalists up at fancy hotels, and then arranges a series of closely monitored interviews with the "talent" (most often the stars and the director). The journalists are then expected to go home and write puff pieces about the movies in question, run in newspapers and magazines as either reportage or as a classy form of "film criticism." If these journalists don't oblige—and sometimes obliging entails not only favorable coverage, but articles with particular emphases set by publicists, articles that screen out certain forbidden topics and hone in on certain others—then the studios won't invite them back to future junkets.

There are probably more of these kinds of articles about new or forthcoming movies in newspapers and magazines than any other kind, and many entertainment writers—including a number who also double as film reviewers—make a veritable profession out of these junkets. The stories that result are obviously meant to be read and enjoyed as news rather than as promotion, and most newspaper editors seem to have few qualms about fostering this false impression. It's often standard procedure, in fact, for publicists to work directly with editors and get particular journalists assigned to write particular pieces, which means in effect that the articles are commissioned by the studios (or distributors) and then whipped into the desired shape by the editors and writers.

And it wouldn't be fair to ascribe this sort of practice only to the big-time players in the industry; even marginal distributors sometimes get into the act as well. I was once approached by the distributor of a film by Jean-Luc Godard about writing something for *The New Yorker* to promote its release; the distributor had already been in touch with an editor there and was trying to set something up. Given my sympathy for the film, the offer seemed irresistible, and I obligingly sent off a letter of proposal to the editor in question. If memory serves, the final piece — which wound up as a small item in the magazine's listings section — wound up being written by the editor himself.

The only full-scale junket I ever participated in was in late 1981, when an old college friend who was an editor at *Omni* arranged for me to visit British Columbia, where John Carpenter's remake of *The Thing* was being shot. The offer came almost immediately after I was fired from the *Soho News*, a Manhattan weekly where I had been working for over a year as a film and book reviewer — my main source of income at the time — so it was hard to turn down this opportunity, especially because I didn't have any other easily discernible way of paying my next month's rent in Hoboken. So I flew to Seattle in mid-December, staying over in a hotel at my own expense (with the promise of an eventual refund), then caught a 7:10 A.M. flight on Alaskan Airlines to Ketchikan. From there I took a bus to Stewart, a B.C.-Alaska border town in the cold heart of the Klondike, where I first discovered the 100-proof Canadian liqueur Yukon Jack (bottled in Connecticut) and was put up at a local motel along with the only other journalist on that particular junket, Bob Martin, who edited three teenage magazines (*Starlog*, *Fangoria*, and *Twilight Zone*). The next morning, we rode in the darkness up a mountain, were given special jumpsuits to prevent us from freezing, and led to the remote site where Carpenter, cast, and crew were shooting, assisted by artificial wind and snow machines to make it all look more authentic. Martin and I got to witness the explosion of a cabin and say hello to the star, Kurt Russell, but Carpenter was too busy to talk to us. This proved to be no problem as far as my article for *Omni* was concerned; as soon as I returned to Hoboken, Carpenter phoned me for a proper interview, and all I was expected to do according to junket protocol was pretend that whatever he said to me was said on location. (Getting my refund for the Seattle hotel room was a dicier matter until I became more aggressive about placing collect calls at odd hours to the publicist, and eventually to the producer.)

Junkets and what they produce have never been a secret, but some commentators who've stumbled accidentally upon them act as if they were. Even as sophisticated a writer as *Time* art critic Robert Hughes was shocked in the spring of 1999 when he went to see *The Phantom Menace* with his girlfriend's kids and discovered that it wasn't what the hoopla promised. Amazed at how George Lucas's "decadence as a film-maker resonates and, in that depressing term, 'synergizes' with the decadence of movie coverage in the American media," he went on to complain in the May 16 issue of the *New York Daily News*:

> He has managed to broker, or more exactly, enforce, a situation by which hundreds of thousands of promotional words have been churned out and published about *The Phantom Menace* by writers who were specifically forbidden by Lucas to see it; and the said writers went right along with it, because, in the end, the tail of Hollywood was wagging the ass, if not the whole dog, of journalism.

Though belated recognition is always preferable to no recognition at all, what seems surprising about Hughes's outrage is the implication that if all these journalists had seen *The Phantom Menace* weeks in advance, they might not have written the same sort of promotional blather about it. For by bringing the entertainment press to its knees, Lucas proved that a critical reading of the movie was irrelevant to what the mass media saw as its duty. To my mind, this was no more egregious or grotesque than the front-page coverage accorded to, say, Oliver Stone's *JFK* and the American Film Institute's "One Hundred Best American Films" in *The New York Times,* or the kind of promotional reviews *Schindler's List* and *Saving Private Ryan* received almost every-where in the United States when they came out. Media overkill of this kind was fully operational well before *The Phantom Menace* was a gleam in George Lucas's eye, so it's possible that what made the differ-ence for some observers like Hughes is simply that it became more obvious with the Lucas movie. After all, the same month, *Newsweek* ran a cover story on *The Phantom Menace* complaining about the media overkill while fully acknowledging that it was part of that overkill—unlike Hughes's own magazine, *Time*, which simply went along with the drift.

If you've ever wondered where all the enthusiastic superlatives from reviewers in movie ads come from, you might be surprised to learn that many of these quotes are not extracts from longer reviews but blurbs supplied by professional blurb writers—some of whom go to the trouble of writing their own blurbs, while others actually commission blurbs from writers who attend the press screenings. It's also been reported more than once that studios often suggest several possible blurbs to these writers and invite them to select one, apparently in order to make their job less taxing. If such practices naturally lower the credibility of film criticism as a whole, I'm inclined to regard this as a healthy rather than negative development, if only because it encourages more skepticism toward infotainment in general—an industry that, realistically speaking, includes most film reviewing as well as most so-called film journalism.

It also includes such things as TV coverage of film festivals. I've never attended Telluride, but I'll never forget the national TV report on that event a few years back when members of the cast and crew of Oliver Stone's *U-Turn*, including Stone, were seated outdoors in a semicircle hawking their movie and incidentally commenting on how pleasant the festival was because you didn't have to "do" press there. This provided a Proustian flashback to a remote memory of mine from my teens in Alabama: paging through an issue of *Photoplay*, which my grandmother subscribed to, and coming across a photo spread devoted to Fabian's very first date as a star without the interference or presence of any press or photographers. In point of fact, the infotainment industry has been around as long as movies, and was fully in place back in the fifties, even if it didn't have a label back then. Whether it masks its operations any more smoothly today than it did half a century ago is debatable.

* * *

One of my oldest and dearest friends, Meredith Brody, is a cinephile who's as addicted to movie lists as I am. We met at the Cinémathèque in Paris in the early seventies and usually see each other every year at the Toronto Film Festival. She lives in Hollywood and works mainly as a restaurant critic, though she also writes frequently about movies.

When I first met Meredith, she was keeping a list of all the films she saw in Paris. These days, in L.A., she keeps a kind of scrapbook devoted to all the films opening locally that she doesn't see — pasting in newspaper ads of each of them that she later removes if and when she sees the picture.

While I was visiting her over a weekend in December 1998, she started to read aloud some of the titles in her scrapbook, all of them pasted in over the previous six months. Most if not all of these movies had played in Chicago, which meant that even if I hadn't seen them I'd read some promotional material about them, assigned them to the second-string reviewer at my paper, and read her subsequent capsule review — or else written a descriptive capsule myself. Yet the curious and disturbing thing about Meredith's list of titles was that whether I had seen them or not and regardless of whether or not they had shown in Chicago and I had read anything about them, a good eighty percent of them were absolutely opaque and lacking in any resonance for me, even after Meredith read aloud their ad copy.

Could this be explained by premature senility on my part, an incapacity to remember anything in my mid-fifties? I doubt it, because hearing a list of random commercial titles from the forties, fifties, sixties, seventies, or eighties wouldn't draw the same blank from me — or from Meredith either, who's still in her forties. (Some might argue that it's easy to forget how many wretched movies were made during those earlier decades, when the task of furnishing theaters with product on a more regular basis made the likelihood of indifferent and unmemorable work even higher. But I'm sure I would still remember more of the lesser movies of 1956 than the bulk of the 1998 output.) The fact is, movies can get away with being terrible these days without causing any crisis in the film industry, because no matter how much the capacity to make movies that matter has been impaired, the capacity to advertise, market, and disseminate them has only improved. From a business standpoint, this is far more important than whether or not we care about these movies.

How, one may ask, could this possibly be true? If movies today have become as terrible as I'm implying, wouldn't people stop seeing them?

Maybe they would if the will of the people were as decisive a cultural influence as we like to believe it is, but I'm beginning to have my doubts. Much as the imposed and enforced "consensus" of the Stalinist state made it impossible to figure out what Soviet citizens really wanted until the state power was phased out—and I daresay it remains a somewhat cloudy issue today—finding out what the American public "really" thinks about movies apart from the fancies of corporate executives and journalists is no less difficult. And we can't turn to journalism for a definitive answer because the profession is mainly devoted to spreading and running minor variations on the corporate cover stories.

Consider what might happen if Roger Ebert couldn't find a single movie to recommend on one of his weekly shows. Or let's assume that this has already happened once or twice. How much freedom would he have to assign a thumbs-down to everything three or four weeks in a row without getting his show canceled? And for all the unusual amount of freedom I enjoy at the *Chicago Reader*, how long could I keep my job if I had nothing to recommend week after week? For just as Communist film critics were "free" to write whatever they wanted as long as they supported the Communist state, most capitalist film critics today are "free" to write anything as long as it promotes the products of multicorporations; the minute they decide to step beyond this agreed-upon canon of "correct" items, they're likely to get into trouble with their editors and publishers.

This isn't to say that critics aren't free to express their dislike for certain expensive studio productions; what they aren't free to do, in most cases, is to ignore these releases entirely or focus too much of their attention on films whose advertising budgets automatically make them marginal in relation to the mainstream media. The fact that I'm able to do this considerably more than the majority of my colleagues is merely the exception that proves the rule, and it only applies to my writing for the *Chicago Reader*. The only two times I've appeared on Chicago's nightly TV talk show *Chicago Tonight*, I've been forced to speak almost exclusively about studio releases. The first time, in 1994, was around the time of Oscar night; the second time was the day after Christmas two years later, and, weary of being obliged to promote only movies that were "important" because of the studio muscle behind them, I agreed to appear only if I'd be allowed to speak about a couple of foreign and independent pictures. This privilege was eventually granted to me—after a show devoted exclusively to promoting garbage like *Evita*—over the brief closing credits, and it's why I'm unlikely ever to agree to appear on the show again.[1]

No less typical was the refusal of *The New Yorker* to give even capsule reviews to either Jim Jarmusch's *Dead Man* or André Téchiné's *Thieves*, two of the most important U.S. releases of 1996—and, coincidentally, the two movies I wanted to discuss but couldn't on *Chicago Tonight* because prime time had to be reserved exclusively for the forgettable "big" movies of the moment, no matter how awful. (Such restrictions can lead to a lot of wishful thinking: one colleague on the show explained how *Evita* reminded him of Bertolt Brecht.)

The reasons for the neglect of these two features in *The New Yorker* are probably not identical, apart from the fact that in both cases they weren't deemed important enough by its film reviewers. *Dead Man* was distributed by Miramax and *Thieves* by Sony Classics, a comparably large company. I don't think Sony Classics could be blamed for *The New Yorker* overlooking *Thieves*—a neglect that undoubtedly has mainly to do with an overall neglect of foreign-language movies that was spearheaded by Pauline Kael during her last years as critic there but has become commonplace in virtually all mainstream magazines since then. But in the case of *Dead Man*, I don't think it would be an exaggeration to say that Miramax played a role in the film's neglect, especially when one considers that this was the first of Jarmusch's features

----

[1] I had a much happier experience appearing on Roger Ebert's TV show, along with fellow Chicago reviewers Dan Gire, Ray Pride, and Michael Wilmington, on a special show devoted to Stanley Kubrick's *Eyes Wide Shut* (July 17 and 18, 1999)—a film that all of us liked, in contrast to most of our New York colleagues. This experience confirmed my suspicion that network television is paradoxically more open to alternative points of view than PBS. Although the issue of speaking about independent and foreign films wasn't relevant in this case and the constraints of the show's format clearly limited what we could say, I did feel that the final editing of Ebert's show fairly and accurately represented what we said during the lengthy taping. There was certainly no sense of being censored, as there has been in all my dealings with *Chicago Tonight*.

to have been snubbed by *The New Yorker* in this fashion. (That it also happens to be the best of Jarmusch's features, in my opinion, is a point worth arguing.) As soon as it became apparent that Jarmusch, protected by his contract and by his ownership of the film's negative, refused to allow Miramax to recut *Dead Man* for its American release, the distributor's lack of enthusiasm for the film became obvious, and manifested itself in a number of ways. When, for instance, the programmer of a Jarmusch retrospective contacted Miramax about showing the film, he was advised not to because it was lousy. Jarmusch himself publicly denounced Miramax's handling of the film when he accepted an award for Robby Müller's cinematography at the New York Film Critics Circle's annual dinner, and was subsequently supported in his protest at the same event by Albert Brooks—who had dark stories of his own about how his own first feature, *Real Life*, had been handled by its distributor.

A good example of the sort of film Miramax puts its muscle behind is *The Wings of the Dove*; among the major films it has chosen to dump over the past few years even more flagrantly than *Dead Man* are Abbas Kiarostami's *Through the Olive Trees*, the color version of Jacques Tati's *Jour de fête*, and the restoration of Jacques Demy's *The Young Girls of Rochefort*. The fact that *The Wings of the Dove* was treated with vastly more respect and attention by the national press than any of these pictures—which implied that a soft-core, middlebrow reduction and distortion of a late Henry James novel was vastly more important than key works by four of our greatest filmmakers—was almost entirely a function of the message sent out by its distributor, both in terms of advertising dollars and in terms of overall handling. The insulting implication that this emphasis accurately reflected the taste of the public is of course impossible to prove (or disprove); to say that Miramax's campaign "worked" on the public as well as on the critics doesn't mean that a comparable campaign on behalf of the color *Jour de fête* wouldn't have worked as well, even if the targeted audience would have been substantially different.

From the vantage point of Chicago, *Jour de fête* and *The Young Girls of Rochefort* received limited runs only because the Music Box, the principal independent Chicago art theater showing foreign-language pictures, made repeated requests to show them; when Miramax finally agreed, it stipulated that no money be spent advertising these pictures. In the case of *Through the Olive Trees,* which received an even more limited run at the Art Institute's Film Center, no advance screenings for the press were permitted and even requests for videos for preview purposes were denied. Is it any surprise, therefore, that none of these three pictures was reviewed on Gene Siskel and Roger Ebert's TV show? The fact that Disney owns Miramax and produced the Siskel-Ebert show might prompt conspiracy theories about this process, but in fact no conspiracies are necessary to explain this neglect. (On other occasions, I should add, Siskel and Ebert went out of their way to support relatively independent efforts such as Jon Jost's *All the Vermeers in New York.*) Miramax has the clout to dictate which of its releases are important and which are not, simply due to a radical failure of nerve, imagination, knowledge, and intelligence on the part of magazine and newspaper editors, TV producers, and reviewers—none of whom expect to be called on their decisions because these are virtually invisible to the public.

The whole notion of expertise in film criticism is cripplingly tautological: according to current practice in the United States, a "film expert" is someone who writes or broadcasts about film, full stop, yet most "film experts" are hired not on the basis of their knowledge about film but because of their capacity to reflect the existing tastes of the public. The late Serge Daney understood this phenomenon perfectly—and made it clear that it was far from exclusively American—when he remarked that the media "ask those who know nothing to represent the ignorance of the public and, in so doing, to legitimize it."

Case in point: Chicago film critics who often attended the same screenings as Roger Ebert and Gene Siskel were aware that the former is a hardcore film buff and the latter, who died in early 1999, was someone whose interest in film, at least to all appearances, was almost exclusively professional. (When Siskel first started writing for the *Chicago Tribune,* his main beat was real estate.) For instance, Ebert attends several film festivals every year and Siskel generally made it to few or none. After attending Cannes only once, as a TV reviewer in 1990, Siskel showed no interest in returning, and one could surmise that his relatively low recognition factor abroad might have been partially to blame. Ebert reviews a good many film books, and to my knowledge Siskel never did; if he ever read any books about film on his own, it would have surprised me. Inside the profession, Siskel was famous for making so many gaffes about movies in his weekly print reviews that Neil Tesser in the *Chicago Reader* used to run a weekly feature that inventoried them, entitled "Siskel Watch," long before I came to Chicago; later, I was told Siskel's mistakes became fewer after his copy began to be regularly and extensively checked by others.

This doesn't necessarily mean that I wound up agreeing with Ebert's judgments more than Siskel's on their TV show. Gene's own strength was a commonsensical approach based on his own extensive experience as a reviewer, and it often served him well. But if one mentioned the discrepancy in backgrounds, orientations, and apparent interests between Siskel and Ebert to a nonspecialized viewer of their show—noting simply that one of them was clearly an enthusiastic film buff while the other just as clearly wasn't—the most common response was to query which one was the enthusiastic film buff. In other words, though I regard Siskel and Ebert as the best by far of the TV reviewers, the show's format made it virtually impossible to recognize informed opinion or expertise; matters of film history and aesthetics were virtually beside the point.

So it wasn't surprising to hear it said of Siskel, shortly after he died, that he "loved movies"—an assertion made on the cover of *TV Guide*, by Whoopi Goldberg on the 1999 Academy Awards telecast, by Janet Maslin in the *New York Times* (whose own disinterest in movies, apart from the movie business, may even surpass Siskel's), and in many comparable places and circumstances. If in fact he did love movies independently of his professional duties, he did a superb job of hiding this fact from his colleagues. The only extended conversations I ever had with him were on the subjects of Anita Hill (at the time of the Clarence Thomas hearings) and his own show, and I never heard about him casually discussing any movie, new or old, with any other colleague.

Yet the potency of Gene's TV profile was such that in July 2000— five months before the new, expanded, and more prominent headquarters of the Art Institute's Film Center, Chicago's principal nontheatrical film venue, was scheduled to open—it was announced with some fanfare that it would be renamed The Gene Siskel Film Center. And it was equally telling that this new name was widely perceived within Chicago as a sort of cosmopolitan calling card that would make the Film Center better known outside the United States; as Tony Jones, president of the School of the Art Institute, expressed it, "We think it is a fitting tribute to Gene because he helped focus the international entertainment spotlight on Chicago."

But did Siskel actually do that? If the Film Center's new name makes its cultural agenda more user-friendly for a wider public, then the renaming would be justified—even if it still might foster a certain amount of confusion, as renaming the Art Institute the Entertainment Institute undoubtedly would. On the other hand, whether it would enhance the institution's international reputation is questionable, for outside the highly circumscribed world of U.S. television, Siskel's name is no more meaningful than that of, say, O. J. Simpson. And even within the world of Chicago, Gene was far from being the Film Center's most faithful supporter, at least as a journalist. According to Chicago writer Patrick McGavin, Siskel reviewed only one Film Center program between 1986 and 1998—in contrast to the hundred or so pieces done by Dave Kehr over seven years, or the 341 published by Michael Wilmington in only five years, both for the same paper.

Ebert and Siskel's show may well have represented one of the many points in our film culture where reviewing shades off into promotion and coverage becomes more important than evaluation. Given the huge promotional budgets of most studio releases, this is probably inevitable; the furnishing of clips for a TV review or for a TV preview is not necessarily the same process, but to the untrained viewer it often looks like the same thing, and in many cases it *is* virtually the same thing. By the same token, the newspaper reader who can't easily distinguish between film criticism and film promotion—between the reviews of movies and the news stories about them—isn't so much naive as hip to what's going on.

* * *

The first contemporary film critic I ever read regularly with admiration was Dwight Macdonald, who wrote a monthly column for *Esquire* between 1960 and 1966. I was between the ages of seventeen and twenty-three during this period, and for the first couple of those years became friendly with one of Macdonald's sons, Nick (who subsequently became a filmmaker, and once persuaded me to run off to see Jean Renoir's *The Rules of the Game* for the first time, in New York, during one of our school breaks). Towards the end of Dwight Macdonald's stint at *Esquire*, when I was an undergraduate at Bard College and running the Friday night film series on campus, I invited him to give a lecture there, and spent an enjoyable evening with him.

Though I can't say I agreed with Macdonald's taste about everything—my favorite film in the mid-sixties, F. W. Murnau's *Sunrise*, was something that bored him to tears—he provided much of my initial route into film as an art form, and I was as enthusiastic about his polemical prose style as I was about his taste and critical perceptions. Yet by the time he collected his film pieces in the late sixties, in a collection called *On Movies*, my feeling about his work was already becoming modified. Part of this seemed to be due to a change in Macdonald's own positions; after all, he had essentially launched his *Esquire* column by heralding and defending Alain Resnais's *Hiroshima, mon amour*, Jean-Luc Godard's *Breathless*, John Cassavetes's *Shadows*, and Michelangelo Antonioni's *L'avventura*, and concluded his stint as a film reviewer by denouncing Resnais's *Muriel*, Antonioni's *Eclipse*, and Orson Welles's *The Trial*, among other films, while ignoring the subsequent films of Godard. But part of it came from a growing suspicion that Macdonald's grasp of film history was partial and in some ways superficial.

This was eventually brought home to me by the juxtaposition of two statements in *On Movies*. The first, which begins the second paragraph of the book's "Forenotes," is, "I know something about cinema after forty years, and being a congenital critic, I know what I like and why." The second occurs seventeen pages later, in the fourth paragraph of the book's first essay, "Agee on the Movies." It's a passing remark on a letter James Agee sent him in 1927 that Macdonald has just quoted from: "'Why was movie jargon puzzling?' [Agee] begins and proceeds to explain the 'lap dissolve' (which I must confess it's taken me forty years to realize doesn't refer to holding the camera in the lap but to over*lapping*; should have read his letter more carefully). . . ."[2]

---

[2] *Dwight Macdonald on Movies*, New York: Da Capo, 1981, pp. ix and 5.

Though it's characteristically refreshing of Macdonald to cheerfully concede his ignorance about a technical term, it's still highly revealing what his candor exposes about what's expected from film critics, and what many film critics expect from themselves. Try to imagine, if you can, a respected literary critic at the end of his career writing, "I know something about literature after forty years," and then confessing without embarrassment, a few pages later, "I've just discovered that a semicolon is something other than half of part of the lower intestine that extends from the cecum to the rectum."

It might be argued, I suppose, that the importance of the semicolon in relation to literature exceeds the importance of the lap dissolve in relation to cinema, but even this position is somewhat debatable. I would counter that the lap dissolve is every bit as important to the work of Josef von Sternberg (a director, incidentally, that Macdonald treats fairly dismissively) as the semicolon is to the work of Henry James. I would further argue that the importance of lap dissolves and superimposed images in *Sunrise* is fundamental to the art of Murnau in that film. This doesn't mean that an acquaintance with the term "lap dissolve" would have necessarily altered Macdonald's appreciation for *Sunrise*, but it *does* at the very least suggest that his objections could have been voiced in a more sophisticated and intelligible fashion.

Magazine and newspaper editors, book publishers, and TV producers seem to deem a certain basic knowledge about the medium—considered obligatory to informed writing in our culture about painting, sculpture, theater, dance, architecture, literature, history, psychology, and countless other disciplines, not to mention sports—inessential when it comes to film. Consequently, Macdonald's passionate if imprecise engagement with cinema was every bit as unexceptional as Siskel's "love of movies." And both are reflected in the haphazard way in which *The New York Times Book Review*, *The New York Review of Books*, and the *Times Literary Supplement* assign reviewers to books about film, which isn't the case with books about the above subjects. (In the *Times Book Review*, Janet Maslin's review of David Thomson's *Rosebud* and Alexander Stille's review of Tag Gallagher's *The Adventures of Roberto Rossellini* are two examples of what I mean.)

Why? Part of the reason is that movies are regarded as a "democratic art," which means that anyone and everyone is entitled to have an opinion about them—a position that I am not in the least bit interested in contesting, at least insofar as I believe in democratic values. But problems begin when this democratic ideal becomes confused with issues of expertise—when, in short, anyone is proclaimed an expert precisely because he or she is publicly stating an opinion. I don't mean to suggest by this that either a Siskel or a Macdonald qualifies as an "anyone"; as I've already implied, both had their areas of competence as well as distinction. So do other colleagues whom I think even less of—respected reviewers who either hate what they're doing or feel so alienated by it that they wind up writing about not what they like but what they think or assume their readers will like.

It's clear that even alienated labor of this kind can provide helpful services to some people. But I object to turning this kind of alienation into a norm of criticism, which is what I see happening all around me—and to factoring in low estimations of the audience as a way of rationalizing low expectations on the part of reviewers. When alienation of this kind enters reviewing, a whole set of agendas apart from the movies themselves wind up determining much of the shape and drift of the critical discourse. Preconceptions set up by ads and promotional campaigns launched months in advance determine more of what the reviews say than anything in the movies themselves, and it's often felt that the major job of reviewers should be to ratify such preconceptions rather than attempt to refute them. The following chapter examines in detail one clear instance of how this gets played out.

Chapter Four
At War with Cultural Violence:
The Critical Reception of *Small Soldiers*

During the spring of 1998, not long before the American release of *Small Soldiers*, I happened upon "The Toys of Peace," a wise and wicked tale by Saki included in A. S. Byatt's recent collection, *The Oxford Book of English Short Stories*. Set in 1914, it recounts the noble and doomed efforts of the hero to interest his two nephews, aged nine and ten, in "peace toys": models of a municipal dustbin and the Manchester branch of the YWCA, lead figurines of John Stuart Mill, Robert Raikes (the founder of Sunday schools), a sanitary inspector, and a district councillor. Forty minutes later, he looks in on the boys and finds that they've converted these objects into war toys: the municipal dustbin punctured with holes to accommodate the muzzles of imaginary cannons, Mill dipped in red ink to approximate an eighteenth-century French colonel, with a grisly game plan mapped out to yield a maximum amount of bloodshed, including the remainder of the red ink splashed against the side of the YWCA building.

A mordant rejoinder to PC child rearing in 1914 England, Saki's story testifies to the long-standing lure of make-believe war to boys. Even more wicked and wise in some ways is Joe Dante's *Small Soldiers*—a trenchant satire rude enough to suggest that some of the make-believe wars boys like to play turn out to be the real ones, including those in Vietnam and the Persian Gulf. The sentiments and fabrications underlying such escapades, as this movie sees it, are not so different from those underlying the games little boys play. This is especially true for civilian spectators who watch the battles from afar, accepting the mise en scène of newscasters and governments the same way that kids accept the game plans of toy manufacturers. But it also applies to some of the participants—the eager enlistees programmed by movies to see warfare as a glorified form of kicking butt. Garry Wills's recent book, *John Wayne's America*, hypothesizes that it was our fantasies about a movie star that got us into Vietnam in the first place. And couldn't one argue that the two most successful American exports, movies and weapons, are both aggressive, fantasy-driven toys?

Small Soldiers opened in the United States in early July 1998, only two weeks prior to the release of *Saving Private Ryan*—a feature from the same Hollywood studio, DreamWorks, and directed by the man, Steven Spielberg, who effectively produced *Small Soldiers*—adding pertinence to the satire for anyone who cared to connect it with contemporary reality. To my way of thinking, Spielberg's film represented a sophisticated form of warmongering, motored by clever, mainstream adaptations of practically every war film he'd ever seen; yet although his own discourse was every bit as cross-referenced to other war films as Dante's, this fact seemed far from apparent to the American press, which applauded Spielberg's film precisely for its freshness and originality. Spielberg drew on second-degree memories of *All Quiet on the Western Front*, Fuller's war films, Kubrick's war films, *The Bridge on the River Kwai*, third-degree memories of John Ford's war films, and many others—complete with little kernels of wisdom culled from each of these sources—while *Small Soldiers* parodied *The Dirty Dozen* and *Apocalypse Now*, among others. But the same critical establishment that deemed *Small Soldiers* both old hat and commercially crass, a remake of either *Gremlins* or *Toy Story* (or, in some cases, improbably both) motivated by simple greed, declared *Saving Private Ryan* to be brand-new and morally enlightening. The impact of the extreme violence of the Normandy Beach landing near the beginning silenced criticism in the same way that shouting can sometimes win an argument.

In short, the media profiles accorded these two releases were so radically different that the relevance of Dante's film to Spielberg's went virtually unnoticed. As far as most of the public was concerned, *Small Soldiers* was anything but an auteur film: the name "Joe Dante," barely known in the first place among American filmgoers, was given so little emphasis in the film's advance publicity that I failed to notice it myself and came very close to missing the Chicago press screening, even though I've been a passionate fan of Dante's work at least since *Gremlins*. One way of partially accounting for this confusion was the deceptive nature of the ads—which I was later surprised to discover Dante had approved, perhaps as one way of negotiating and rationalizing his ambiguous alliance with the movie's intricate tie-ins with Burger King and the sale of various war toys. These ads foregrounded the toy soldiers known as the Commando Elite as if they were the movie's unironic heroes rather than its pathetically programmed comic villains, falsely equating the movie's essence with the crassness of Commando Elite's manufacturer in the movie, known as Globotech. Until I noted in the ads' fine print that Dante was the director, I came close to skipping the film myself thanks to this cheesy promo.

But don't we all tend to lay critical grids over most films before we see them? A year or so ago I discovered in *The Realist*, Paul Krassner's humor magazine, that the Chinese title of Oliver Stone's *Nixon* was *The Big Liar*—which led me to speculate that if Stone had had the balls to give his movie that title in English, I probably would have hated it less. (I also have to admit that the aura of hushed respect surrounding *Saving Private Ryan* already made me approach it with some suspicion; for that matter, I'm wary of trusting the rhetoric of any director who chooses to begin and end a picture with the waving of an American flag—even a somewhat grey and tarnished American flag, as in this case, still sounds a note of sanctity.)

Perceived almost exclusively as a summer release for small children with multiple commercial tie-ins, *Small Soldiers* was for the most part reviewed as such, and even though the two multiplex audiences I saw it with in Chicago—as well as the thousands of spectators at the outdoor piazza screening of the Locarno International Film Festival on August 7, 1998, a month after its U.S. opening, where it showed on a double bill with *There's Something About Mary*—appeared to fully understand and appreciate it as a satire, the same appreciation in the U.S. media was at best scattered, perhaps because the ads spoke louder than the movie itself. (This is often the case with high-profile studio releases. *Austin Powers: The Spy Who Shagged Me*, which had a production budget of $35 million, was said to have an advertising budget of between $35 and $40 million.)

By contrast, the same media perceived *Saving Private Ryan* almost immediately as a serious art film; like *Schindler's List* and *Amistad*, it was earmarked, long before any reviewers saw it, as a prestige item, a highly personal project, and consequently a brave commercial risk on the part of both Spielberg and DreamWorks. The fact that *The New Yorker* advertised a promotional interview with Spielberg on its cover by describing *Saving Private Ryan* as the film "to end all wars" was emblematic of the responses to the film elsewhere. Reviewers found it to be both serious and adult—further evidence of Spielberg's growing maturity as a film-maker, and a far cry from the money-grubbing cynicism and exploitative nature of something like *Small Soldiers*, which many of the most influential American film critics criticized for its violence, hypocrisy, and capacity to traumatize small children. No such criticism was waged against *Saving Private Ryan* because the much more graphic violence of the Normandy Beach sequence was taken to be a healthy jolt of reality, traumatizing only in a favorable sense by shocking the (supposedly adult) audience into a perception of the truth.

A characteristic phrase from *New York* magazine's capsule review by David Denby—the film critic who can be counted on most regularly to express American doublethink with the least amount of self-consciousness—is the assertion that *Saving Private Ryan* "blows every other World War II film out of the water." The use of a violent military metaphor to justify a supposedly pacifist or at least semi-pacifist war film should be connected ideologically and syntactically with *The New Yorker*'s previously cited cover blurb—i.e., "the film to end all wars that blows every other World War II film out of the water"—in order to understand more precisely the sort of hypocrisy that Dante's film exposes.

But I don't mean to suggest that the dismissal of Dante's work was exclusively the consequence of American publicity. An appreciation of the ethical force of *Small Soldiers* depends not only on a recognition of Joe Dante as a particular kind of satirist, but also on a sharing of certain generational attitudes, as well as on the timing of the release of *Saving Private Ryan*, which gave Dante's film a pointed relevance for me. Put somewhat differently, *Small Soldiers* thrives on its contextual references whereas *Saving Private Ryan* succeeds with audiences only when its own contextual references are overlooked. The media was inattentive to the references to other war movies in both cases because these went against the critical profiles these films were supposed to have—crass business motives in the case of *Small Soldiers*, heartfelt reflections of real-life experiences in the case of *Saving Private Ryan*.

The essential auteur of *Small Soldiers* was perceived by many American spectators to be Burger King, a not-unreasonable assumption given the film's promotional tie-in deals, not to mention the fact that, as I eventually discovered from Dante himself, Burger King had the final cut. In Locarno, the only hint of a tie-in or promotional gimmick came with the free hair gel handed out to spectators as a joke in conjunction with *There's Something About Mary*, so audiences were freer to respond to the movie on its own terms.

If Burger King indeed qualifies as the film's auteur and Dante is merely its struggling *metteur en scène*, *Small Soldiers* can indeed be read as hypocritical; if the movie exists mainly to sell war toys and Dante can only work in the margins of this project by ridiculing selling war toys—and selling, buying, and consuming wars—then the whole enterprise has to be regarded as a machine turned against itself. So the question of how adept some critics were in screening out the ridicule has to be joined with the question of how defenders such as myself managed to screen out Burger King's ad copy. In the final analysis, the heart of the matter is the question of what a movie consists of— a viewing experience or the central object in a marketing campaign. *Saving Private Ryan* was mainly treated as the former and *Small Soldiers* the latter, which accounts in part not only for the discrepancy between the two responses but also for the overall failure of the press to perceive any meaningful relationship between the two movies.

The following remarks are an attempt to chart that discrepancy and failure via my own particular reading of *Small Soldiers*.

* * *

Beginning with a TV commercial for Globotech, a huge conglomerate that boasts converting weaponry into peaceful uses—"beating swords into plowshares for you and your family"—*Small Soldiers* whisks us off to the first meeting of Globotech's CEO (Denis Leary) with two toy designers working for his latest acquisition, Heartland Play Systems. One of these designers, nerdy Irwin (David Cross)—a rough equivalent of Saki's idealist hero—believes in making educational, non-violent toys and has come up with a blueprint for benign, noble monsters known as the Gorgonites, creatures searching peacefully for Gorgon, their ancestral home. The other designer, hyper Larry (Jay Mohr), proposes the Commando Elite, a hard-ass squad of killer soldiers.

Scoffing at Irwin's qualms about violence and rationalizing his own preferences in movie-entertainment terms ("Don't call it violence—call it action. Kids love action"), the CEO combines these two projects into a single line of products by designating the mainly white Commandos, miniature Schwarzeneggers and Van Dammes, as good, old-fashioned American destroyers and the Gorgonites as their multiracial targets and victims, then sends both designers off to produce high-tech toys within six months. Eager to please his new boss, Larry filches Irwin's computer password and with it manages to acquire a microchip from the U.S. Defense Department, thereby empowering his Commandos with all the "action" they need.

When an early shipment of Commandos and Gorgonites is getting trucked through a small town in Ohio, a rebellious teenager named Alan (Gregory Smith), minding his father's New Age toy store, the Inner Child, persuades the trucker (Dick Miller) to turn over one set of the new products on consignment, despite the fact that his father (Kevin Dunn) won't stock war toys. Knowing that he can turn an easy buck by selling these toys on the sly while his father's away at a seminar on small businesses, Alan represents another version of Larry and the CEO—let's call it the entrepreneurial spirit—while his ineffectual father represents Irwin's bumbling idealism. But once both Commandos and Gorgonites break out of their boxes and become engaged in a full-scale war—the Commandos programmed to search and destroy, the Gorgonites programmed to hide and eventually lose—the humans in Alan's house and the family next door, including Christy (Kirsten Dunst), the girl Alan is pursuing—become caught in the crossfire and are forced to take sides. As the Commandos convert everyday domestic objects and appliances into weaponry, the grim undersides of consumer culture and kick-ass ideology come together in riotous, carnivalesque splendor.

Dante's satire doesn't simply target war and warmongering but the everyday cultural violence that encompasses them, by which I mean the violence *in* pop culture as well as the violence *of* pop culture. With the possible exception of *Inner Space,* just about all of Dante's best work is concerned with this cultural violence—cuddly Spielbergian pets in *Gremlins;* animated cartoons in "It's a Good Life," his segment of *Twilight Zone—The Movie;* TV in the finale of *The Explorers* and practically all of *The Second Civil War* (his prescient and neglected 1997 made-for-cable satire); xenophobia in *The 'Burbs* (despite the confusing ending); war fever in *Matinee;* corporate merchandising in *Gremlins 2: The New Batch*—and part of the exciting achievement of *Small Soldiers* is to combine all of these concerns into one streamlined statement.

Part of the kick of Dante's cheerful scorn is that it takes on not only the more obvious targets like *The Dirty Dozen* (by employing members of the original cast to speak the voices of the Commandos), but also the less obvious ones, like *Apocalypse Now*—already perceived by many as an antiwar film and hence something of a sacred cow, even in the nineties—while adroitly exposing the innate childishness of the overblown epic and heroic stances in all of them. The self-importance of a supposedly "balanced" portrait like *Patton* (Richard Nixon's favorite movie) is made to seem just as ludicrous as an imperialist adventure like *Rambo,* and the consumerist aspect of war films in general is kept in the foreground. This pointedly includes the hypocrisy of such flag-waving "history lessons" as the exploded and severed body parts in *Saving Private Ryan,* which are contrived simultaneously to sell tickets and to provide moral correctives to other war movies—though the movies being corrected often upped the violence quotient in their own eras with identical rationalizations and mixed motives.

An ironic syndrome: every time a director decides to make a war film more graphic in its violence than its predecessors, the argument seems to be, "This'll make someone think twice about wanting to go to war," but the apparent result is to make young male spectators even more eager to prove their mettle by diving into such bloodbaths. It's another version of the syndrome described in the Saki story, and one that has understandably prompted some critics to claim that there's no such thing as an antiwar war movie—though Spielberg, perennial exploitation apologist, has recently claimed the reverse, that "every war movie, good or bad, is an antiwar movie" (presumably including *Sands of Iwo Jima* and *The Green Berets*).

It might be argued that self-deception is central to Spielberg's achievements, as central to them as deceiving the public, because the two activities ultimately amount to the same thing. (Perhaps the apparent national desire to make Spielberg America's official guru and poet laureate is predicated on an implicit understanding that he's every bit as innocent about his motives as his audience—meaning that the audience knows it can safely remain innocent as long as he's the grown-up in charge.) Audiences wouldn't be nearly so susceptible to accepting the seriousness of Spielberg's "grown-up" projects if he weren't so adept at doing con jobs on himself. It surely takes a combination of innocence and show-biz smarts to convince an audience to contemplate the Holocaust by first getting them to identify with a Nazi who enjoys going to ritzy nightclubs. The same mentality led Spielberg to tell Stephen Schiff in *The New Yorker* that he received an enormous amount of pleasure from giving money to charities without telling anyone—without telling anyone, that is, except Schiff and his millions of readers. That's why the same man capable of claiming that *Jaws* was "his" Vietnam and that "every war movie, good or bad, is an antiwar movie" can convince other people that *Saving Private Ryan* is something other than one more recruiting film.

I'll never forget the experience I had escorting the late Samuel Fuller, the much-decorated World War II hero and maverick filmmaker, to a multiplex screening of *Full Metal Jacket*, along with fellow critic Bill Krohn, in Santa Barbara thirteen years ago. Though Fuller courteously stayed with us to the end, he declared afterward that as far as he was concerned, it was another goddam recruiting film—that teenage boys who went to see Kubrick's picture with their girlfriends would come out thinking that wartime combat was neat. Krohn and I were both somewhat flabbergasted by his response at the time, but in hindsight I think his point was irrefutable. There are still legitimate reasons for defending *Full Metal Jacket*, in my opinion—as a radical statement about what conditioning does to intelligence and personality, as a meditation on what the denial of femininity does to masculine definitions of civilization, as a deeply disturbing experiment in sprung and unsprung narrative, and no doubt as other things as well. But as a piece of propaganda against warfare, it remains specious and dubious, providing one more link in an endless chain of generic macho self-deceptions on the subject. And for all its technical flair, it might be argued that the principal achievement of *Saving Private Ryan* is to extend that sort of self-deception into the nineties.

* * *

Attempting to tabulate the forty-seven American reviews of *Small Soldiers* that I've read—a file that omits my own favorable review in the *Chicago Reader*, a few portions of which are recycled here—I note first of all that there's an almost even split: twenty-two are unfavorable, eighteen are favorable, and seven are mixed. But what constitutes "favorable," "unfavorable," and "mixed" is largely a matter of interpretation and hardly means the same thing to any two reviewers. For instance, Eric Layton's review for *Entertainment Today*, which I've identified as "mixed," concludes, "To fully enjoy *Small Soldiers*, ignore its murky political messages and just enjoy the exceedingly special effects—sort of like you did during *Armageddon*." Layton also argues, "Adam Rifkin's script is ostensibly a meditation on the dangers of military technology and the senselessness of war, but *Small Soldiers* is so immersed in violence, all moralizing is rendered moot." Rita Kempley voiced similar misgivings in the *Washington Post*, not because of the violence but because of the audience it addresses: although the movie's "message is more sophisticated than it seems . . . the target audience of 6-, 7- and 8-year-olds aren't about to read anything into this rowdy, repetitious war game. And they certainly aren't going to notice the hypocrisy inherent in a movie built around the violent children's entertainment it pretends to condemn." But Steve Murray in the *Atlanta Journal-Constitution* based his own mixed reactions on finding the film too derivative of *Toy Story*, *The Indian in the Cupboard*, the made-for-TV feature *Trilogy of Terror*, and, most of all, *Gremlins*: "That 1984 flick was also directed by Joe Dante, but he can't sue himself."

Perhaps a more meaningful tabulation would be how many of the reviews perceived the film as satirical, at least in its intentions, regardless of whether they were favorable or not. My rough estimate is that about two-thirds did, though interestingly enough the third that didn't included most of the reviews that appeared nationally and reached the largest number of readers, including, among others, those of Gene Siskel in the *Chicago Tribune,* Peter Travers in *Rolling Stone,* Joe Morgenstern in *The Wall Street Journal,* Peter Rainer in *New Times,* Leonard Klady in *Variety,* and David Ansen in *Newsweek.* And not even this imposing lineup includes the *Chicago Tribune's* Michael Wilmington, who alluded to the film's unfulfilled "satiric potential," but only in relation to toys; Roger Ebert (both in the *Chicago Sun-Times* and syndicated elsewhere), who noted a "satirical purpose" only in the evisceration of a member of the Commando Elite by a lawn mower; Dennis Lim in the *Village Voice,* who saw the satire directed exclusively against capitalism; Kenneth Turin in the *Los Angeles Times,* who noted only that Dante "does bring sweetness and a sense of satiric comedy to the human relationships"; and Janet Maslin in *The New York Times,* who criticized the film for directing "well-deserved satire at the toy industry" at the beginning and then "forgetting" to include any more of it later. (It's worth adding that Maslin's "mixed" notice, in keeping with many of her reviews, echoes *Variety* by judging the film largely as a business venture; it begins, "Nothing beats a plaything when it comes to comandeering the attention of children, so Joe Dante's *Small Soldiers* should have had the makings of a sure thing." Many of the other reviews, for that matter, underline the degree to which, even outside trade publications, present-day film reviewing often conflates business judgments with aesthetic evaluations.) In short, none of these dozen reviewers gave the slightest indication that *Small Soldiers* had anything to say about war or war films, and because they set the tone of the film's overall critical reception, the possible relevance of Dante's film to *Saving Private Ryan* became a lot easier to miss.

Two recurring references in most of these reviews, especially the unfavorable ones, are to the late Phil Hartman, whose last screen performance is in the film, and to *Toy Story,* the Disney computer animation hit. Hartman, murdered by his girlfriend while the film was still in production, plays the hero's next-door neighbor, a compulsive TV buff who at one point utters a memorable line to his wife — "World War II is my favorite war" — that one can easily imagine being attributed to Spielberg. Though the film is dedicated to Hartman in its closing credits (featuring a brief outtake of him as a tribute) and his role in the film is relatively minor, many reviewers were disturbed by his presence; one considered it an act of bad taste by DreamWorks to have released the film at all, and Travers in *Rolling Stone* structured his entire short review around the complaint that *Small Soldiers* was unworthy of Hartman's talent.

Toy Story, by virtue of using toys as characters, was most frequently mentioned as a film that *Small Soldiers* either ripped off or tried unsuccessfully to emulate. The late Gene Siskel complained on the weekly TV show that he shared with Ebert that he expected something more "cutting edge" from *Small Soldiers*, like *Toy Story*—apparently thinking of the technology involved in that cartoon feature, without any reference to its content—and many other reviewers, including Ebert, decried Dante's violence as harmful and disturbing to children, again in comparison to *Toy Story*. (On their TV show, they jointly concluded that the film was too dumb for adults and too violent for children, making it not worth seeing for anyone.) But the only cutting edges I can recall from that earlier movie are the ones used to gouge out the eyes of toy figures, perhaps because I find it difficult to isolate technology from what it's being used for. I don't have children of my own, but it's hard for me to see how an exercise in good-natured, across-the-board ridicule of warmongering could traumatize the same kids who are packed off to enjoy the squeezed-out eyes and severed limbs of *Toy Story* without qualm. One parent has assured me that the violence of *Toy Story* wasn't perceived by his little boy as violence but rather as a visceral rush of images. It's hard to know how to quarrel with this, but I would argue that just as kids are perfectly able to distinguish between animation and live action (which amounts to the usual defense of *Toy Story* as a harmless children's movie), they're also able to distinguish between toys and human beings. In any event, the subsequent wide popularity of *Small Soldiers* with small children on home video, which briefly encouraged DreamWorks to envision a sequel, hasn't to the best of my knowledge—based on the experiences of various parents and babysitters I've spoken with—resulted in any traumas.

The strongest element of censure in the reviews by both Ebert and Klady is the charge of mean-spiritedness, which deserves to be examined in greater detail. Here are the most relevant passages from the two reviews:

EBERT:

Small Soldiers is a family picture on the outside, and a mean, violent action picture on the inside. Since most of the violence happens to toys, I guess we're supposed to give it a pass, but I dunno: The toys are presented as individuals who can think for themselves, and there are believable heroes and villains among them. For smaller children, this could be a terrifying experience. . . .

In *Small Soldiers*, toys have unspeakable things happen to them, and many of them end up looking like horror props. Chip Hazard [a member of the Commando Elite] meets an especially gruesome end. What bothered me most about *Small Soldiers* is that it didn't tell me where to stand or what attitude to adopt. In movies for adults, I like that quality.

But here is a movie being sold to kids, with a lot of toy tie-ins and ads on the children's TV channels. Below a certain age, they like to know what they can count on. When Barbie clones are being sliced and diced by a lawn mower, are they going to understand the satirical purpose?

KLADY (opening paragraph of review):

The notion of technology running amok fuels *Small Soldiers*. When children's action toys, implanted with faulty military microchips, begin to move, speak and learn, they turn on their human owners with a lethal vengeance. It's an adult's paranoid dream come to life, so setting it in a juvenile context may have inadvertently undone the foundation of the story. And while pic's sense of a toy store turned upside-down, courtesy of dazzling f/x, will draw young viewers, ultimately the film's mean-spiritedness and serious underpinnings will turn off its core audience. The result will be rapid commercial erosion and disappointing theatrical box office; ancillary movement, particularly on video, could provide the pic with a more vital afterlife.

In order to counter Ebert's and Klady's objections, some of the facts in their reviews need to be disputed: Klady's claim that "the action toys . . . turn on their human owners with a lethal vengeance" obscures the facts that the targets of the Commando Elite are actually the Gorgonites, who are programmed to hide and to lose, and that the human "owners" of both toys are at risk only when they get in the way or shelter the Gorgonites. Similarly, Ebert's description obscures the fact that many of the Gorgonites "[look] like horror props" from the outset, and this is what makes them the heroes of the film. Moreover, the affection expressed by the film toward these noble underdogs and the fear and derision expressed toward the Commando Elite, represented unambiguously as unthinking and merciless killing machines, provides precisely the moral positioning that Ebert finds absent—an indication both of "where to stand" and "what attitude to adopt," though this clearly *is* an indication rather than a set of moral directives.

Given such faulty descriptions, the charge of mean-spiritedness becomes comprehensible. The sense of recoil conveyed by both reviews suggests that a serious grappling with the issue of enjoying warfare as spectacle *is* indeed "mean-spirited" if the viewer's own impulses in that direction become the target of the ridicule. And though Ebert is provocative enough to suggest that allowing the viewer a certain amount of moral freedom is commendable in a movie for adults but reprehensible in a movie for children, it might be argued that the only partially concealed moral directives and biases of *Saving Private Ryan* make Spielberg's film in Ebert's terms a film for children, not adults.

The fact that these reviewers and others didn't perceive Dante's efforts as satire about the consumption of war as spectacle or art is unfortunate but not entirely unprecedented. Dante's major predecessor in American pop cinema, the late Frank Tashlin, was equally misunderstood in the United States. Tashlin's own vision of cultural violence was grounded in animated cartoons—he began as a cartoonist and animator—but the objects of his satirical and parodic scorn were somewhat different, tied to what was most aggressive about American pop culture in the fifties: comic books (*Arists and Models*); Hollywood (*Hollywood or Bust*); rock 'n' roll (*The Girl Can't Help It*); advertising (*Will Success Spoil Rock Hunter?*); television (*Rock-a-Bye Baby*); all kinds of media excess, sexual hysteria, loud colors, and gadgets (passim).

As a fan and aficionado of horror and SF movies as well as cartoons, Dante has a different spin on cultural aggression and what it consists of, but his fascination with the pop materials that he mocks and synthesizes rivals Tashlin's, leading some commentators to conclude that he's too invested in these materials to qualify as a satirist. Just as some critics found Tashlin too vulgar to qualify as a satirist of vulgarity, some critics today find Dante's movies too violent to qualify as satires about violence. I would argue in both cases that the extreme stylization of both directors creates a sense of detachment about what they're showing that is the true source of disturbance. Nothing is ever perceived as real in their comic fantasies, which means that viewers who want to participate are forced to reflect on their own reactions to what they're watching, examine their own reflexes, and consider how much they're the targets of what's being satirized.

Small Soldiers doesn't represent the first time that Joe Dante has been misunderstood, nor, I suspect, will it be the last. His previous theatrical release in the United States, the 1993 *Matinee*, was about war fever, and reviewers who saw any connection between the Cuban missile crisis and the periodic eviscerations of Bagdad in the early nineties were few and far between. Though virtually all of Dante's movies are about the ethics and ramifications of spectatorship, he prefers to keep a low profile within the studio system and works without a personal publicist—the most obvious reason why a good many reviewers resist treating him like an auteur.

No doubt part of the failure of many American critics to perceive *Small Soldiers* as satire can be attributed to the habit of perceiving satire strictly according to the Swiftian model—the contempt for humanity in general and the audience in particular that infects, for instance, *Dr. Strangelove, Wag the Dog,* and *The Truman Show,* all relative favorites with critics and other industry "insiders" who pride themselves on their "media savvy." The character played by Ed Harris in *The Truman Show* epitomizes this self-regarding image—a deity in the clouds who understands what the audience needs and wants with the proper amount of lofty condescension; the fact that Harris was honored with an Academy Award nomination for this performance only underlines the flattery.

From this standpoint, one of the most elucidating as well as disconcerting aspects of *The Second Civil War*—the middle film in Dante's war trilogy that started with *Matinee,* regrettably seen only on cable in the United States (though shown theatrically in Europe)—is the degree to which Dante refuses to show contempt for any of his human characters, no matter how monstrous and misconceived their behavior might be. The contradiction in *The Second Civil War* between the dangerous xenophobia of the policies of the governor (Beau Bridges) and the affection he expresses for both his Mexican mistress (Elizabeth Pena) and Mexican food may be blatantly hypocritical, but rather than heap scorn on this character, Dante actually appears to like him; in effect it's only the xenophobia that gets fully ridiculed. A similar refusal to treat any characters as pure villains characterizes the work of Tashlin, and the generational attitude associated with Dante's satire is part of Tashlin's legacy. It's a legacy of both skepticism about and distance from the complex joys and perils of spectatorship—a legacy suggesting that Tashlin's origins as a cartoonist and Dante's as a film critic may represent two versions of the same basic impulse.

Small children seemed to have a much easier time picking up the satiric message of *Small Soldiers* than many of this country's most prestigious film critics, suggesting the problem that "noise"—represented in this case by advertising and Burger King tie-ins, both of which helped to occlude Dante's creative input—presents in assessing movies. Or maybe a likelier reason that film critics missed the point is their desire to assent to Spielberg's patriotic warmongering, which *Small Soldiers* exposes with cheerful derision.

Chapter Five
Communications Problems and Canons

In 1998, Water Bearer Video issued in a boxed set of four cassettes the complete, ten-episode silent French serial *Les vampires*. Directed by Louis Feuillade in 1915 and 1916 and starring the great actress Musidora as the mysterious Irma Vep, this monumental and exciting crime fantasy is one of the key works in the history of cinema—seminal in its influence on moviemaking as a whole, and to my mind considerably more watchable, pleasurable, and even modern from certain perspectives than the contemporaneous long features of D. W. Griffith, *The Birth of a Nation* and *Intolerance*. Yet astonishingly, this major work had been unavailable in the United States for over eighty years, ever since it ran commercially as a serial in American movie houses; apart from a few exceptional archive and festival showings from the sixties onward, not a single episode was distributed in any form. Maybe this was due to a problem regarding copyright and was not simply a matter of protracted neglect; in any case, as a consequence of this unavailability, American film history courses routinely elided Louis Feuillade's work from their syllabi—an oeuvre comprising several hundred films, including several other serials, some of them of comparable interest: *Fantomas* (1913–14), *Judex* (1916), *La nouvelle mission de Judex* (1917), *Tih Minh* (my own personal favorite, 1918), *Barrabas* (1919), and seven lesser known serials of the early twenties. (Shortly before *Les vampires* became available on video in the United States, it achieved a certain amount of public currency through the release of Oliver Assayas's wonderful 1996 feature *Irma Vep*—a comedy about a contemporary French remake of Les vampires starring Hong Kong actress Maggie Cheung that contained a few short video clips from the Feuillade serial.)

When I taught a semester of silent film history at the University of California, Santa Barbara in the early eighties, I was shocked to discover that not a single one of my predecessors had ever included Feuillade in the syllabus. In order to have done so, they would have had to rent, as I did, an hour-long episode from Fantômas that was available in 16-millimeter from the Museum of Modern Art—not an ideal solution, but the only possibility unless one had access to prints or videos from abroad. By the late eighties I had a VCR that allowed me to play European videos on an American monitor, and after I finally obtained a video of Les vampires from abroad, I showed a few early episodes in a film theory course I was teaching at the School of the Art Institute in 1995, and discovered to my delight that the film was every bit as fascinating and engrossing to my students as it was to me.

So the eventual release of Les vampires on video in the United States in 1998 was major news in the film world, and even more gratifying, major sectors of mainstream media treated it as such. In Time magazine, critic Richard Corliss devoted a special story to the video release, calling it the major film event of the year, and a subsequent article appeared in the Arts and Leisure section of the Sunday New York Times. By early 1999, and perhaps sooner than that, it was a routine matter to come across boxed sets of Les vampires in mainstream video stores; thanks to the efforts of Corliss and others, Feuillade's masterpiece had triumphantly entered the mainstream of American culture and commerce—or, more precisely, reentered that mainstream for the first time since the teens. And even though the likelihood remains remote of this leading to the availability of actual prints of Feuillade serials in the United States, it's heartening to discover that such a major cultural gap can eventually be filled.

* * *

Why did it take eighty years for most people to realize that such a gap existed in the first place? One factor is the different discourses found in at least three separate sectors of American film culture—the mainstream, the film industry, and academia—each of which tends to screen out one or two of the others. Although film industry jargon has increasingly entered the mainstream in recent years thanks to the info-tainment of magazines like *Premiere* and *Movieline* and TV shows like *Entertainment Tonight,* trade publications such as *Variety* and *Holly-wood Reporter* still typically speak a somewhat different language from the mainstream press, and the language of academic film studies exists far beyond the borders of either. Indeed, the divisions created by theo-retical jargon are so substantial that they can't be restricted by any means to American film culture. When I was living in Paris in the late sixties and early seventies, endless debates were being waged in the pages of the two major film magazines, *Cahiers du cinéma* and *Positif,* about the terminologies employed by film critics under the sway of Louis Althusser and Jacques Lacan, and comparable battles took place in such British magazines as *Sight and Sound, Movie,* and *Screen* when I was living in London in the mid-seventies. Even today, some of the residue of such debates persists in various forms, though it is still pos-sible for a French or English film theorist to speak on occasion within a relatively mainstream forum—a situation that remains virtually unthinkable in America.

The splintering effect of these three separate discourses in Ameri-can film culture guarantees not only the absence of a single commu-nity with common interests but the present impossibility of conceiving of such a community. Instead of a public forum, what we all share is essentially the same multimillion-dollar ad campaigns designed to move the same limited corpus of products. Some academics may have gotten the word about *Les vampires* becoming available on video—although I know a few sophisticated professors who found out a few months later than the readers of *Time*— but there's no question that they're every bit as inundated with material about *Titanic, Saving Pri-vate Ryan,* and *The Phantom Empire* as everyone else. And though all we share is a discourse of promotion—which none of us entirely believes in, though none of us can avoid it—the possibilities for using this discourse as a means of communication between individuals with common interests is extremely limited. Turn to most movie reviews and entertainment news and you see the implications of those limita-tions in all their force.

The fact that the film cultures of France and the U.K. (to cite only two examples) are vastly more interactive and interconnected than ours can be attributed to a good many factors, ranging from government-supported institutions (such as the Cinémathèque Française and the British Film Institute) to the smaller size of these countries, not to mention an overall centralization of resources. A film critic from Paris or London who wants to watch the shooting of a studio film has to travel to the suburbs, but a film critic from New York who wants to do the same thing generally has to fly to the West Coast. Moreover, a French or British film academic is likely to be in closer proximity to the resources of Paris or London than a film scholar in Iowa City, Iowa or Madison, Wisconsin is to either New York or Los Angeles.

In some respects, the film culture in England can be interactive to a fault: when I lived in London, I was shocked to discover that some film teachers were so dependent on the film extracts made available by the British Film Institute that they didn't always bother to see the complete features they were extracted from. For instance, I used to chide a friend who taught the "Diamonds Are a Girl's Best Friend" number from *Gentlemen Prefer Blondes*—a respected contributor to *Screen* and *Screen Education*—for her ignorance about and relative indifference to the film as a whole. And the extreme factionalism found in the film communities of both England and France has had its crippling aspects as well—not only partisans of *Cahiers du cinéma* who refuse to read *Positif* (and vice versa), but enemies of *Sight and Sound* who have constructed elaborate histories of English-language film criticism that are shaped and inflected by the unstated determination to exclude references to everything that magazine ever published. (The original edition of Pam Cook's *The Cinema Book*—I haven't yet seen the updated version—is one such example.) And after the departure of *Sight and Sound*'s longtime editor Penelope Houston, this kind of neo-Stalinist suppression became reconfigured after anthologies of the new *Sight and Sound* started to appear; henceforth, it became acceptable for *Sight and Sound* to enter the history of English film criticism, but only the post-Houston version of that magazine. In other words, sustained turf wars in both England and France lead to highly skewed accounts of the history of film criticism, not to mention film history in general.

One also has to factor in the less marginalized status of cultural events and intellectuals in the public life of most European countries. In Italy, intellectuals like Umberto Eco write regularly for the daily newspapers (as did the late Italo Calvino), and most of the articles by Roland Barthes comprising *Mythologies* originally appeared in mainstream French magazines such as *Le nouvel observateur*. In 1992, I participated in a highly specialized conference on Orson Welles in Rome attended by about fifty people, the sort of event that probably wouldn't have merited even a mention in the local press if it had occurred in New York, Los Angeles, or Chicago; in Italy it was treated as major news and reported extensively in national magazines and newspapers. Pretty much the same thing happened in 1999 when I participated in two Welles-related events at the Munich Film Archive for a few hundred spectators.

* * *

In the past, a university education was the best or at least the most typical way of acquiring some knowledge about what an art form had to offer. It wasn't the way I pursued my own self-education about film history, because when I started out as a film critic in the late sixties and early seventies, I had already reached the end of my own formal education in literature, and the opportunities for studying film academically in the states at that time were few and far between. I had to opt instead for a program of self-education carried out through reading and attending films in New York, Paris, and London. This is where the special rewards of the Cinémathèque Française and the British Film Institute became apparent to me. In the seventies the former offered six to eight film programs a day at two auditoriums at opposite ends of Paris, comprising a more rich and diversified survey of film history than could—or still can—be found in any American institution; it was this same adventurous programming, spearheaded by the Cinémathèque's remarkable cofounder, Henri Langlois, that had educated the directors of the French New Wave in the fifties. (Today the same institution has several screening sites in Paris and a good many seminars in addition to film programs.) And even though London's National Film Theatre was more comparable to New York's Museum of Modern Art, the

British Film Institute also published two first-rate magazines, both of which I worked for, as well as perhaps the best reference library of film books and periodicals to be found anywhere. (Back then, this library was available to every paying member of the National Film Theatre, which operated like a film club. More recently, it became much harder for members to gain access to it; the two magazines merged and became taken over by individuals whose knowledge of film history was comparatively meager; and today, in many respects, the British Film Institute, though more responsive to the interests of film academics, survives as a pale shadow of what it was until the early eighties.)

These were the main unofficial "film schools" I attended, either as a customer or as an employee, during my many years of living abroad. But prior to that, and for better and for worse, a university education had a lot to do with my sense of what the greatest literature, painting, and classical music consisted of when I was in my mid-twenties.

Although I can't speak with any authority about whether one can still learn this kind of information about painting and classical music from an American university, I'm quite confident that the chances of encountering canons devoted to literature and film in American universities nowadays are relatively low, because canons themselves are regarded with a great deal of suspicion. In English and literature departments, a mistrust of canons devoted mainly to the works of "dead white males" has clearly diminished the possibility of teaching literature from a literary standpoint; the social sciences have taken over the study of fiction and poetry to a crippling degree, and in a way this has only completed the damage often done in grammar school and high school by neglecting to enforce grammar for related ideological reasons. Some perceptive recent remarks by Michel Chaouli, assistant professor of German and of Comparative Literature at Harvard, in the *Times Literary Supplement*, are telling:

> The wider the range of objects of study, the more specific and specifically policed the style of presentation becomes. This may be one reason why in our graduate curriculum the literary canon is being inexorably displaced by a rather narrow theoretical canon. If during the reign of the literary canon one lived in fear of having one's work labelled "trivial", today's dreaded word must be "untheorized".
>
> In its intelligent versions, cultural studies urges literature departments not to promulgate the norms of the cultural elite by promoting a canon

indebted to the notion of the romantic genius, but rather to devote themselves to studying the ordinary without abandoning the value of value. But
given the workings of our field, a democracy of objects of study may easily be vitiated by an aristocracy of subjects. The trade-off is quite clear: the
more ordinary the object of inquiry, the more extraordinary the critic; all
the cultural capital that is given up in choice of object flows back in the
breathtaking creativity with which meaning can be made to appear anywhere. The romantic genius returns, this time not as poet, but as critic.[1]

As for film canons, the popularity of auteurism in seventies film
studies took a nosedive once the ideological construction of authorship
started getting interrogated by writers like Roland Barthes and Michel
Foucault—writers who, as Chaouli implies, became canonized, along
with Louis Althusser, Jacques Lacan, and others, at the same time that
filmmakers and their works were rapidly becoming decanonized.
Although the demurrals of these writers and others were certainly
worth paying attention to, the increasing inclination of American film
studies to favor approaches based on the social sciences and to mistrust
aesthetics made the erection of film canons a much more precarious
undertaking, with the lamentable result that most film academics
essentially gave up on the activity. Unless the film in question figured
as a centerpiece in an important theoretical text—which was the case,
for instance, with *Young Mr. Lincoln*, canonized as a collective text by
the editors of *Cahiers du Cinéma* that appeared first in *Cahiers du
Cinéma* no. 223 (1970), then in English translation in *Screen* vol. 13, no.
3 (1972) and numerous subsequent academic anthologies—it often
couldn't find a privileged place in a classroom.

This didn't mean, however, that a certain amount of de facto can-
onization didn't continue to creep into film studies by the back door.
An increasing interest in the study of melodrama, for instance, led to
the singling out of such films as *Mildred Pierce, Now, Voyager*, and *Imitation of Life* as key texts, and because the latter of these films was
directed by a former auteurist favorite, Douglas Sirk, a modified form
of auteurism might still be employed when a Sirk film got discussed in
class. But the increasing distrust of supporting aesthetic canons, even

---

[1] "What Do Literary Studies Teach?: A Vast Unravelling," by Michel
Chaouli, *Times Literary Supplement*, February 26, 1999, p. 14.

after it eliminated or at least modified many of the claims of auteurism, generally led to the practice of viewing films as symptoms of social formations, economic conditions, or psychological predilections, rather than as aesthetic objects. And since the mainstream continued to go about its promotional business in elevating certain films as aesthetic objects, the relation of academic film study to this process became mainly passive and complicitous, in spite of its better impulses. The desire of some professors to get large enrollments, for instance, has encouraged them to validate such topics as the mythological underpinnings of the *Star Wars* cycle—which have already been extensively validated in George Lucas's own press campaigns—rather than interrogate, say, the ideological functions of these myths in launching wars, which might cut back on those same enrollments.

In some respects, the "democracy of objects" and "aristocracy of subjects" alluded to by Chaouli—corresponding to a mistrust of aesthetic hierarchies and a dependence on (mainly European) theoretical models—yields not so much an absence of canons when it comes to film studies as a canon that exists by default, what Harold Bloom calls a survivor's list:

> We have not had an official high culture in this country since about 1800, a generation after the American Revolution. Cultural unity is a French phenomenon, and to some degree a German matter, but hardly an American reality in either the nineteenth century or the twentieth. In our context and from our perspective, the Western Canon is a kind of survivor's list.[2]

Bloom is of course referring to a canon of literary works rather than films, but there's enough carryover in attitudes to make portions of his argument applicable. There was never an "official high culture" relating to film in this country, but for a brief period in the sixties there was a faint evocation of the possibility of one, largely imported from France, that combined a reevaluation of Hollywood cinema with a kind of modernist reevaluation of contemporary cinema tied to the French New Wave. It was enough of an evocation, at any rate, to strike

---

[2] Harold Bloom, *The Western Canon*, New York/San Diego/London: Harcourt Brace & Company, 1994, p. 38.

terror in a number of academic orthodoxies, and the fact that it was occurring around the same time that many film studies programs were being established produced a number of contradictory effects. A skeptical form of auteurism began to enter the academy, but the political and ideological qualifiers to this auteurism quickly began to overtake them, so that a canonizing of theoretical texts became paramount and a canonizing of filmmakers and films became secondary. Then, over time, thanks to a growing mistrust of aesthetic canons as well as aesthetic theories, the treatment of films as social, economic, and psychological symptoms began to dominate. Effectively this meant that the aesthetic positions of mainstream critics were allotted a clear and unchallenged playing field; each sphere of criticism was expected to stick to its own turf and mind its own field, and the most pronounced form of interchange between the two spheres was a growing disdain and mutual lack of respect. What might have figured in a more interactive film culture as some sort of dialectic and polemical struggle became instead a kind of reciprocal alienation.

Again and again, one witnesses in contemporary film courses a weary acceptance of the priorities of the media as an unalterable fact of nature, priorities that have to be adopted rather than questioned or undermined in order to solicit the interest of students; and the very same priorities, alas, hold with equal firmness in publications such as *The New York Review of Books*. The philosophy behind this attitude appears to be that we can alter our culture only by boring from within; and the fact that George Lucas operates according to the same principle isn't very encouraging if one considers that the resources at his own disposal to "bore from within" are astronomically greater than that of all the film professors in the world combined.

* * *

Although I've been suggesting throughout this chapter that academic film study often operates in a state of denial, I haven't yet broached the single area where that denial can be said to be most cripplingly in force: the profound difference between watching a film and watching a video. The simultaneous phasing out of 16-millimeter film distribution and the rapid spread of movies on video have combined to make the study of films *on film* a luxury that most of the film departments in this country can no longer afford. With a few notable exceptions—which usually turn out to be the most sophisticated as well as the best endowed film study programs and departments—films are now screened and studied principally on video, laser disc, and DVD formats. Most professors have little choice in the matter, so it would be pointless to blame them for pursuing this alternative. Where denial comes into the picture is in the commonly held pretense that watching a video, laser disc, or DVD is essentially the same thing as watching a film.

In other words, expediency has unconsciously created and subsequently intensified an ongoing imposture. It's a demonstrable fact that video and film are not even remotely interchangeable in relation to such basic factors as light, projection, definition, shape and texture of image, and interaction of sound and image—to start with only a short list, and overlooking the problem of cropping and scanning on video that eliminates roughly a third of the image of most anamorphic wide-screen films and usually alters the editing of those films as well. Indeed, the fact that film critic Fred Camper—who reviews films with some regularity for the *Chicago Reader* and publishes film criticism in many other outlets—categorically refuses to preview any film on video stems directly from this important distinction. For the same reason, Camper refuses to show films on video whenever he teaches film courses.

But Camper is the exception, not the rule, in film reviewing and film teaching alike. Given the logistical difficulty of proceeding otherwise, most other film teachers wind up showing films on video to their students and then discussing them as films. Even if they want to discuss what they show as videos and not as films, the corpus of available written material about this distinction is too minuscule to make such an approach practical for most film academics. As I note in Chapter Eight, the late French film critic Serge Daney—who wrote interestingly and at length about the ramifications of watching films on television, and who might provide an interesting starting point for a pedagogical way of dealing with some of the problems involved—has not yet been translated into English. And without a theoretical or practical guide for coping with the differences between film and video, film teachers typically wind up circumventing and ignoring most of those differences in order to concentrate on other matters: alienation in a nutshell. In the not-too-distant future, when film may disappear entirely from what we now refer to as movie houses and may survive only in museums and other specialized institutions, the theoretical work done on the phenomenology and aesthetics of film throughout the twentieth century may be ground underfoot in favor of less differentiated standards. Indeed, if video aesthetics eventually replace film aesthetics, this may only become fully understood and theorized after the present transitional period is over, when the confusing impasse of treating the two media as interchangeable is no longer seen as a necessary evil.

It's a truism that the technological and material limitations of the equipment used in teaching tend to define the limitations of what's being taught, so it doesn't seem accidental that the relative disfavor in recent years of aesthetics in academic film study and the increasing popularity of the social sciences coincides precisely with some of the conditions of watching films on video. By the same token, one could argue that the interest in stars over directors that is already emphasized in the mass media has often been reflected in academic film study for the same reason—because stars are more immediately visible and recognizable on TV screens than directorial styles. And in the case of certain films where the material relations of sound and image are crucial—such as the features of Robert Bresson and many experimental works—it can easily be argued that the value of such works is effectively eliminated on video. In Chapter Six, I discuss the overwhelming success of a recent touring retrospective of Bresson's films in 35-millimeter prints. Most of these films lose their aesthetic impact on video, which obviously had some connection with this success: attempting to "teach" Bresson on video is a losing proposition from the start, making the impact of his films on film a good deal stronger than it might have been otherwise.

In other words, although academic film study should ideally focus on the most salient attributes of films that are ignored in the culture at large, the logistics of teaching film courses usually obliges most teachers to replicate the same omissions and curtailments and perpetuate the same problems. However useful videos, laser discs, and DVDs are as tools in analyzing sequences, their omnipresence in film departments as textual substitutions for film are as crippling in some ways as using Cliff's Notes instead of texts in literature courses. The fact that many students nowadays can't even identify what they're watching as a projected film or a projected video or laser disc—something I've heard about repeatedly from teacher friends as well as observed firsthand—is symptomatic of the kind of alienation that the surrounding culture has already imposed on education.

* * *

Like it or not, one of the major activities of any film culture is a labeling of certain films as good and others as bad, and no academic approach can eliminate this activity entirely. At best it can hope to offer some critical training in understanding that activity; at worst it becomes victimized by it. By adopting the stance that the formation of aesthetic canons is beneath its more "scientific" interests, academic film study effectively clears the way for mainstream huckmeisters to carry out this work without interference or fear of contradiction. It thus becomes all the easier for an organization like the American Film Institute to join forces with the studios in carrying out work that universities should have attended to decades earlier—the subject of my next chapter.

Chapter Six
The AFI's Contribution to Movie Hell
or, How I Learned to Stop Worrying
and Love American Movies

Just about everyone I've spoken to regarding the American Film Institute's list of the one hundred greatest American movies in 1998—presented on a stultifyingly vacuous three-hour CBS special in June—was
depressed about it, in a hang-dog sort of fashion. Not only was the list lack-
luster, the show completely failed to offer any interesting justifications for
any of the selected titles. But this depression wasn't at all the sort of defla-
tion that comes when outsized hopes are dashed. Rather, it was a kind of
grim acknowledgment that what we call "business as usual" these days
automatically follows a law of diminishing returns, yielding an increasing
dumbing down of film culture that outpaces our already shrinking expectations. "Of course it's going to keep getting worse and worse," we all
assume, and then it gets to be even worse than we imagined.

Was the list simply a brute commercial ploy dreamed up by a con-
sortium of marketers to repackage familiar goods, or was it a legitimate
cultural intervention that was somehow supposed to improve the quality of our lives? For that matter, are we still capable of distinguishing
between the two? If it was the former, then surely it qualified as front-
page news (which it widely received) only if we're living in the equivalent of Stalinist Russia. If it was the latter, then why does the list contain
so many movies that lie—movies that lie about Vietnam (*The Deer
Hunter, Apocalypse Now*), about racism (*The Birth of a Nation, Taxi*

Driver, Pulp Fiction), about countless other matters? Why are so many of the entries aesthetically bland or worse while recapitulating all the worst habits of Hollywood self-infatuation, liberal (*Guess Who's Coming to Dinner*) as well as conservative (*Forrest Gump*)? *Shane* to my taste was already bad enough, but why did *Butch Cassidy and the Sundance Kid* have to make the cut as well, along with (choke) *Dances with Wolves*? I yield to no one in my love for James Cagney, but did he ever make a less interesting picture than *Yankee Doodle Dandy*, the only one on the list?

But let's stop and consider what we're working with. Unlike every other comparable national institution on the globe, which considers world cinema of national importance, the American Film Institute restricts its focus to films of its own nationality. (The organization was launched during the Johnson administration, when patriots must have been concerned about Americans seeing too many foreign pictures.) This means that a mere survey of the best hundred movies, full stop, is a lot more than the AFI can handle, and a recycling of already overtouted product has to be delivered to our doorsteps all over again, just to prove what fine citizens we are. To make matters worse, as Michael Wilmington pointed out in the *Chicago Tribune*, "The battle-weary NEA, which used to supply the AFI with several million dollars in annual grants, now gives about $100,000. By contrast, Britain supports its own Film Institute to the tune of over $60 million a year."

Yet on reflection, I doubt whether the AFI can justify getting even two cents on its present agenda. When they recently shut down their art theater at the Kennedy Center in Washington, the AFI's director, Jean Firstenberg, said to the press that video made repertory programming unnecessary; if she meant what she said, I'd rather see the same funds used to reduce the AFI to rubble. Given its egregious industry ass-kissing throughout its existence, I'm tempted to conclude that the AFI's only substantial contribution to film culture—American *or* global—is the fact that David Lynch's *Eraserhead* was produced at its film school. Certainly if you compare what it has recently done—in restorations, revivals, documentaries about film history, or presenting foreign-language movies—to what a private-sector enterprise like Turner Classic Movies routinely does every week, there isn't any contest.

But the malaise I'm talking about, provoked by the aforementioned list of one hundred movies, isn't just a response to the long-term uselessness of the AFI; it's about the increasing lack of any viable distinction between corporate greed and what used to be called public works. It doesn't really matter whether in the present circumstances this has grown out of a holy or unholy alliance between the AFI, Blockbuster Video, CBS, TNT, Turner Classic Movies, and the home video divisions of thirteen film studios—all of which planned a summerful of jolly hoopla around this tacky list to promote their joint efforts. What matters is the rise of corporate cultural initiatives bent on selling and reselling what we already know and have, making every alternative appear more scarce and esoteric, and not even attempting to expand or illuminate the choices made in the process. (As an academic friend points out, it's almost as if most of the masterpieces in the Louvre were cleared out to make room for the work of Sunday painters.)

It's surely indicative of the perceived "success" of the AFI's crass venture that it went on in June 1999 to mount a similar if even more meaningless media onslaught devoted to the one hundred "greatest screen legends" in American movies. "'AFI's 100 Years . . . 100 Stars,'" claimed a publicity handout, "also includes a major national video program aimed at encouraging movie fans to introduce and reintroduce themselves to film classics"—aimed, in other words, at making more money in video sales and rentals. If teaching the audience anything were the true aim of such an enterprise, the AFI might have focused this attention on directors or screenwriters rather than stars, although I'm sure even then its polling procedures would have yielded only more ways to resell us movies by Spielberg, Lucas, and other AFI "discoveries."

Let me hasten to add that if I were drawing up my own list of the hundred greatest American movies from scratch, roughly a quarter of the AFI's list would be on it.[1] But it seems more useful to offer an alternative

---

[1] These are—in order of their ranking on the AFI list, but with no implied ranking on my part—*Citizen Kane, Singin' in the Rain, Sunset Boulevard, All About Eve, 2001: A Space Odyssey, Dr. Strangelove, Bonnie and Clyde, The Best Years of Our Lives, North by Northwest, Rear Window, King Kong, The Birth of a Nation, A Streetcar Named Desire, All Quiet on the Western Front, The Third Man* (although it isn't American), *Rebel Without a Cause, Vertigo, Stagecoach, The Manchurian Candidate, The Gold Rush, City Lights, The Wild Bunch, Modern Times, Duck Soup,* and *The Searchers.*

list of one hundred features rather than an unwieldy composite of the twenty-five or so AFI titles I can live with and seventy-five others. I've also decided to list my choices alphabetically rather than impose any kind of order based on merit, which would be like ranking oranges over apples and declaring Wednesday superior to Monday. For if these lists have any purpose at all from our standpoint (as opposed to the interests of the merchandisers), this is surely to rouse us out of our boredom and stupor, not to ratify our already foreshortened definitions and perspectives.

Above all, the impulse to provide another list is to defend the breadth, richness, and intelligence of the American cinema against its self-appointed custodians, who seem to want to lock us into an eternity of Oscar nights. And the most salient fact about my own list is that it's far from exhaustive; I haven't even found room on it for such miracles as *Adam's Rib*, *The Band Wagon*, *The Bitter Tea of General Yen*, *Blonde Crazy*, John Ford's Cavalry trilogy (*Fort Apache*, *She Wore a Yellow Ribbon*, *Rio Grande*), *Crumb*, *Dog Day Afternoon*, *Duel in the Sun*, *Family Plot*, *Gun Crazy*, *Ice*, *Lives of Performers*, *Me and My Gal*, *The Old Dark House*, *Paths of Glory*, *Pickup on South Street*, *Point of Order*, *Rope*, *Ruggles of Red Gap*, *Safe*, *Salt of the Earth*, *The Sun Shines Bright*, *Two Lane Blacktop*, and God knows what else.

For all the ranting and raving I do about the absence of foreign movies from American screens—exacerbated by the fact that the only American cable channel to show many of them, BRAVO, systematically recuts them all—I have to admit that of all the national cinemas I know, the American cinema is almost certainly the richest. That's what makes the historical and aesthetic paltriness of the AFI list so stupefying.

Given the stringent limitations placed on what kind of American movies can be financed, made, exhibited, and marketed today, it's especially poignant that a brilliant industry aberration like *Citizen Kane* should head the AFI list, just as it's headed every comparable list over the past thirty-odd years—a movie that clearly couldn't get bankrolled today (it's in black-and-white), much less survive test-marketing previews, and which failed to turn a profit when it came out. The persistence of *Kane* as a favorite is ample proof, if proof were ever needed, that viewers—even "film professionals"—are smarter than they're usually cracked up to be. (*Kane* was the first of Orson Welles's Hollywood films, and one reason why I've refrained from including his last, *Touch of Evil,* on my own list is my personal involvement as consultant on a version reedited according to Welles's instructions, released in 1998.)

Viewers are perhaps less smart at rooting out the American masterpieces that currently don't enjoy as much mainstream visibility—ones that require some alertness to what plays fleetingly at alternative venues and the sort of initiative that's needed to get to them. The lax attitude that "anything" can eventually be caught up with on video is a debilitating illusion—not only because it's literally untrue, but also because none of these masterpieces was ever designed to be seen that way, any more than any great novel was ever written in order to be skimmed or read with various pages torn out.

The vicissitudes of availability (read: access) always play a major role in developing film tastes and canons, and if the AFI and its business cronies had wanted to do something genuinely useful, they might have polled the same group about the one hundred most *neglected* American movies and then made an effort to make them available, on film *and* on video. I can't say I'd agree with all the results, and some of the most neglected films are experimental works that wouldn't work on video anyway. But it's emblematic of how far we are from any reasonable film culture that, even if the AFI and company had elected to make the first ten or twenty-five films on its own list available in new 35-millimeter prints, to be shown in theaters across the country, a revolution would have to occur in the studios to make such an occurrence possible.

* * *

Being landlocked is a major part of the problem. Twenty-one years ago, I participated in a similar "revaluation" of American cinema conducted by the Royal Film Archive of Belgium that polled one hundred and sixteen Americans and eighty-seven non-Americans from two dozen countries. The results, contained in a fascinating volume called *The Most Important and Misappreciated American Films Since the Beginning of Cinema,* were much more substantial and lively, and not only because the 1925 *Ben-Hur* garnered more votes in that survey than the 1959 version. (Truthfully, I haven't seen either, but at least the silent version piques my curiosity.) Thirty-six movies in the AFI list made it into the RFA's top hundred, and *Citizen Kane* topped both lists.

But even after one takes into account the fifteen titles in the AFI list made since 1977 (the year of the RFA survey), the differences are extremely telling. The films in the RFA list that came in second, third, and fourth—*Sunrise*, *Greed*, and *Intolerance*—don't figure at all in the AFI pantheon, and not far below those essential works were movies by such key figures as Robert Flaherty, Buster Keaton, King Vidor, Ernst Lubitsch, Victor Seastrom, Preston Sturges, and Josef von Sternberg, all unrepresented in the AFI's corny hit parade.

Should one snobbishly conclude from this that non-Americans are necessarily more intelligent and discerning when it comes to American movies? I wouldn't. It's important to bear in mind that the RFA polled two hundred and three film professionals—historians, critics, archivists, directors, teachers, and even a few students—whereas the AFI polled over fifteen hundred Americans of every conceivable stripe in terms of their knowledge about film. (If memory serves, I was one of them.) One should add that the RFA's and the AFI's notions of what a "film professional" is couldn't be more disparate: in this country, where familiarity with film history rarely plays any role in the hiring of reviewers, "film professionals" tend to get defined in tautological terms as people who write about films. (Combined with institutional validation, this produces all sorts of strange anomalies—such as the process by which, say, Pauline Kael and Daphne Merkin, two film critics for *The New Yorker*, might be regarded as sisters under the skin.) The differences between Americans and non-Americans in judging American movies are basically matters of access and cultural conditioning—not taste or intelligence in isolation from these factors—and the consequences of these differences can be staggering.

Let me cite a couple of examples of what I mean, both drawn from recent experience. Two nights before I tried to watch the AFI's three-hour special, I was in a hotel room in downtown Helsinki, having just returned from the four-day Midnight Sun International Film Festival in Lapland, and when I did some channel-surfing, I found two films playing on Finnish TV, both in pristine prints—Ingmar Bergman's *Wild Strawberries* and Robert Bresson's *Lancelot du lac*. When I mentioned this the next morning to Peter von Bagh, director of the Midnight Sun Festival, he was miffed that the local TV programmers were so thoughtless that they could screen both films at once, meaning that local film buffs couldn't tape both of them.

Another example, four days earlier: When I arrived on a bus with the other guests at Sodankyla—the remote village in the Arctic Circle where the Midnight Sun Festival has been held since its inception thirteen years ago—the first thing I saw on the main street was a couple of new street signs that said, "Samuel Fuller's Street." An hour later, von Bagh—a professional film historian who was one of the eighty-seven non-Americans polled by the RFA in 1977—was officially and permanently renaming the street at an impromptu ceremony. For those who need to know, Fuller is a major Hollywood filmmaker who died in November 1997 and is unrepresented not only in the AFI's top hundred, but also in its top four hundred (though he gets two slots in my list); he attended the festival its first year and subsequently starred in *Tigrero*, a film made by one of the festival's cofounders, Mikka Kaurismaki. This year, the festival showed a feature-length documentary about Fuller, Fuller's *Underworld, U.S.A.*, and *Tigrero* as well. And given the force and complexity of what Fuller's films had to say about American racism from the early fifties onward, it was more than a little disconcerting to fly back to Chicago, turn on the TV, and hear Jack Valenti praise the mediocre and relatively gutless *To Kill a Mockingbird* (1962)—number thirty-four on the AFI list—as the first Hollywood film to deal honestly with racial issues. It made me wonder if Valenti had been living on the moon; if so, he might have rocketed down to the Arctic Circle for some enlightenment.

Robert Mulligan, who directed *To Kill a Mockingbird*, is a talented filmmaker, but better pictures by him would have found their way onto the list if his mise en scène were the issue. One can safely bet that the inclusion of *To Kill a Mockingbird*—like the preference for *Guess Who's Coming to Dinner?* over the infinitely superior Tracy-Hepburn vehicle *Adam's Rib*—is merely a function of the kind of liberal self-congratulation that brings standing ovations to Oscar nights and tears to Valenti's eyes. It has nothing to do with either the art of cinema or the reality of America—check out *The Phenix City Story* if you want to learn something about Alabama, as opposed to Gregory Peck's virtue—but a great deal to do with the industry's guilty conscience. Indeed, what the AFI in one of its press releases has called a "celebration of the one-hundredth anniversary of American movies" reminds me of Haven Hamilton's glib country-western national anthem at the beginning of Robert Altman's *Nashville*: "We must be doing something right to last two hundred years." If this piss-poor representation of the best that American cinema can do is all we have to celebrate, we must be doing something wrong.

✳ ✳ ✳

One proof of how landlocked we are is the inclusion on the AFI list of British films like *Lawrence of Arabia* (number five), *The Bridge on the River Kwai* (number thirteen), *Doctor Zhivago* (number thirty-nine), *The Third Man* (number fifty-seven), and, more arguably, *A Clockwork Orange* (number forty-six)—a gesture no doubt of unconscious imperialism on the part of those polled, apparently justified by the tentacles of American finance and/or a few Hollywood actors. (Why *The Third Man* turns up according to these rules but not *The Thief of Bagdad* is anyone's guess. But in part as a riposte to *A Clockwork Orange*, Kubrick's most dubious feature, I've included Andy Warhol's remarkable adaptation of the same English novel, *Vinyl*, on my own list.)

Last summer, for a retrospective of "neglected" American movies selected by American directors held at the Locarno film festival, Steven Spielberg had either the cheek or the innocence to select *Lawrence of Arabia*—a neglected American movie if there ever was one. But back in 1977, only four stray participants in the RFA survey thought to include any of the David Lean films cited above, three of whom were American (and one of whom was a member of the AFI's board of trustees), and not one of the two hundred and three had the nerve to select *The Third Man*. So maybe a gradual slippage in our understanding of what is and isn't American is part of the trouble. For my own list, I've grappled long and hard with the existential issue of national identity posed by such ambiguous masterpieces as F. W. Murnau's *Tabu*, Luis Buñuel's *The Young One*, Albert Lewin's *Pandora and the Flying Dutchman*, Josef von Sternberg's *The Saga of Anatahan*, Michael Snow's *Wavelength* and *Back and Forth*, and David Cronenberg's *Naked Lunch*, and have finally wound up excluding all of them because of my serious doubts.

Rightly or wrongly, I've also refrained from including some of my favorite films by high-profile directors who are well represented on the AFI list, even if their best films aren't. For the record, I prefer *The King of Comedy* and *Kundun* to *Taxi Driver* and *Raging Bull*, *The Conversation* to either of the *Godfathers*, and *Dumbo* to *Snow White and the Seven Dwarfs* and *Fantasia*; but even though I had some regrets about excluding these favorites, I have no doubt that readers can find them without my prodding. (Though one might quarrel with my excluding animated features entirely from my list—just as I would quarrel with the absence of independents like Cassavetes and experimental filmmakers like Brakhage from the AFI's—I would argue that the most remarkable animation in American cinema, from Tex Avery to Robert Breer, is generally found in short films. For that matter, the absence of shorts as an arbitrary ground rule is what explains my exclusion of Maya Deren as well.)

I've deliberately sought to make my list conservative rather than provocative, and grounded in pleasure rather than any dutiful sense of historical importance. But since I've already stressed the significance of access and cultural conditioning in forming tastes, I should clarify the nature of my own background, which inevitably slants my list in a particular direction. Twenty-five of my selections were released in the fifties, while I was growing up, and my acquaintance with American cinema was based on two atypical forms of access that determined my cultural conditioning. The first came from being the grandson of a man who ran a chain of movie theaters in Alabama and the son of a man who worked for the chain, which meant that I had virtually unlimited access to Hollywood movies throughout most of the fifties, seeing practically everything that came out without having to pay admission. And the second form of access came from living in Paris and London between 1969 and 1977, when the American movies I saw in both places—bolstered in Paris by the Cinémathèque and numerous revival houses, and in London by the British Film Institute, where I was an employee—were not always the same things that one could see in New York and Chicago. And apart from this kind of access, the criticism I was reading in both cities was reeducating me on the subject of American movies, because French and English critics were discovering important things about these movies that my cultural conditioning in Alabama didn't reveal. Discoveries of this kind are still going on across the world, illuminating certain aspects of American film history that we're still catching up on—though we might never pick up on the signals if all we're listening to is the American film industry and its deputies.

Am I saying that the fifties were the most plentiful decade in American movies? That's what my own access and cultural conditioning tells me, because what I find there, in spite of all that period's repression — and maybe in part because of it — is an unparalleled grappling with this country's social reality that other decades, including the present one, can't begin to match. But I can easily imagine a critic like Manny Farber who grew up during the thirties making an equally strong case for that decade; and a more recent generation of critics who grew up during the seventies — including Kent Jones in the United States, Nicole Brenez in France, Alexander Horwath in Austria, and Adrian Martin in Australia — have recently been offering some powerful arguments on behalf of American movies from that era. (For the record, I've wound up including sixteen films from the seventies, fifteen from the forties, fourteen from the thirties, eleven from the twenties, and ten from the sixties, whereas the teens, eighties, and nineties get only token representation.)

In the final analysis, selecting America's hundred greatest movies has to be an ongoing act of exploration — which can only happen if we stop to consider what we still don't know about the subject and try to set up some channels for educating ourselves. The sad news about the AFI's version is that it proposes we stop looking, go home, and proceed to pick more lint out of our navels for the next few decades.

A note regarding the two lists to follow: directors (along with dates) are appended to each title strictly for purposes of identification, not necessarily as an indication of who was the most important creative individual on each film. Hence the relative anomalies of Alan Crosland (*The Jazz Singer*), Charles Vidor (*Gilda*), and Mark Robson (*The Seventh Victim*), among others.

THE AMERICAN FILM INSTITUTE'S TOP ONE HUNDRED

1. *Citizen Kane* (Orson Welles, 1941)
2. *Casablanca* (Michael Curtiz, 1942)
3. *The Godfather* (Francis Coppola, 1972)

4. *Gone with the Wind* (Victor Fleming, 1939)
5. *Lawrence of Arabia* (David Lean, 1962)
6. *The Wizard of Oz* (Victor Fleming, 1939)
7. *The Graduate* (Mike Nichols, 1967)
8. *On the Waterfront* (Elia Kazan, 1954)
9. *Schindler's List* (Steven Spielberg, 1993)
10. *Singin' in the Rain* (Stanley Donen and Gene Kelly, 1952)
11. *It's a Wonderful Life* (Frank Capra, 1946)
12. *Sunset Boulevard* (Billy Wilder, 1950)
13. *The Bridge on the River Kwai* (David Lean, 1957)
14. *Some Like It Hot* (Billy Wilder, 1959)
15. *Star Wars* (George Lucas, 1977)
16. *All About Eve* (Joseph L. Mankiewicz, 1950)
17. *The African Queen* (John Huston, 1951)
18. *Psycho* (Alfred Hitchcock, 1960)
19. *Chinatown* (Roman Polanski, 1974)
20. *One Flew Over the Cuckoo's Nest* (Milos Forman, 1975)
21. *The Grapes of Wrath* (John Ford, 1940)
22. *2001: A Space Odyssey* (Stanley Kubrick, 1968)
23. *The Maltese Falcon* (John Huston, 1941)
24. *Raging Bull* (Martin Scorsese, 1980)
25. *E.T. the Extra-Terrestial* (Steven Spielberg, 1982)
26. *Dr. Strangelove* (Stanley Kubrick, 1964)
27. *Bonnie and Clyde* (Arthur Penn, 1967)
28. *Apocalypse Now* (Francis Coppola, 1979)
29. *Mr. Smith Goes to Washington* (Frank Capra, 1939)
30. *The Treasure of the Sierra Madre* (John Huston, 1948)
31. *Annie Hall* (Woody Allen, 1977)
32. *The Godfather, Part II* (Francis Coppola, 1974)
33. *High Noon* (Fred Zinnemann, 1952)
34. *To Kill a Mockingbird* (Robert Mulligan, 1962)
35. *It Happened One Night* (Frank Capra, 1934)
36. *Midnight Cowboy* (John Schlesinger, 1969)
37. *The Best Years of Our Lives* (William Wyler, 1946)
38. *Double Indemnity* (Billy Wilder, 1944)
39. *Doctor Zhivago* (David Lean, 1965)
40. *North by Northwest* (Alfred Hitchcock, 1959)

41. *West Side Story* (Robert Wise, 1961)
42. *Rear Window* (Alfred Hitchcock, 1954)
43. *King Kong* (Merian C. Cooper and Ernest B. Schoedsack, 1933)
44. *The Birth of a Nation* (D. W. Griffith, 1915)
45. *A Streetcar Named Desire* (Elia Kazan, 1951)
46. *A Clockwork Orange* (Stanley Kubrick, 1971)
47. *Taxi Driver* (Martin Scorsese, 1976)
48. *Jaws* (Steven Spielberg, 1975)
49. *Snow White and the Seven Dwarfs* (Walt Disney, 1937)
50. *Butch Cassidy and the Sundance Kid* (George Roy Hill, 1969)
51. *The Philadelphia Story* (George Cukor, 1940)
52. *From Here to Eternity* (Fred Zinnemann, 1953)
53. *Amadeus* (Milos Forman, 1984)
54. *All Quiet on the Western Front* (Lewis Milestone, 1930)
55. *The Sound of Music* (Robert Wise, 1965)
56. *M*A*S*H* (Robert Altman, 1970)
57. *The Third Man* (Carol Reed, 1949)
58. *Fantasia* (Walt Disney, 1940)
59. *Rebel Without a Cause* (Nicholas Ray, 1955)
60. *Raiders of the Lost Ark* (Steven Spielberg, 1981)
61. *Vertigo* (Alfred Hitchcock, 1958)
62. *Tootsie* (Sydney Pollock, 1982)
63. *Stagecoach* (John Ford, 1939)
64. *Close Encounters of the Third Kind* (Steven Spielberg, 1977)
65. *The Silence of the Lambs* (Jonathan Demme, 1991)
66. *Network* (Sidney Lumet, 1976)
67. *The Manchurian Candidate* (John Frankenheimer, 1962)
68. *An American in Paris* (Vincente Minnelli, 1951)
69. *Shane* (George Stevens, 1953)
70. *The French Connection* (William Friedkin, 1971)
71. *Forrest Gump* (Robert Zemeckis, 1994)
72. *Ben-Hur* (William Wyler, 1959)
73. *Wuthering Heights* (William Wyler, 1939)
74. *The Gold Rush* (Charlie Chaplin, 1925)
75. *Dances with Wolves* (Kevin Costner, 1990)
76. *City Lights* (Charlie Chaplin, 1931)
77. *American Graffiti* (George Lucas, 1973)

78. *Rocky* (John G. Avildsen, 1976)
79. *The Deer Hunter* (Michael Cimino, 1978)
80. *The Wild Bunch* (Sam Peckinpah, 1969)
81. *Modern Times* (Charlie Chaplin, 1936)
82. *Giant* (George Stevens, 1956)
83. *Platoon* (Oliver Stone, 1986)
84. *Fargo* (Joel Coen, 1996)
85. *Duck Soup* (Leo McCarey, 1933)
86. *Mutiny on the Bounty* (Frank Lloyd, 1935)
87. *Frankenstein* (James Whale, 1931)
88. *Easy Rider* (Dennis Hopper, 1969)
89. *Patton* (Franklin Schaffner, 1970)
90. *The Jazz Singer* (Alan Crosland, 1927)
91. *My Fair Lady* (George Cukor, 1964)
92. *A Place in the Sun* (George Cukor, 1951)
93. *The Apartment* (Billy Wilder, 1960)
94. *GoodFellas* (Martin Scorsese, 1990)
95. *Pulp Fiction* (Quentin Tarantino, 1994)
96. *The Searchers* (John Ford, 1956)
97. *Bringing Up Baby* (Howard Hawks, 1938)
98. *Unforgiven* (Clint Eastwood, 1992)
99. *Guess Who's Coming to Dinner* (Stanley Kramer, 1967)
100. *Yankee Doodle Dandy* (Michael Curtiz, 1942)

ROSENBAUM'S ALTERNATE ONE HUNDRED

1. *Ace in the Hole/The Big Carnival* (Billy Wilder, 1951)
2. *An Affair to Remember* (Leo McCarey, 1957)
3. *Anatomy of a Murder* (Otto Preminger, 1959)
4. *Avanti!* (Billy Wilder, 1972)
5. *The Barefoot Contessa* (Joseph L. Mankiewicz, 1954)
6. *Bigger than Life* (Nicholas Ray, 1956)
7. *The Big Sky* (Howard Hawks, 1952)
8. *The Black Cat* (Edgar G. Ulmer, 1934)
9. *Bride of Frankenstein* (James Whale, 1935)
10. *Broken Blossoms* (D. W. Griffith, 1919)

11. *Cat People* (Jacques Tourneur, 1942)
12. *Christmas in July* (Preston Sturges, 1940)
13. *Confessions of an Opium Eater* (Albert Zugsmith, 1962)
14. *The Crowd* (King Vidor, 1928)
15. *Dead Man* (Jim Jarmusch, 1995)
16. *Docks of New York* (Josef von Sternberg, 1928)
17. *Do the Right Thing* (Spike Lee, 1989)
18. *Eadweard Muybridge, Zoopraxographer* (Thom Andersen, 1974)
19. *11 x 14* (James Benning, 1976)
20. *Eraserhead* (David Lynch, 1978)
21. *Foolish Wives* (Erich von Stroheim, 1922)
22. *Force of Evil* (Abraham Polonsky, 1948)
23. *Freaks* (Tod Browning, 1932)
24. *The General* (Buster Keaton, 1927)
25. *Gentlemen Prefer Blondes* (Howard Hawks, 1953)
26. *Gilda* (Charles Vidor, 1946)
27. *The Great Garrick* (James Whale, 1937)
28. *Greed* (Erich von Stroheim, 1925)
29. *Hallelujah, I'm a Bum* (Lewis Milestone, 1933)
30. *The Heartbreak Kid* (Elaine May, 1972)
31. *Housekeeping* (Bill Forsyth, 1987)
32. *The Hustler* (Robert Rossen, 1961)
33. *Intolerance* (D. W. Griffith, 1916)
34. *Johnny Guitar* (Nicholas Ray, 1954)
35. *Judge Priest* (John Ford, 1934)
36. *Killer of Sheep* (Charles Burnett, 1977)
37. *The Killing* (Stanley Kubrick, 1956)
38. *The Killing of a Chinese Bookie* (John Cassavetes, 1976)
39. *Kiss Me Deadly* (Robert Aldrich, 1955)
40. *The Ladies Man* (Jerry Lewis, 1961)
41. *The Lady from Shanghai* (Orson Welles, 1948)
42. *Last Chants for a Slow Dance* (Jon Jost, 1977)
43. *Laughter* (Harry d'Arrast, 1930)
44. *Letter from an Unknown Woman* (Max Ophuls, 1948)
45. *Lonesome* (Paul Fejos, 1929)
46. *Love Me Tonight* (Rouben Mamoulian, 1932)
47. *Love Streams* (John Cassavetes, 1984)

48. *The Magnificent Ambersons* (Orson Welles, 1942)
49. *Make Way for Tomorrow* (Leo McCarey, 1937)
50. *Man's Castle* (Frank Borzage, 1933)
51. *The Man Who Shot Liberty Valance* (John Ford, 1962)
52. *McCabe and Mrs. Miller* (Robert Altman, 1971)
53. *Meet Me in St. Louis* (Vincente Minnelli, 1944)
54. *Mikey and Nicky* (Elaine May, 1976)
55. *Monsieur Verdoux* (Charlie Chaplin, 1947)
56. *My Son John* (Leo McCarey, 1952)
57. *The Naked Spur* (Anthony Mann, 1953)
58. *Nanook of the North* (Robert Flaherty, 1922)
59. *The Night of the Hunter* (Charles Laughton, 1955)
60. *The Nutty Professor* (Jerry Lewis, 1963)
61. *The Palm Beach Story* (Preston Sturges, 1942)
62. *Panic in the Streets* (Elia Kazan, 1950)
63. *Park Row* (Samuel Fuller, 1952)
64. *The Phenix City Story* (Phil Karlson, 1955)
65. *Point Blank* (John Boorman, 1967)
66. *Real Life* (Albert Brooks, 1979)
67. *Reminiscences of a Journey to Lithuania* (Jonas Mekas, 1971)
68. *Rio Bravo* (Howard Hawks, 1959)
69. *Scarface* (Howard Hawks, 1932)
70. *The Scarlet Empress* (Josef von Sternberg, 1934)
71. *Scarlet Street* (Fritz Lang, 1945)
72. *Scenes from Under Childhood* (Stan Brakhage, 1967)
73. *The Scenic Route* (Mark Rappaport, 1978)
74. *The Seventh Victim* (Mark Robson, 1943)
75. *Shadows* (John Cassavetes, 1960)
76. *Sherlock Jr.* (Buster Keaton, 1924)
77. *The Shooting* (Monte Hellman, 1967)
78. *The Shop Around the Corner* (Ernst Lubitsch, 1940)
79. *The Sound of Fury/Try and Get Me!* (Cy Endfield, 1951)
80. *Stars in My Crown* (Jacques Tourneur, 1950)
81. *The Steel Helmet* (Samuel Fuller, 1951)
82. *Stranger than Paradise* (Jim Jarmusch, 1984)
83. *The Strawberry Blonde* (Raoul Walsh, 1941)
84. *Sunrise* (F. W. Murnau, 1927)

85. *Sylvia Scarlett* (George Cukor, 1935)
86. *The Tarnished Angels* (Douglas Sirk, 1958)
87. *That's Entertainment! III* (Bud Friedgen and Michael J. Sheridan, 1994)
88. *This Land Is Mine* (Jean Renoir, 1943)
89. *Thunderbolt* (Josef von Sternberg, 1929)
90. *Tom, Tom, the Piper's Son* (Ken Jacobs, 1969)
91. *To Sleep with Anger* (Charles Burnett, 1990)
92. *Track of the Cat* (William Wellman, 1954)
93. *Trouble in Paradise* (Ernst Lubitsch, 1932)
94. *Vinyl* (Andy Warhol, 1965)
95. *Wanda* (Barbara Loden, 1971)
96. *While the City Sleeps* (Fritz Lang, 1956)
97. *Will Success Spoil Rock Hunter?* (Frank Tashlin, 1957)
98. *Woodstock* (Michael Wadleigh, 1970)
99. *The Wrong Man* (Alfred Hitchcock, 1956)
100. *Zabriskie Point* (Michelangelo Antonioni, 1970)

Chapter Seven
Isolationism as a Control System

Is it possible that because of the rise of the new media, which have given us the ability to manufacture what we call virtual reality, we are now able, without quite knowing what we are doing, to create a secondary world that we are liable to mistake for the primary world given to our senses at birth? If so, the prime need it serves is probably not political at all but the one Freud identified as the chief motive for dreaming: wish fulfillment—a need catered to both by our luxuriously proliferating sources of entertainment and the means of their support, namely, advertisement of consumer products. In our variant of self-deception, pleasure plays the role that terror plays under totalitarianism.

—Jonathan Schell, "Land of Dreams,"
The Nation, January 11/18, 1999

This chapter and the next explore complementary and mutually alienating attitudes: the desire to keep out foreign influences in order to preserve American "purity," and the fact that what we consider American "purity" is often composed of foreign influences. In other words, our desire to keep our movies American doesn't make sense if we no longer have a clear idea of what "American" is. Globalization is the major reason for this confusion, though it goes under different names and affects us through different manifestations.

I recently heard about an American teenager visiting Wales who insisted on calling all the Welsh people she met English. When it was pointed out to her that the Welsh didn't like being identified that way, she said she was sorry but that's what she was taught in school and at this point it was too complicated for her to change, regardless of how Welsh people happened to feel.

The fact that she's a teenager is probably pertinent; raging hormones make it even harder than usual to deal with ambiguities. But why is it that only an American can readily be imagined making such a remark, or arriving at such a conclusion? Maybe it's because once you're taught to view everything outside the United States as somewhat unreal—and every other country as a failed or imperfect version of the United States—anything becomes possible, including this special brand of solipsism. There are plenty of other kinds as well—such as Americans who wouldn't be caught dead in an American art museum making tracks for the Louvre as soon as they hit Paris, presumably so they won't have to confront too many Parisians. And not so many years ago, President George Bush made his case against national health by claiming that it was an obvious failure in Canada—the sort of statement that can confidently be made only to some innocent Americans who never set foot outside this country.

Precisely for this reason, even bad or mediocre foreign movies have important things to teach us. Consider them cultural CARE packages, precious news bulletins, breaths of air (fresh or stale) from diverse corners of the globe; however you look at them, they're proof positive that Americans aren't the only human beings and that the decisions we make about how to live our lives aren't the only options available—at least not yet.

As strange as it sounds, this is fast becoming an endangered position. I assume that writer-director Kevin Smith was well past his teens when he told an interviewer a few years back, "I don't feel that I have to go back and view European or other foreign films because I feel like these guys [i.e., Jim Jarmusch and others] have already done it for me, and I'm getting it filtered through them. That ethic works for me." It shouldn't be surprising that Jarmusch was as appalled by Smith's statement as I was, if only for what it reveals about a certain kind of landlocked naiveté—the kind that assumes that world cinema, and therefore the world, can be categorized and summarized so simply. But it isn't all that different, really, from the kind of sweeping judgments that can easily pass for cleverness in our culture. "One of the extraordinary advantages of growing up French," began David Denby's review of Catherine Breillat's *Romance* in *The New Yorker*, "is that you can be absurd without ever quite knowing it"—an advantage presumably denied to world-weary Americans such as himself. To find such a statement funny and/or true, it helps if you glide past the fact that it's describing fifty-eight million living people, none of whom Denby evidently imagines reading his sentence. If a French critic made the same statement about growing up American, I wager that most of us would find the remark stupid. But too many Americans feel licensed to define the rest of the world, cheerfully and without shame, in terms of their own limitations.

About a decade ago, when I was looking for a VCR that would play foreign videos in PAL and SECAM formats on an American NTSC monitor, I came across some interesting fliers describing these machines. While arguing how useful such VCRs were, the ad writers invariably assumed that the only reason an American would want one was to convert NTSC videos to PAL or SECAM formats so they could be sent overseas. The idea that an American might actually want to look at videos from overseas seemed so unlikely that the notion of attracting such individuals never came up.

That a good many Americans are interested in seeing foreign movies, including some that exist only overseas, isn't really a matter of dispute. I get e-mails from such people every week inquiring where they can find certain foreign films on video and sometimes proposing various swaps, and there are many specialized video sale outlets— Facets Multimedia in Chicago and Video Search of Miami, for example—catering principally to that market. Of course, these people are generally only interested in finding films discussed in books and magazines; as a service to its customers, Video Search of Miami, which specializes in cult genre movies, lists twenty such magazines, ranging from *Asian Cult Cinema* to *Video Watchdog*.

But people can only be interested in films that they know about, and given the lack of interest in the mass media in anything that isn't already omnipresent, the range of what people are likely to know about is shrinking rapidly. That's why the themes of innocence and ignorance strike a chord in young audiences despite the supposed cynicism that the press keeps attributing to them. On some level Americans are aware of their own isolation from the rest of the world as well as their crippling lack of information, and *The Blair Witch Project*—the independent, no-budget horror feature that became a runaway hit during the summer of 1999—may have derived much of its power from that implicit recognition, expressed in the mounting sense of helplessness experienced by a trio of film students lost in the woods.

Apart from the film's capacity to allegorize this sense of isolation and ignorance, using an audience's own imagination as paint box, one might have thought that its unexpected commercial success might have been celebrated in the press as a welcome challenge to the dominance of special effects and other production values foisted on the public by the studios. After all, this was a clear sign that the audience wasn't simply kowtowing to the limited options offered by blockbusters like *The Phantom Menace*. Yet the national press perversely chose to extract the reverse meaning out of this grassroots expression. In a provocative article in the *New York Observer* (August 23, 1999), "*Blair Witch* Innocence Scares Media Fatheads," Philip Weiss noted that

> *Time* and *Newsweek* both put *Blair Witch* on the cover four weeks after it premiered and tried to argue that some calculated acts of hype had created the phenomenon. Their articles talk about Sundance, a giant team of marketers, the Internet and some cool TV shows. *The New York Times* also said that the Internet had been used skillfully to push the film.
>
> But all this is a self-justifying media delusion: Something can only succeed by cagey manipulation of the media. *Time* even ended its timeline of the marketing of *Blair Witch* with the Aug. 16 *Time* cover—as if that were part of the plan. The cover of *Time* would have killed this picture. Any big hype would have killed it. There wouldn't have been a *Time* cover in the first place. All the 40ish editors in the mainstream would have checked their watches—as I did—through the movie.
>
> The media are just playing catch-up to the viewers. The response to *Blair Witch* is a populist response that has nothing to do with hype.

As Weiss suggests, the media have a vested interest in proving that the audience is just as corrupt as their own coverage of movies implies. And the moment the audience dares to confound this stereotype and think for itself, a concerted effort is made to demonstrate that the gullible public is merely responding to hype. Consequently, the critical backlash against the popularity of *The Blair Witch Project*, a backlash that essentially equated popularity with hype, came even from such unexpected quarters as Stuart Klawans in *The Nation* and maverick independent filmmaker Jon Jost on the Internet.

***

A 1999 traveling retrospective of the complete works of French filmmaker Robert Bresson—omitting only his first film, *Affaires publiques*

(1934), which preceded his first feature by nine years, at Bresson's own request (largely because it survives only in incomplete form)—offered another encouraging sign that the audience wasn't half as jaded as it was cracked up to be. Throughout his career, stretching from *Les anges du péché* in 1943 to *L'argent* in 1983, and encompassing thirteen features, Bresson has been widely and correctly regarded as one of the essential figures in the history of world cinema, but getting Americans into theaters to see his films was generally believed to be almost impossible. I don't mean to suggest by this that his films fared especially well elsewhere, even in France; apart from his third and fourth features, *Diary of a Country Priest* (1951) and *A Man Escaped* (1956), which did respectably as art-house releases around the world, he was fatally considered an esoteric director whose films audiences found boring, stilted, and pretentious. In part because of Bresson's refusal, starting with his third feature, to employ professional actors, as well as his insistence on directing his "models" (as he called them) to read their lines as tonelessly as possible, the public ridiculed, when it did not ignore, his work; and only a small band of enthusiasts—including a significant number of other filmmakers—persisted in defending his films. Needless to say, the fact that all these features were foreign and subtitled— excepting only an English-dubbed version of *Diary of a Country Priest* that circulated in 16-millimeter—only made things worse.

So one might have supposed that when James Quandt, the ambitious director of the Cinémathèque Ontario in Toronto, began organizing a substantial Bresson retrospective, with brand-new 35-millimeter prints struck of all the features, he was doomed to fight the same uphill battle. Yet this series of thirteen features was a big success practically everywhere it showed in the United States, attracting turn-away crowds in New York, Chicago, Los Angeles, and Washington, D.C., and showing in fifteen separate venues nationwide before returning to some of those cities for encore engagements. (According to Quandt's most recent gleanings, apparently only Houston failed to attract a sizable audience.)

What brought about this substantial change in Bresson's popularity? Some would argue that it was merely a matter of time, and it's certainly true that the cumulative spadework of critics who were Bresson enthusiasts over the years undoubtedly led to more mainstream articles about him in *The New Yorker* and *The New York Times* when the Bresson restrospective was launched in New York. (The latter of these, by Dave Kehr, was substantially more sophisticated than the former, by Anthony Lane, but both performed the invaluable job of getting the word out.) Another reason might be the industry truism that in order for a film or series of films to be commercially successful, it has to have the status of an "event"—meaning, I suppose, that a retrospective with new prints qualifies as an event and that the prior commercial release of a single Bresson masterpiece (say, *Au hasard Balthazar*) apparently doesn't. The overall critical consensus greeting the retrospective was something relatively new; none of Bresson's individual features had received that sort of universal acclaim when they first appeared. And it was cheering to discover that the traditional role of journalistic criticism in simply bringing the news can still pay off with a foreign director as supposedly difficult and as esoteric as Bresson—another strong indication that the alleged dimness and crassness of the American public is simply a matter of guilt by association that deflects from the responsibility of critics, distributors, and exhibitors.

* * *

Ten years ago, I flew all the way from Chicago to the San Francisco Film Festival for a weekend to see Bresson's first film—which had been discovered in incomplete form at the Cinémathèque Française, bearing the title *Béby Inauguré*. Shorn of three of its musical numbers and now totaling twenty-three minutes, this rather elaborate piece of slapstick and surrealist tomfoolery was written and directed by Bresson and released in 1934, a full nine years before shooting started on his first feature, *Les Anges du péché*, and I had been hearing about it for years as an irretrievably lost curiosity. When asked in some interview what the film was like, Bresson had reportedly replied, "Like Buster Keaton, only much, much worse." But then, after the incomplete print was found, I heard that he was pleased rather than appalled about the recovery.

Prior to the festival screening, the director and screenwriter Paul Schrader, who hadn't yet seen the film either, offered a detailed introduction that outlined his transcendental interpretation of Bresson's work. And in a way this totally irrelevant and incongruous preparation for *Affaires Publiques* proved to be almost as hilarious as the film itself, as if one of the royal dignitaries ridiculed by Bresson in the film had offered his own thumbnail sketch of the proceedings. Though a sense of humor has never been one of Schrader's strong points—even if one discounts the apparently unconscious humor of the newspaper headline "Fall from Grace" in *Late Sleeper,* one of his better movies—his dogged efforts to enforce a metaphysical reading of one of the world's most physical filmmakers were completely derailed by the film itself, which is a good deal closer to *Million Dollar Legs, Duck Soup,* and Jean Vigo's *Zéro de conduite* in spirit—not to mention Alfred Jarry's *Ubu roi*—than it is to either *Diary of a Country Priest* or *Pickpocket.*

As it happens, Schrader's wasn't the only blatant critical gaffe I encountered at the festival that year. The same weekend, I was lucky enough to see Souleymane Cissé's sublime *Yeelen* for the first time, and was shocked to learn from Michael Sragow that this film as well as Tian Zhuangzhuang's remarkable *The Horse Thief* demonstrated that the San Francisco Film Festival was more interested in ethnography than in art. To my mind, both misreadings ultimately stem from a reluctance to deal with film in terms of sound and image; Schrader's spiritual grid and Sragow's ethnocentric (i.e., racist) grid both derive from personal agendas that factor out much of what the filmmakers are doing.

Part of the problem we have in seeing (and hearing) Bresson clearly is that we tend to stereotype him in relation to a system. A similar conundrum haunts our simplistic and idealistic readings of Yasujiro Ozu, and the bracing lucidity of Shigehiko Hasumi's groundbreaking 1983 book on Ozu, a French translation and adaptation of which was published in 1998 by *Cahiers du cinéma,* points beyond these limits. Explicitly countering the transcendental readings of Ozu by Schrader, Donald Richie, and others, Hasumi also seeks to liberate Ozu from the negative descriptions that have encrusted most of the criticism about his work and the characterizations of that work as "typically" Japanese. The final chapter of Hasumi's book, "Sunny Skies," is available in English in the collection of essays on *Tokyo Story* edited by David Desser for Cambridge University Press (1997), and one sentence in particular seems equally applicable to Bresson: "Ozu's talent lies in choosing an image that can function poetically at a particular moment by being assimilated into the film, not by affixing to the film the image of an object that is considered poetic in a domain outside the film."

***

The other day I received an e-mail from someone wanting to know how I could have described *The Tree of Wooden Clogs* as Marxist when it was so clearly a religious film. Actually it was Dave Kehr who had written the *Chicago Reader*'s capsule review of Ermanno Olmi's feature in 1985, two years before I'd started work on that paper, but I hastily e-mailed back that any Italian would tell you that Marxism could easily be seen as a form of religion. Afterward I realized that this response was flip. It would have been better to say that Catholicism and Marxism have had a long and complex coexistence in Italy, and it was unrealistic to expect that they would be mutually exclusive as systems of belief; the career of Pier Paolo Pasolini is proof of how intimately the two can be intertwined, regardless of the contradictions involved. That led me to think about how the similar characterizations of European Marxism in this country foster such confusion. Shortly after this I happened to read André Bazin's description of *The Bicycle Thief* as one of the great Communist films—an aspect of the film I suspect couldn't have been apparent to American audiences when it won the Oscar for best foreign film in 1949.

Given our extreme isolationism—arguably even greater today than it was half a century ago—it's logical that we should think of foreigners in stereotypical terms because we have so little information and experience to draw upon; similarly, we often think of non-Americans as wannabe Americans. So, out of necessity, we wind up thinking about much of the rest of the world in shorthand: Communists are nonreligious, the French worship Jerry Lewis, Iranians are subject to heavy censorship in the arts, the Chinese produce fortune cookies. That there are plenty of religious Communists, that most contemporary French viewers prefer Woody Allen to Jerry Lewis, that Iranians tend to revere artists more than we do, and that Chinese fortune cookies are strictly for export are lesser-known facts because they interfere with our ready-made formulas. At most such data offers fleeting clues about what usually escapes our radar, and unless we can combine them with additional information, they're likely to be helpful only as counter-stereotypes, not as understandings of these foreign cultures.

Dimness about geography and dimness about history often go hand in hand. When I recently taught a class on Luis Buñuel's *The Discreet Charm of the Bourgeoisie*, the main stumbling block for the students— most of whom were adults rather than teenagers—appeared to be historical rather than geographical. That is, the problem wasn't that the filmmaker was Spanish or that the dialogue was in French but that this radically discontinuous and unorthodox narrative feature had won the Oscar for best foreign film in 1972. Considering how impossible this would have been had the same feature been released in 1999, the students—most of whom had been alive and conscious of what was happening in the world back in 1972—couldn't figure out how and why things had changed so much since then.

* * *

TRANSATLANTIC REALITY AVOIDANCE: A REPORT FROM THE FRONT (MAY 1999)

"'I think, therefore I am,'" reads the opening epigraph of *The Thirteenth Floor*, the fourth virtual-reality thriller I saw in Chicago in as many weeks in the spring of 1999, followed by the quotation's source, "Descartes (1596–1650)." It's an especially pompous beginning for a movie whose characters scarcely think, much less exist, but not an unexpected one given the metaphysical claims and pronouncements that usually inform these thrillers.

If any thought at all can be deemed the source of these pictures cropping up one after the other—with the exception of David Cronenberg's *eXistenZ*, a film with a lot more than generic commercial kicks on its mind—this might be an especially low estimation of what an audience is looking for at the movies. The assumed desire might be expressed in infantile and emotional terms: "I don't like the world, take it away." In other words, the virtual-reality thriller seems to solve the puzzle of how to address an audience assumed to be interested only in escaping without reminding them of what they're supposed to be escaping from. It smacks of significance by indulging in glib self-referential hints that movies are just a form of dreaming anyway, implies that anything that suggests the real world is—or might as well be—a hallucination, and is usually "thoughtful" enough to include gobs of violence on the assumption that even if the world is no longer desirable, kicking ass for any reason at all is. And in the cases of *The Matrix* and *The Thirteenth Floor*, the two studio blockbusters in the batch (the other two being the Spanish movie *Open Your Eyes* and *eXistenZ*), a worshipful attitude towards digital technology appears to be the only factor that justifies the conceits about alternative realities in terms of science fiction rather than a less prestigious and more hybrid form like science fantasy. As the press book for *The Thirteenth Floor* eagerly puts it, "Over two thousand years ago, Plato postulated that the 'real' world exists only in our imagination. The technology of modern society has begun to prove Plato's point." Thanks a lot, modern society; tough luck, Kosovo Albanian and Serb civilians.

The only point at which I differ from Jonathan Schell's remarks about virtual reality at the beginning of this chapter ("In our variant of self-deception, pleasure plays the role that terror plays under totalitarianism") is his suggestion that "the prime need it serves is probably not political at all," which my European-trained bias is tempted to label Famous Last Words. This is because avoidance of politics qualifies as a political position just like any other, and the desire to avoid politics in American life, however primal, stems from political suppositions, often unacknowledged as such. Accepting and/or submitting to the status quo is commonly regarded as a "neutral" position, but the twentieth century has already amply taught us that neutrality in certain contexts amounts to defeat or alienation at best, complicity at worst.

At the beginning of most movies, including quite a few bad ones, there's a period of grace when exciting possibilities still hover. The same feeling of both mystery and potentiality presides at the beginning of film festivals—the titles, directors, actors, countries, and catalogue descriptions portend all sorts of things. Disappointment generally follows when the promises aren't kept and the anticipatory dreams go unfulfilled, except for those interesting occasions when expectations get revised on the spot (or a few days afterward) and unforeseen pleasures start to emerge. More often, the exciting possibilities gradually become narrowed down into familiar, shopworn routines—the kind that our experts inform us are the only sure-fire things that sell (except for when they don't).

So I have to admit that *The Thirteenth Floor* kept me hoping for the first half-hour or so, before it turned into another virtual-reality boondoggle. The press screening was held the morning after the prizes at the 1999 Cannes film festival were announced, and because this was the first year since 1993 that I didn't attend at least part of that event, I still had months or in some cases years to wait before the movies there that interested me the most had even a chance to disappoint me. You might say that this is my own virtual-reality game, playable in different ways in terms of both *The Thirteenth Floor* and the Cannes festival I didn't attend, though the difference between waiting half an hour and waiting several months is not to be sneezed at: in the latter case, for instance, I had to worry more about all the misinformation that was likely to gum up my expectations in the interim.

I don't mean to suggest that virtual-reality thrillers are the only form of virtual reality in our midst. All four that appeared in the space of a month roughly coincided with the Cannes festival, including its preliminaries and immediate aftermath, and the American coverage of that event seemed boxed in by a comparable set of assumptions. The ruling philosophy behind most of this coverage seemed to be, why should we be interested in new films from all over the world unless it's to ratify what we already know? Why, for instance, didn't they show *Star Wars, Episode I—The Phantom Menace*? Why weren't there any more Hollywood blockbusters? ("Cannes picks dour pix, snubs H'w'd," trumpeted a *Variety* headline before the festival even started.) And, most important of all, how happy or unhappy is or was Harvey Weinstein, cochairman of Miramax, about the festival as a whole?

The happiness or unhappiness of Harvey has become the main theme of North American film festival coverage in recent years; it's equally prominent in reports from Sundance, and whenever Oscar night rolls around you can bet that cameras will be poised to discover how he's feeling at various selected moments—especially those that confirm whether the Oscars he's worked and paid for get delivered or not. At Cannes, where the focus is supposedly on hundreds of movies rather than a handful of box-office favorites, and supposedly on artistic merit rather than in-house industry popularity, the American press gets indignant if Oscar-night results aren't approximated, Harvey's beam of approval included. This year, the attitude appeared to be, "I don't like the world, take it away"—a complaint seemingly addressed to Harvey, who presumably knows how to take it away and even where to take it.

Unfortunately for the American press, this wasn't the year when Harvey could take charge. He seemed pretty unhappy when the Cannes prizes were being announced—most of them, incidentally, to filmmakers I admire a good deal more than most of the pets in his stable—and his fans in the press seemed incensed that his tastes weren't being honored. But since Harvey's displeasure invariably bolsters my faith in the future of world cinema, Cannes's 1999 winners seemed to be a pretty invigorating bunch.

The argument is that Weinstein dominates the stateside distribution of specialized movies—he's supposed to be the Nero or Caligula with the thumbs up or thumbs down perogative—but how he manages to maintain this dominance is discussed less often. Critics who call him the distributor most responsible for enabling us to see foreign films aren't doing simple arithmetic. Because Miramax picks up over twice as many films as it releases—keeping most of its unreleased pictures in perpetual limbo, shaping and recutting most of its favorites, and marginalizing most of the others so that only a handful of people ever get to see them—there's statistically *less* chance of the public ever having access to a movie if Miramax acquires it. (Why are all of Abbas Kiarostami's recent features except for *Through the Olive Trees* available for rental on video? Guess which one Miramax "distributes." And why did most Americans never get a chance to see either the color version of *Jour de fête* or the restoration of *The Young Girls of Rochefort*? Guess again. It's been speculated that one reason why Miramax picks up so many films is in order to prevent other distributors from acquiring them; if this is true, then I guess we're supposed to conclude that Miramax's profit motive is more important than the desire of many people to see these and other films that are kept out of reach.) Yet if you follow the drift of *The New York Times*, the *Chicago Sun-Times*, the *Chicago Tribune*, *Variety*, and comparable publications, Harvey's disposition at any given moment appears to be a useful shorthand for the overall health and direction of world cinema. It's certainly a lot easier to track than what a bunch of difficult foreign filmmakers have to say about the state of the world and what an unpredictable international jury—headed in 1999, as it happens, by David Cronenberg—decides is most valuable. So why not conclude that Harvey's mood is more interesting and important as well?

On the other hand, if it's a question of selling a feel-good Holocaust comedy like *Life Is Beautiful,* it's hard to deny that Miramax conquers markets that true independent distributors are unable to penetrate. Visiting my home town recently, I discovered that *Life Is Beautiful* was playing even in Florence, Alabama; it may have been the first time a subtitled film had shown there theatrically in four decades, ever since my family's former chain of theaters became reluctantly independent.

Seeing a subtitled feel-good Holocaust movie may be better than not seeing any subtitled movies at all—just as seeing a virtual-reality thriller may be better than seeing no SF thrillers of any kind. A bird in the hand is worth two in the bush, and if the bushwhackers at Cannes want to send home something ready for the microwave, they may feel they have to depend on a Harveyburger rather than on anything more exotic. But if that's the case, they have an opinion of their public that's not dissimilar from that of the people churning out virtual-reality thrillers. What's happening in the world outside of virtual reality is a lot more complicated than what's happening inside, and if the inside is all we're equipped to deal with, then we can't be very well equipped.

Certainly not equipped to cope with the film that won the jury prize at Cannes, Manoel De Oliveira's *The Letter*—his adaptation of the first great short novel in French, Madame de Lafayette's *La princesse de Clèves* (not *Madam de Cleeves,* as the *Tribune* had it, or *La princesse de Cleeves,* as BRAVO's Cannes coverage pronounced it). I haven't liked all of De Oliveira's films—even if he's incontestably the greatest of all Portuguese filmmakers as well as the oldest filmmaker anywhere currently at work, and the only one left who started out in silent cinema. His last feature, *Inquiètude,* placed first on my 1998 ten-best list, but it's theoretically possible, if I'd attended Cannes in 1999, that I might have concluded, along with Roger Ebert's colleagues (as reported in one of his Cannes dispatches), that *The Letter* was "the second or third worst film in the festival." (Could it have been those same esteemed colleagues who noisily walked out at Cannes during the exquisite final shots of Terence Davies's *The Neon Bible,* or who chastised Jim Jarmusch for not letting Harvey recut *Dead Man*?) I also might have concluded that a jury comprising, among others, Cronenberg, Holly Hunter, George Miller, and André Téchiné might have something to teach me, so their verdicts might have at least piqued my curiosity.

And what about the other disputed Cannes prizewinners? The Palme d'Or went to *Rosetta* by Luc and Jean-Pierre Dardenne, the Belgian brothers who made *La promesse*; the grand jury prize, best actor, and half of the best actress award went to *L'humanité* by Bruno Dumont, the French filmmaker who made *La vie de Jésus*; the other half of the best actress award went to Emilie Dequenne in *Rosetta* (apparently increasing the outrage was the fact that all three acting awards went to nonprofessionals); best screenplay went to the Russian-German coproduction *Moloch* by Russian filmmaker Aleksandr Sokurov, another major artist generally shunned or else jeered at by the Miramax hounds. Relatively undisputed by the American press was the best director prize to Pedro Almodovar for his Spanish crowd-pleaser *All About My Mother* and best set design prize to Chen Kaige's *The Emperor and the Assassin.* (Chen's previous film, the initially hypnotic *Autumn Moon,* was reedited into indigestible chopped liver by Harvey, which I assume is what makes him acceptable to large portions of the American press.)

Bearing in mind that some Cannes awards are compromises rather than unanimous choices, there's still a discernible profile that emerges from the dominance of films by gifted regionalists that is clarified by some remarks made by Austrian critic Alexander Horwath a couple of years ago, to which I've added a couple of tentative amplifications:

> In the framework of film-cultural globalization two fake alternatives have evolved: the Miramax idea of U.S. "indies" and the reduction of European art cinema to a few "masters" who can transcend all national borders and dance in all markets (Kieslowski and Zhang Yimou might be two good examples [to which one might add Almodovar and Chen]). I am much more interested in filmmakers who speak in concrete words and voices, from a concrete place, about concrete places and characters. I like the image of the brothers Dardenne . . . standing somewhere in the middle of industrial Belgium, looking around and saying, "All these landscapes make up our language" [which also might be said of Dumont standing somewhere in rural France]. Next to the filmmakers we've often discussed (like Ferrara, Assayas, Egoyan, Wong Kar-wai, et al.) there are many more if lesser-known examples of such a kind of cinema.

Their dialects are much too specific to fit into the global commerce of goods—in Austria: Wolfgang Murnberger (today), John Cook (in the 1970s); in Germany, Michael Klier, Helge Schneider. Or in Kazakhstan: Darezhan Omirbaev. And even in Hollywood: Albert Brooks.[1]

The fact that I recognize only the two last names in Horwath's final list gives me further cause for hope, but from the looks of things, the same evocation of untapped pleasures beyond the Miramax radar is more likely to elicit groans and consternation from the American press. The tension between art and commerce at Cannes has always been fierce, but in past years a certain amount of strained coexistence has always been possible. I expect it's still that way, but judging from all the American reports I've encountered from Cannes this year, it sounds like the art contingent has been reduced to the size of a pesky gnat. (Here's *Variety*'s way of putting it: "If the *Rosetta* award was a jolt, things really got out of hand with *L'humanité*, a two-and-a-half-hour account of the slowest murder investigation ever filmed that provoked considerable critical derision from everyone except, perhaps, certain French critics.") The fact that this year the gnat bit Harvey's ass is apparently what's causing all the fuss.

POSTSCRIPT: HARVEY BITES BACK

Three days after I submitted the above article to the *Chicago Reader* and five days before it was published, Janet Maslin eliminated my niggling fears that I might have exaggerated the national press's obsession with Harvey Weinstein at Cannes. In her Sunday "wrap-up" piece about the festival in *The New York Times* (May 30, 1999), Maslin went beyond my previous examples and made Weinstein's distress the only major event deserving extended coverage. After four short and dutiful

---

[1] "Movie Mutations," by Jonathan Rosenbaum, Adrian Martin, Kent Jones, Alexander Horwath, Nicole Brenez, and Raymond Bellour, in *Film Quarterly*, vol. 52, no. 1, fall 1998, p. 46. Note: this is a condensed English version of an article roughly twice as long that first appeared in French in *Trafic* no. 24, 1997, and has also appeared in its full version in Dutch (*Skrien* nos. 221–225, 1998), German (*Meteor* nos. 12 & 13, 1998), and Italian (*Close Up* no. 4, 1998). The full version can be found in English on the University of California Press Web site: *http://www.ucpress.edu/journals/fq/critic.html*.

paragraphs devoted to the prizes given to "two intense, painful French-language films dealing with hard lives in lonely surroundings" (i.e., *Rosetta* and *L'humanité*), she devoted the following eight paragraphs to what clearly mattered most to her about the festival (I've italicized three of her sentences in order to make points about them later):

> In any case, this was the year that Harvey Weinstein of Miramax declared war. Weinstein has long been galled by this event's elitism and its predilection for dull, irrelevant films and he thinks it's time for a change. "There's something wrong with Cannes, and it needs to be fixed," he said angrily by telephone from the closing night party. "The luster of the festival is completely submerged. *It's losing its place in film history. It has the potential to be so much more than it is now, the potential to be so much more serious and less political.* I've reached the frustration point, and I'm not scared to say so any more."
>
> Of course Weinstein could be accused of sour grapes. Miramax's version of Oscar Wilde's *Ideal Husband* was this year's closing night film and Kevin Smith's *Dogma* was an out-of-competition hot potato. (Miramax bought back *Dogma* to shield Disney, its parent company, from possible protests against the film's views on Catholicism.)
>
> But otherwise, the usually unstoppable Miramax team was practically AWOL. Then again, the big American studios were also missing with the notable exception of Disney, which was attached to films by David Lynch, Tim Robbins and Spike Lee.
>
> "I feel a very sentimental attachment to Cannes, but I'm tired of begging," said Weinstein, who had no luck getting *Dogma* into the main competition, though there was room for a two and a half hour soap opera (*Our Happy Lives*) about a group of star-crossed French characters. "I'm tired of fighting for obvious choices." (Among Miramax's previous rejects for Cannes' main competition are *My Left Foot* and *The Crying Game*.)
>
> So he spent much of this year's festival stirring up producers, directors and financiers of his acquaintance. Maybe they will be able to offset the doldrums that are especially extreme. *When the* Variety *critic Todd McCarthy fired off a salvo against overlong films of no interest to anyone but their creators, his column was more popular than most of the movies in town.*
>
> And if nothing changes? "Then I won't come," Weinstein said.
>
> If that sounds like a no-prisoner stance, it's also an indication of what an extreme sport Cannes can be from a business standpoint. That's what it amounts to for the small club of distributors who dominate American art-house fare.

This was followed by seven more paragraphs—the first two devoted to which American distributors other than Miramax picked up half a dozen films for distribution, clearly the subject that interested her least in the article, and the last five devoted to the gear employed by those distributors in Cannes—e.g., a bicycle for Sony Classics' Tom Bernard, hiking boots for Fine Line Features' Mark Ordesky—which captured substantially more of her attention and apparent interest.

I suspect an entire book could be written about the meanings of both "film history" and "political" as Weinstein understands those terms, but it's not a book I would ever care to write or even research. In order to contemplate the first, I suspect I'd have to ignore a good 95 percent of the films I care about the most and concentrate on items like *The Crying Game* and *My Left Foot* that made Harvey a lot of money. And in order to write about "political" in contradistinction to "serious," an American yahoo specialty, I'd have to ignore everything I learned about politics over nearly eight years of living in Paris and London—an education that started with the premise that politics were involved with everything that improved the quality of one's life, society, and environment[2], not merely with the results of an election or a festival jury's vote that improved one distributor's bank account.

Anyone who's ever attended the Cannes festival knows that one can carve about as many publics as one wishes out of the hordes of people attending. (After all, Cannes is only the world of film in miniature, and as Oscar Wilde once aptly noted, "There are as many publics as there are personalities.") So I'm not unduly surprised when Maslin reports that Todd McCarthy's own attack on the 1999 Cannes selection "was more popular than most of the movies in town"—even if she's the only one I've encountered so far who has voiced that sentiment or anything close to it—because all critics, myself included, tend to find what they go looking for. But I can't help but conclude that she's living in a very

---

[2] A perfect illustration of this premise is *Rosetta* itself, especially if one considers that the film inspired a new Belgian law known as "Plan Rosetta," passed on November 12, 1999, prohibiting employers from paying teenage workers less than the minimum wage. To the best of my knowledge, this fact went unreported in the American press apart from my own *Chicago Reader* review (January 14, 2000)—which isn't surprising given the usual tendency to treat audiences like servants of Disney rather than citizens of the world. But judging by discussions I had with two separate Chicago audiences who saw the film, the film's political, visceral, and emotional power registered loud and clear.

different universe from mine. Even Weinstein, I presume, might have preferred his own two films at the festival to McCarthy's column, though here I'm strictly second-guessing this Dickensian character.

As a rule, Maslin during her visits to Cannes attended only the films in competition and a few high-profile special events, and often missed several of these (such as *Taste of Cherry* during the last year I attended Cannes as a critic). So what she described as "most of the movies in town" was an expedient fiction that suited her temperament and inclination to see as little of the range of what Cannes has to offer as she could manage to get away with. (Truthfully, no single human being could comment intelligently or even intelligibly on "most of the movies in town" when several dozen are screened daily.) It's also evident that she had little desire to hang out with critics more interested and knowledgeable about movies than she was, because this might make her at least faintly aware that she might be missing something. (I'm ruling out some of the titles that interest me the most, like Jean-Marie Straub and Danièle Huillet's *Sicilia!*, because I couldn't imagine her sitting through them, but surely there were other, less demanding items she might have enjoyed.)

Most of my friends attend dozens of other screenings in the numerous other sections of the festival, and practically all of them reported back that the 1999 Cannes festival was full of interesting and exciting things to see, including several of the films in competition. None of them, I should add, showed any interest in what Harvey Weinstein had to say about these movies—unless this was related to whether American viewers would ever get to see them or not. (In most cases, it wasn't.) Much more relevant to this issue was whether or not they might have been selected by the film festivals in New York, San Francisco, and Toronto, among many others.

As a postscript, it's worth adding that David Cronenberg's response to Harvey Weinstein has so far—to the best of my knowledge, judging by the reach of my computer's search engines—appeared only in French, a significant fact in itself. An interview with Cronenberg by Laurent Rigoulet appeared in the June 2, 1999 issue of *Libération,* entitled "Cronenberg contre-attaque." Some of Cronenberg's points—such as his insistence that his jury's prizes aren't supposed to be popularity contests—are similar to mine. (He also emphasizes that the jury found the films in competition exciting even when they were failures "because

they attempted something," and compared the experience favorably to
the "depressing" experience of being sent videos of Oscar-nominated
films every year, "essentially a minifestival of American movies . . .
where one sees the same strategy everywhere and feels pitifully grateful
towards the minor film that tries to find a slightly different approach.")
But it's only fair to note his claim that there were no conscious political
or intellectual motives behind his jury's decisions. (He also stressed that
the decision to award two acting prizes to the nonprofessionals in *L'humanité* was based strictly on the quality of the performances, not on the
biographies or filmographies of the actors.) Dismissing McCarthy's
attack in *Variety* as "pure Hollywood propaganda," he adds (the translation is again mine), "You have to understand that Cannes has become
an insult to the Americans. They find this festival marvelous and they
want to make it their own. And since they haven't succeeded in taking
it over, they've begun to hate it. They say that the festival has lost its reason for existing, that it's 'irrelevant.' That's a wonderful word for the films
we've chosen. What does it mean? I believe that's the way Harvey Weinstein, the boss of Miramax, put it. I'd love for him to explain to me what
makes *Shakespeare in Love* more relevant than *Rosetta*. What does it
mean that a feel-good comedy set in Elizabethan England represents for
him an artistic film whereas *Rosetta* lacks relevance?"

***

The apparent conviction of so many American "experts" in Cannes
that foreign material is somehow contaminated unless it gets the Weinstein seal of approval (and the editing "polish" that usually goes with it)
seems analogous to the blinkers that define what's plausible in relation
to class-bound assumptions. We often tend to forget that what we call
realism, from Emile Zola to David Denby, almost invariably derives
from a class position. One very useful aspect of Denby's film criticism,
apart from the beautifully chiseled construction of his prose style, is the
way it reliably and sometimes hilariously reflects middle-class or
upscale blindness to the world that everyone else inhabits. In his review
of *Eyes Wide Shut*, for example, we discover in the course of his reality
lessons that "a prostitute who picks up [the hero] and takes him home
is patently too beautiful and well educated to be working the pave-
ments." When I cited this remark to a friend, she replied, "I guess he's

not doing trade." The only on-screen evidence of education I could spot was a sociology textbook and an Oscar Peterson CD; but clearly middle-class constructions of street hookers exclude such workaday possibilities, along with beauty. Woody Allen's uncouth prostitutes and convicts must be more ideologically correct specimens, since they're more apt to use terms like "dem" and "dose." Maybe I'm jumping to conclusions in assuming that Denby has less trouble with these middle-class fantasies of Allen's—all seemingly derived from Warners crime pictures of the thirties—but he certainly wouldn't be alone in this bias; Mia Sorvino actually won an Oscar for playing the cartoon hooker in *Mighty Aphrodite*. (Nobody accused her of being too beautiful for the part, but then again, she wasn't working the streets.)

I could be wrong about this, but I suspect that at least part of what made so many American critics incensed by Kubrick's unfashionable, posthumously released masterpiece was that it was shot overseas by an expatriate, even though it was set in New York. Perhaps because it starred Tom Cruise, carried the Warners logo, and was made by a film-maker who spent roughly the first half of his life in the United States, people went expecting an "American" film of the nineties and got something else—an essentially nationless movie reflecting just about every decade in this century *except* the nineties, which transplanted a remarkable Arthur Schnitzler novella written in 1926 and set in pre-World War I Vienna into a mannerist English studio representation of New York City roughly a century later.[3] Certainly the film was American in some respects, but there were other, equally valid ways in which

---

[3] Some New York critics poignantly inquired how a movie about New York could get so many facts about the city wrong. But the notion that Kubrick's film is "about" New York is absurd to begin with—apparently motivated by these critics' desire to validate themselves as New Yorkers rather than to say anything meaningful about the movie. Nobody would think of claiming that Schnitzler's story was "about" Vienna—its title is *Traumnouvelle*, not *Viennanouvelle*—so it hardly seems reasonable to assume that Kubrick would want to make a movie about a city he hadn't visited at least since the early eighties. Similarly, the insistence of some of these critics that the film remains "unfinished" because Kubrick never completed the sound mixing not only contradicts the testimony of Kubrick's widow, an artist herself, but suggests a curious double standard relative to their treatments of films such as *Mr. Arkadin*, which Orson Welles was unable to finish editing.

it might be regarded as English, Austrian, or, even better, as transnational or multinational—a category that we've so far learned to identify economically but not yet culturally or existentially.

It's worth stressing that a lot of what audiences today routinely regard as "American" isn't—at least not in the way that such a term used to apply to studio releases. (This is the subject of the next chapter, and another pertinent cause of our everyday alienation regarding movies.) We've been trained to confuse labels with contents, and outmoded critical categories and reflexes with contemporary practices—which leads us to discuss videos as if they were movies and the tastes of producers and publicists as if they were the tastes of audiences. So it's only natural that we should wind up considering multinational movies as American if enough American or "American" stars (Arnold Schwarzenegger would qualify) are featured. Never mind that the funding might be foreign, not to mention the director, writers, and/or crew; the whole thing is still supposed to be "ours" even if it belongs to Japanese or Arab investors. And maybe this misperception wouldn't matter so much if we didn't keep applying notions of—and assumptions about—national cinema to releases that confound such categories, so that what constitutes "an American movie" in the year 2000 often has scant relation to what was defined as such in 1950. As suggested earlier, this implies that our isolationism is historical as well as geographical—a condition of being lost in time as well as space.

Chapter Eight
Multinational Pest Control:
Does American Cinema Still Exist?

Independence Day, the first election-year motion picture to receive the endorsement of both major party Presidential candidates, opened to national acclaim on 2 July 1996, the day that alien spacecraft were first sighted. "I recommend it," President Bill Clinton told a crowd the next morning. Hillary, Bill and Chelsea Clinton watched the incineration of the White House on 2 July from the scene of the crime. They were joined by Dean Devlin and Roland Emmerich, who produced, directed and wrote the film, and by the film Chief Executive, Bill Pullman, who sat next to his real-life counterpart. President Clinton comforted his daughter when she took fright at the obliteration of her home; soon after, the on-screen President would comfort his daughter when her mother, who had been away from the White House on business, died from the effects of the blast that leveled Los Angeles.

Hollywood and Washington, twin capitals of the American empire and seats of its international political economy, collaborated to promote the movie that filmed their destruction.

— Michael Rogin, *Independence Day* (1998)[1]

Motion pictures are the most conspicuous of all American exports. They do not lose their identity. They betray their nationality and country of origin. . . .They are demonstrably the single greatest factors in the Americanization of the world and as such fairly may be called the most important and significant of America's exported products.

— The Motion Picture Producers and Distributors Association (1928)[2]

---

[1] London: British Film Institute, p. 9.
[2] Ibid., p. 73.

When did American action blockbusters stop being American? It's hard to define a precise moment in the two decades separating the genocidal adventures in George Lucas's *Star Wars* from those in Paul Verhoeven's *Starship Troopers* (a much more interesting and provocative film), but the differences in national pedigree are palpable, even when it comes to an ostensibly ratified flag-waver like *Independence Day*. Even though the latter film all but busts a gut in declaring its national credentials and *Starship Troopers* is a creative adaptation of an all-American novel (by Robert A. Heinlein), was consciously modeled on Hollywood World War II features (as was much of *Star Wars*), and even boasts a hyperbolically all-American cast that could have sprung full-blown out of a camp classic of Aryan physiognomy like Howard Hawks's *Red Line 7000*, the only state that either can be said to honor or reflect is one of drifting statelessness.

What I mean is that if the alien bugs from Verhoeven's movie wanted to learn what American life and culture was like in 1977, *Star Wars* would serve as a useful and appropriate object of study. It would tell them, among other things, about the video games children played, the voyeuristic distance of most of the population regarding warfare, the puritanical attitudes in 1977 America regarding sex, the attitudes of middle-class American children toward both pets and servants, and the economic power of teen and preteen culture and the sense of entitlement that went with it. But if they wanted to know what American life was like in 1997, *Starship Troopers* wouldn't have nearly as much to tell them, and *Independence Day* would arguably tell them even less about American life in 1996—except, perhaps, for how little life in the remainder of the world is allowed to penetrate our national borders. (Significantly, every time another country needs to be represented in abbreviated form in *Independence Day*, a stereotypical image dating back to the fifties is reverted to.) The confidence of the Motion Picture Producers and Distributors Association seventy years ago is hard to imagine in the multinational globalized money markets of the nineties—in contradistinction to the hoopla reported by Michael Rogin, all of which seems contrived to convince us that an anonymous piece of nostalgic uplift like *Independence Day* is as American as apple pie.

Maybe it is in some way, but whether or not the apple pie served in McDonald's strictly qualifies as "American"—at least for an everyday customer in Beijing—is quite another matter; and whether it's as quintessentially and as exclusively American as we habitually think it is also warrants a certain amount of healthy skepticism. Back in the late sixties, when my youngest brother was living in Nairobi, Kenya, he spent part of his time conversing with members of the Red Guard who were stationed there, and one of the topics of their conversation was the nationality of Coca-Cola. The Red Guard soldiers, who liked Coca-Cola, were convinced that it was a product of Kenya; they refused to believe that a corrupt capitalist and imperialist nation such as the United States could have produced it.

Labels are deceptive: Kentucky Fried Chicken outlets in Tokyo aren't simply or necessarily promoting the Kentucky way of life. If, for example, they sell corn soup the way that McDonald's outlets in Tokyo do—unlike the McDonald's or Kentucky Fried Chicken outlets in Chicago—then they're using American décor to sell a Japanese product and thereby promote the Japanese way of life, which now includes hot cans of corn soup and a brand of canned espresso called Pokka that you can buy everywhere in Japanese vending machines. Pokka Espresso is brewed in American Canyon, California (though if you want to buy it in Chicago you have to go to an Asian supermarket), and the Pokka people can hardly be said to be promoting an Italian way of life.

My point here is that what we—and the Motion Picture Producers and Distributors Association in 1928—tend to automatically assume is American may not necessarily signify the same thing in the same way to other inhabitants of the planet, especially now that the capital controlling the flow of so-called American products is just as likely to come from somewhere else. The question of a film's national identity, which could be posed with a lot more simplicity in 1928, is often not so simple nowadays when the patterns of life created by capitalism in different corners of the world may wind up mattering a great deal more than the particular distinguishing features of nationality. A few years back, a Peruvian film critic in Chicago told me that the contemporary film that had the most to say to him about life in contemporary Peru was Hou Hsiao-hsien's *Goodbye South, Goodbye,* and the fact that he was telling me this in Chicago rather than in Lima or Taipei seemed significant as well—along with the fact that the film is best known under its English title outside the Chinese-speaking world. It's equally pertinent that Wong Kar-wai's *Happy Together*—a film about Hong Kong with an American title derived from a hit record by the Turtles—is set almost entirely in Buenos Aires.

Manoel De Oliveira's Portuguese-French *Voyage to the Beginning of the World*, a meditation on the differences between being Portuguese and being French, uses an Italian actor (Marcello Mastroianni in his last performance) playing De Oliveira to preside over these reflections. Manuel Poirier's French road movie *Western* focuses on a Catalan Spaniard and a Russian immigrant of Italian origin in a small section of Brittany. Even more typical of art movies of the mid-nineties is *The End of Violence*, a French-German-American coproduction with an American subject, setting, and writer, a German director (Wim Wenders), and an Anglo-American cast. For even more recent films, one may well ask which is more modern and contemporary in feeling: Pedro Almodovar's *All About My Mother*, which is all in Spanish (although it deals with a stage production of Tennessee Williams's *A Streetcar Named Desire* and borrows separate portions of its plot from Mankiewicz's *All About Eve* and Cassavetes's *Opening Night*), or Luis Galvao Teles's *Women (Elles)*—a Portuguese film using only French dialogue to accommodate its international cast of Carmen Maura, Miou-Miou, Marisa Berenson, Kathe Keller, Guesh Patti, and Joaquim De Alminda? For all the Europudding limitations of *Elles*, I would still argue that it's the Almodovar film that is relatively out-of-date.

All these movies show not only how much the world is shrinking, but also how the idea of national cinema is beginning to seem inadequate to the films actually being made. And if we except big-budget American movies from this trend, we're ignoring how these movies are financed, made, and received. *Star Wars*, *Independence Day*, and *Starship Troopers* may, to varying degrees, be regarded as American products in most places, but how much these respective movies reflect contemporary everyday American life is another matter entirely. The fact that they're shown dubbed in many non-English-speaking countries removes one layer of what we perceive as their Americanness. And if we factor in the sort of ideological alterations and abridgements that frequently come with subtitling,[3] some of which likely carry over into dubbing as well, it becomes obvious that some of the traits in these movies

---

[3] For an excellent introduction to this subject, see Abé Mark Nornes, "For an Abusive Subtitling," *Film Quarterly*, vol. 52, no. 3, Spring 1999, pp. 17–34.

that we regard as American may not be regarded as such in other corners of the globe. (Western visitors to Asia often observe printed English used as décor rather than as concrete messages in such places as shop signs and taxicab upholstery, much as Chinese and Japanese characters are often used decoratively in Western countries. In keeping with this practice, it appears that in some cases what Westerners perceive as English might be considered simply "Western" by some Asians.)

Loosely speaking, all three movies are odes to American values set in the fanciful future and mixed with the half-remembered, midcentury past, but this similarity is only skin-deep, and not only because Verhoeven hails from the Netherlands and Roland Emmerich, the director and cowriter of *Independence Day*, hails from Germany. (*Starship Troopers* and *Independence Day* are probably even less Dutch and German than they are American.) *Star Wars* was made at a time when American pop cinema still mainly belonged to Americans; now it belongs mainly to global markets and overseas investors, and because so-called "American cinema" is the brand name that sells best in those markets and for those investors, that's what it says on the label. But what's inside the package is something else, and properly speaking, its existential identity is multinational, not national—which in thematic terms involves subtraction more than addition. Maybe that's why loss of identity was the very theme of *Face/Off*—another recent multinational action special, and one that perhaps marked the end of John Woo's career as a director of Hong Kong action films.

Directors who hail from countries deemed marginal in relation to the international film marketplace probably know this better than anyone. Especially for someone as talented, singular, and prescient as Verhoeven, being considered a Dutch filmmaker immediately becomes a commercial liability. There isn't even the consolation of the "one director per country" principle that seems to rule the discourse of most American film critics writing about foreign films, which appears to constitute part of what keeps Almodovar, Benigni, the Kaurismaki brothers, Kitano, and Von Trier afloat as cult figures in American culture. Yet the moment Verhoeven becomes a Hollywood director, he doesn't so much exchange one nationality for another; rather, he hides, dilutes, and/or dissolves his Dutchness into something that calls itself American only because that makes it easier to sell. He differs from

Emmerich as an essentially stateless director in his more satirical and sardonic edge, which he shares with the late Stanley Kubrick: an attitude that on occasion profitably confuses gloating with jeering, celebration with ridicule, and, most importantly, Americanism with anti-Americanism, meanwhile sustaining an elegant clarity of line. And the anti-Americanism he's selling becomes less a portrait of a country than a portrait of whoever buys his product—a look, maybe a sense of entitlement, conceivably even a style, but not exactly a way of life.

This has only a superficial resemblance to the process by which directors ranging from Chaplin to Hitchcock, Maurice Tourneur to René Clair, Stroheim to Lang or Preminger, and Lubitsch to Wilder transformed themselves into American filmmakers, because in each of these cases it was by superimposing a view of the United States from the outside over a view from the inside. In Verhoeven and Emmerich, among others, there's no longer a view from the inside—perhaps because Americans are by now as dependent on external views of America as everyone else; and even the view from the outside, as I've already suggested, is more of an idea of America that has international currency than anything else, a form of promotion more than a form of observation. Like the lingua franca English that currently circles the globe via the Internet, Verhoeven's style functions less like the front line of a particular invading army than like a streamlined highway others can travel down, and maybe even a destroyer of nationality for that reason rather than a purveyor of it.

Can we relate this style to the protest that disrupted the World Trade Organization's Seattle summit during the last month of the millennium, and to the impromptu coalition that made this possible? The progressive shrinking of the planet and the growing irrelevance of nationality to common interests and even common experiences (compared with those of class, race, and ethnicity, for instance) certainly suggest that Verhoeven's evocation of the future may have more to do with global trends than with Heinlein's original Cold War vision.

* * *

It's difficult to make hasty judgments about these kinds of cultural shifts because the results are likely to be both varied and unforeseeable.

Someone who happened to be with the experimental filmmaker, critic, and programmer Jonas Mekas in 1970 when the word came that Nasser had just died, told me that his first response to this news was to ask, "Is this a good thing or a bad thing for cinema?" Similarly, I don't know if the fading and blurring of the concept of national cinema is good or bad for cinema, but I strongly suspect it's both, which makes things especially confusing.

In some circumstances it may be bad for art and good for commerce, but in other circumstances it might be the reverse, because surely there are times when highways are more desirable for art than invading armies. When the British Film Institute commissioned a series of videos about film history a few years ago, their decision to have filmmakers recount the stories of national cinemas went against the grain of my own training as a devotee of Henri Langlois's Cinémathèque programming, where cinema itself was often the only true nationality and the Tower of Babel proved a more worthy model than those bureaucratic inventions called national cinemas. My ambivalence about *Starship Troopers* as entertainment and as art is a direct function of this uncertainty.

I'm also entering treacherous waters by discussing the impressions of audiences in both the United States and abroad—a subject that no one knows much about, least of all the so-called experts. (Because of the self-fulfilling prophecies and voodoo science that rule test marketing and the routinely doctored figures offered by studios regarding weekend grosses and the relative rankings of new movies, most of the "expertise" offered by film industry analysts is little more than an extension of studio propaganda.) But the even vaguer impressions fostered by commentators about what "American" means need to be questioned. Just like the would-be prophets who proclaim that video is replacing film across the globe and don't factor in the countries that have found ways of eluding the domination of Hollywood, we conclude that what we mean by "American" is the same thing as what foreigners mean. Similarly, Western media call the 1989 demonstrations of Chinese students in Beijing "pro-democratic" due to a Cold War assumption that everything that wasn't Communist had to be pro-democratic, when it appears that the students were, in part, protesting government corruption. By the same token, when Americans discuss television in relation to movies across the globe, they often forget how much of television elsewhere tends to be state-run, with positive as well as negative consequences that are rarely considered in the United States.

***

By national cinema, I mean a cinema that expresses something of the soul of the nation that it comes from: the lifestyle, the consciousness, the attitudes. By virtue of coming more from an American individual than either *Starship Troopers* or *Independence Day*, *Star Wars I—The Phantom Menace* surely qualifies as being more American in this respect, if only because its auteur has more power and independence—which in this case may serve as a commercial disadvantage. (Even more alarmingly, it may serve as an artistic disadvantage as well: Lucas feels freer than either Verhoeven or Emmerich to become obsessed with digital effects at the expense of his story, and to re-create the wooden performances of westerns and SF serials that he saw on TV as a boy.) Lucas may depend on multinational markets for much of his merchandising, but in the realm of SF blockbusters he still has an autonomy denied to his competitors. And outside the realm of SF blockbusters, it might be argued that Clint Eastwood has a comparable creative freedom; the fact that he isn't obliged to test-market his movies with preview audiences already places him outside the multinational trends I've been discussing, and insofar as he's relatively free to follow his own inclinations, his movies could be called every bit as American as those of his predecessors John Ford and Howard Hawks.

For that matter, I wouldn't want to quibble with anyone who argues that *Starship Troopers* or *Independence Day* are American in the same way—or to the same degree—that French fries are French. What I mean is something more delicate and complex—a matter of substance more than packaging, yielded to us by most national cinemas over the past century, but no longer available to us in most multinational blockbusters. For a movie to belong to a particular national cinema often means that it's likelier to have a stronger impact on its home turf, as the recent American art movie *In the Company of Men* did: in France, the same film was cursorily dismissed by the two leading critical monthly film magazines, *Positif* and *Cahiers du Cinéma*, while at the Viennale in Austria its impact seemed minimal alongside other current American films the same year, including even Joe Dante's made-for-cable *The Second Civil War.* I suspect this is because taboos against discussing capitalism critically, which gives *In the Company of Men* much of its subversive impact in the United States, don't exist to the same degree in Europe. But a more pseudo-American picture like *Starship Troopers* was likely appreciated (or avoided) for the same reasons by audiences across the planet: spiffy special effects, severed limbs, and lots of nonstop action.

Superficial enjoyment isn't really the issue. I like bug-crunching as well as the next fellow—although this movie dishes out more of it than I could possibly want—and there are undeniable kicks to be had from Verhoeven's sneering use of recruitment ads, his handsome styling of interstellar navigation, and his abbreviated glimpses of future cityscapes. But calling this and most other expensive action-explosion specials "American" only confuses us about our already scattered self-images. And to assume so cavalierly that this is exactly what teenage boys everywhere are itching for is to overlook the contempt for them that this movie dispenses every chance it gets. A lot of grown-up reviewers wondered whether the jeering satire directed at this crowd would sail right past them, but if the Sunday crowd I saw *Starship Troopers* with at Chicago's 600 North Michigan cinema was any indication, the laughter and applause were both sporadic and laced with hints of self-contempt, and the overall enthusiasm seemed to wane toward the end. It seems that we're all too eager to share the movie's disdain for its target audience ("A new kind of enemy, a new kind of war," said some of the ads—as if alien insects and fifty-year-old weaponry were nineties innovations), just as we're much too docile about accepting the blood-lust as specifically American.

Consider what Verhoeven says about *Starship Troopers* in the movie's press book:

> When I came to the United States I felt that initially I wouldn't know enough about American culture to make movies that accurately reflected American society. I felt that I would make a lot of mistakes because I would not be aware of things such as expressions and social behavior.
>
> I felt I could make science fiction movies because I wouldn't have to worry about breaking any rules of American society. Science fiction reflects those rules but does not represent them.

From this point of view, *RoboCop* and *Total Recall* represent successive steps toward *Starship Troopers*, not to mention wacko fantasies like *Basic Instinct* and *Showgirls* (which are science fiction in spirit if not in substance). All five films project different versions of the same dark irony, the same hyperbolic comic-strip iconography, and the same satirically conceived overblown characters without depth. And arguably it was the awkward yet provocative attempt of *Showgirls* to say something about America—Hollywood in particular—that spelled its commercial doom: it's a film that fundamentally said, "We're all whores, aren't we?" and the American public answered, in effect, "Speak for yourself."[4] *Starship Troopers* modified that statement to read, "We're all stupid apes and cannon fodder, aren't we?" and this time audiences all over the world, more accustomed to receiving such epithets as everyday parts of their action kicks, were somewhat more prone to agree (or disagree, depending mainly on gender and age group).

But whether this movie conveys the desired euphoria to potential warmongers, American and otherwise—at least to the same degree that *Star Wars* and its sequels do—is another matter. Wiping out entire planets in the Lucas scheme of things is clean, bloodless fun that never threatens the camaraderie between fuzzy creatures and humans—who trade affectionate wisecracks while zapping enemies from afar—even when this all gets ennobled by mythical conceits derived from Joseph Campbell. (In *The Phantom Menace*, wisecracks were reduced to an absolute minimum and humor was mainly restricted to a digitally generated overgrown lizard with a Jamaican accent named Jar Jar Binks whose principal function was to tell the audience when it was okay to laugh; most of the warfare, moreover, was restricted to earlier forms of combat stretching back to medieval weaponry. But the overall bloodlessness of the warfare remained a constant.) Verhoevian genocide, by

---

[4] Not quite all American viewers—or Western viewers, for that matter— responded to *Showgirls* in quite this fashion. Two of the film's biggest defenders and champions are Jim Jarmusch and Jacques Rivette. In an interview in *Les Inrockuptibles* (no. 144, 1997), Rivette avowed that he'd seen *Starship Troopers* twice: "I like it very much, but I prefer *Showgirls*. *Showgirls* is one of the great American films of the past few years; it's Verhoeven's best American film and his most personal. . . . It's also the one that's closest to his Dutch films." (my translation)

contrast, assumes no such pretensions; it's a messy affair involving extensive dismemberment on both sides, loads of blood and goo, loss of privacy and comfort, and only a modicum of emotional satisfaction—in short, none of the media pleasures offered by demolishing Baghdad. Most of us Americans probably know as little about Iraqis as the starship troopers do about the alien bugs they fight, and the topography of the bug planet, as Dave Kehr pointed out in the *New York Daily News*, "suggests the scene of the Gulf War." But there the similarities end—especially after one factors in the anachronistic weaponry and forms of combat in Verhoeven's movie, most of it derived from forties and fifties war films, and the power of the enemy to retaliate.

The issues that are being fought over are hardly the same either, however rudimentary they appear in both cases. When Luke Skywalker loses his relatives to alien villains, we're invited to commiserate with him for a few seconds in order to validate his desire for revenge. When the parents of Johnny Rico (Casper Van Dien) get nuked, on the other hand—as part of twelve million Earth casualties, no less—what we've already seen of this pair makes them only slightly less repellent than the bugs who wipe them out, so the tragedy and outrage are strictly rhetorical. If this is the life on Earth worth protecting and risking one's neck and limbs for—and just about the only glimpses of private life that we see are restricted to that yammering couple in their home—then the coed showers and twenty minutes allotted for sex between battles, two rare perks of committed army service, are made to seem nominally more attractive. (The lead characters' home base is "Buenos Aires"— a dimly defined setting with no Latin traces whose loss is about as wrenching in this movie's scheme of things as stubbing one's toe.)

The militarized fascist utopia, presented mainly in the form of interactive recruiting commercials, is presented so sketchily that its main virtue ironically seems to be a leveling of class difference for the volunteer soldiers, the only citizens allowed to vote—though who or what any of them might vote for is anyone's guess. Paradoxically, the genuine Americanism of Heinlein's tiresome 1959 novel is a good deal more international than the ersatz Americanism of Verhoeven's movie, but that's because thirty-eight years of American history—including the Cold War, its aftermath, and the passage from both nationalism and internationalism to multinationalism—separate these two versions of the Good Fight. In the novel, the fighting youth in the boot camp of Earth's galactic empire includes the son of a Japanese colonel working on his Black Belt and two Germans with dueling scars; Johnnie Rico himself, also known as Juan, is the son of a Filipino tycoon, and turns out in one of the novel's delayed revelations to be black. The movie's boot camp, by contrast, is basically American white bread with a few multicultural trimmings—a reflection of neither the fifties nor the nineties but an incoherent mishmash of the two—and it's also coed, which is presumably supposed to reflect the future. (The novel also featured women pilots, but not unisex showers and sleeping quarters.)

As critic H. Bruce Franklin points out in his 1980 book *Robert A. Heinlein: America as Science Fiction*, Heinlein's "right-wing" militarism actually corresponded to the liberal ideology of John F. Kennedy, elected president the year after the novel was published, in anticipating the creation of an elite corps like the Green Berets; Kennedy's signature "Ask not what your country can do for you" speech also seems to come straight out of the novel. (Written as Heinlein's thirteenth juvenile novel for Scribner's—a series celebrating the conquest of space, whose first filmic incarnation was the 1950 *Destination Moon*, adapted from *Rocket Ship Galileo*—the book was rejected for its unapologetic and extreme militarism, then published as an "adult" novel by Putnam. The quaint 1959 notion of shielding teenage boys from this sort of thing—minus most of the graphic gore in the movie, which is now aimed at them—is another indication of how much we've changed in thirty-eight years.)

Franklin also points out that Heinlein's novel, as steeped in Cold War ideology as his 1951 *The Puppet Masters*—and in striking contrast to his neohippie and neo-Communist *Stranger in a Strange Land* (1961)—posits the alien bugs as Chinese Communists and another humanoid race that's omitted in the movie, the "Skinnies," as Russian Communists. (The novel is in fact crammed with pompous, didactic lectures about the Communist menace and the errors of Karl Marx, most of them linked to the "hive" mentality of the bugs—which makes it all the more ironic that the classless military utopia proffered as an ideal alternative seems no less socialist and totalitarian. The movie intensifies this paradox by showing how impossible it is for Johnnie to speak to his girlfriend or parents on the videophone without all his coed bunkmates being present.)

Pictorially, the bugs in the movie on their home planet recall the giant ants of *Them!* (another Cold War allegory, 1954) and the attacking natives in *Zulu* (1964). But ideologically, they're boring cyphers without any discernible language, culture, architecture, or technology (apart from their capacities to bomb Earth and suck out individual brains) — creatures of action storyboards rather than anyone's notion of a society. And, this being a Paul Verhoeven film, humanity doesn't fare much better, either on-screen or off.

Chapter Nine
Trafficking in Movies
(Festival-Hopping in the Nineties)

WHY I'VE NEVER ATTENDED SUNDANCE AND TELLURIDE

Let me begin with a confession that immediately deflates the title of this section: one reason why I've never attended the film festivals held annually in Sundance (Park City, Utah) and Telluride (Colorado) is that I've never been invited. As a matter of policy, the *Chicago Reader*, where I've been the main film critic since 1987, doesn't send me to film festivals because my beat is films showing in Chicago rather than elsewhere. On the other hand, they allow me to go to film festivals because a good number of the movies I see there eventually turn up in Chicago; and in recent years, they've also paid for my plane tickets to attend the Toronto Film Festival every September.

In fact, I've attended quite a few film festivals over the years, and in most cases this has been at the invitation of the festivals themselves, who pay for my air tickets and put me up. They include Austin, Berlin (twice), Cannes (eight times), Chicago (a dozen times), Denver (twice), Edinburgh (twice), the Golden Horse Awards (in Taipei, where I was already on the jury of the Asian Pacific Film Festival), Hong Kong, Honolulu, Locarno (seven times), London (twice), New York (countless times), Pesaro (twice), Rotterdam (thirteen times), San Francisco (twice), San Sebastian (twice), Sodankyla (in Finland), Thessaloniki (in Greece), Torino (in Italy), Toronto (twenty times),

Vancouver, Venice, and Vienna (three times). This totals at least a hundred festivals since the early seventies.

But I've never sought to be invited to either Sundance or Telluride—widely regarded as two of the "hottest" festivals in the United States. The reason in the first case should be clear from the previous chapters. An industry-run affair that is misleadingly represented in much of the press as a celebration of independence, Sundance is the only festival I know where, judging from the reports of colleagues who do attend, audience members are prone to carry on conversations on their cellular phones during the screenings. As for Telluride, which sounds substantially more attractive, I've been put off by the cost of flying to a weekend event, the reports I've heard or read about the groupie ambiance, and the restrictions placed on the annual guest programmers by the festival directors, among other things.

One reason this chapter is called "Trafficking in Movies" is that most of it is adapted from articles I've written for the French quarterly *Trafic*, a magazine launched by the late Serge Daney in 1991. In the previous chapters of this book, I've made an effort to pose my arguments within a specifically American context; what follows, by virtue of having been originally written for cinéphiles who read French, opens out into a somewhat wider context: although my positions are the same, they often look different because I'm expressing them for an audience that has different reference points. I've cut and revised the four pieces used, to help focus and clarify them.

I apologize for the references to and discussions of certain relatively unfamiliar films in spite of these modifications. For whatever it's worth, many of these names and titles are equally unfamiliar to most French readers, but they point toward the acknowledgment and tolerance of a wider range of film references than is acceptable in most circles outside France. Personally I like to encounter mysterious references of this kind—my own film education of the sixties and seventies was virtually forged out of them—because they show that the film world is richer than it's usually cracked up to be, and highlight the discoveries to be made.

***

CANNES, 1995–1997

May 16, 1995:[1] From 1970 to 1973, when I was living in Paris, it was still possible to write Cannes coverage for two magazines, stay in a cheap hotel, and not lose too much money, and last year I was able to start attending again thanks to being on the selection committee of the New York Film Festival. Despite the opening of a new Palais des Festivals in 1983 and the closing or remodeling of various cinemas, the most significant changes to be found here after two decades could arguably be summed up in a single phrase: what we mean when we say "contemporary cinema," entailing not only what we include but what we leave out. In theory, all the beauty and horrors, the contradictions and paradoxes of world cinema are crammed in two weeks over a few city blocks. But in practice, how can we say with any confidence that Cannes is an accurate précis of anything except the international film business (which includes the press)?

Perhaps the biggest difference between the seventies and nineties in Cannes is the matter of whose opinions count the most. In the seventies, I, at least, had the illusion that it was those of the festival director, the programmers, or the jury. Today, it appears to be the opinions of Bob and Harvey Weinstein, the aggressive directors of Miramax — a company owned by Disney that seems to control a near-monopoly of important festival films, as producers, as distributors, or as both. Among their many past possessions are *The Crying Game, The Piano, Pulp Fiction, Queen Margot* (which they substantially recut), *The Glass Shield* (which they obliged Charles Burnett to write and shoot a new ending for before releasing), *Ready-to-Wear* (which they retitled from *Prêt-à-porter*, even after screening the film for the press), Krzysztof Kieslowski's trilogy (*Blue, White,* and *Red*), and *Priest* (recut to placate the ratings board). They are the ones who most often determine which films will be altered (and how), when (or if) these films will open commercially, and how they will be advertised, exploited, and even written about, so "What do Bob and Harvey think?" is a question with vastly

---

[1] Adapted from "Journal de Cannes," translated by Jean-Luc Mengus, *Trafic* no. 15, été 1995, pp. 5–13.

more ramifications than the opinions of, say, festival director Gilles Jacob or the head of this year's jury, Jeanne Moreau.

In the early seventies, it was possible to see films here by Jean-Marie Straub and Danièle Huillet, Luc Moullet, Jean-Daniel Pollet, Edgardo Cozarinsky, Werner Schroeter, and the now mainly forgotten Carmelo Bene and Pedro Portabella, most often in the Director's Fortnight or on the Market (though Bene's *One Hamlet Less* actually turned up in the Palais in 1973.) Such options generally seem much less likely now. One of the key elements in this change is, of course, video and television — each realm a vast continent that siphons off much of what would formerly be considered "cinema." The situation of Mark Rappaport in the United States is instructive: several years ago, he switched from 16-millimeter to video after funding for his features evaporated, but then he discovered that he couldn't get his videos shown or reviewed unless they were transferred to film and then shown in that format at festivals.

Certain haphazard rhyme effects between the seventies and nineties point up this problem in other ways. I still harbor fond memories of seeing *Valparaiso . . .Valparaiso*, Pascal Aubier's satire about leftist myopia, at the Fortnight in 1973. But in order to see Aubier's touching new comedy, *The Son of Gascogne*, at Cannes in 1995, it will be necessary to turn on a TV during one of the final evenings of this festival, which few critics here seem willing to do. Fortunately, I already saw this feature at the Berlin Film Festival's Panorama in February, but for most of my colleagues, *The Son of Gascogne* will never be, even marginally, part of the French cinema of 1995 in the same way that *Valparaiso . . . Valparaiso* was part of the French cinema in 1973. This seems a pity, because if memories are to be trusted, the two films are complementary in significant respects: both are about elaborate hoaxes, and both are eloquent testimonies to some of the more cherished fantasy projections of their separate epochs.

In the more recent film, Aubier's allegory about the myth of the Nouvelle Vague and the meaning of postmodernist pastiche seems a good deal more tender and forgiving than its predecessor, asking us to sympathize not only with the romanticism of an older generation but the frustrations of a younger one reduced to bluff and imitation in trying to live up to that heritage. It's a good deal sadder as well, and in ways that seem directly relevant to Cannes—if only it were around as a reference point, as it once might have been. The same might be said for Cozarinsky's *Citizen Langlois*, also seen in Berlin, a documentary that offers a polemical response to the nationalistic regulation of film history by state bureaucrats—a trend observable in most of the British Film Institute's *A Century of Cinema* series at Cannes (aside from Godard's *2 × 50 Years of French Cinema*, which critiques the same project from within)—by justly treating Henri Langlois, the late cofounder and director of the Cinémathèque Française, as an antibureaucrat for whom cinema itself was the ultimate nationality.

But, judging from the other films shown in Cannes this year, including those in the market, personal essays—and indeed, most other kinds of nonfiction films, especially unconventional ones—are no longer part of "contemporary cinema." (Could this help to explain why Françoise Romand's extraordinary *Mix-up*, made ten years ago, is still so little known in France?) The commercial consensus appears to be that fiction films are universal and documentaries are parochial, with the result that the most universal testimonies that we have on certain subjects—Marker's *The Last Bolshevik*, for example—get treated as marginal in Europe and the United States alike.

Everywhere one looks, unconscious exclusions rule today's film culture. Today, for instance, I purchased a copy of Gilbert Adair's highly entertaining *Flickers: An Illustrated Celebration of 100 Years of Cinema*, just published by Faber and Faber—a personal selection of a hundred stills with accompanying commentaries, each representing a separate year—and read the following in Adair's Introduction: "There are . . . of necessity, numerous, regrettable injustices: no *L'Atalante*, no *Night of the Hunter*, no Dovzhenko, Guitry, Wilder, Sirk, Mankiewicz, Kurosawa, Kiarostami or Nicholas Ray; no Garbo, Monroe or James Dean; no African or Latin American cinema at all." It's an intelligent list of exclusions, so it may seem carping to cite the absence of any of the Taiwanese or Hong Kong masters—Hou Hsiao-hsien, Edward Yang, Stanley Kwan, Wong Kar-wai—from Adair's list of inclusions *or* his "injustices." Indeed, over the past few years, whenever I hear friends tell me that the art of cinema is virtually over, Taiwan and Hong Kong never seem to figure as part of their reckoning.

May 22: The role played by publicity in informing, inflecting, and sometimes even replacing criticism is seldom acknowledged in print, yet our critical reading of many films would be radically different without its influence. A case in point is the construction of Larry Clark's *Kids* as a "critical" site by Miramax over the first four months of 1995. Towards the end of the Sundance Festival in January, a special midnight screening was held of this cautionary, sensationalized, and very depressing first feature by an accomplished still photographer about casual teenage sex and AIDS in Manhattan, and the hyperbolic press responses that ensued seemed manufactured by Miramax's sense of melodrama and its accurate gauging of American puritanism—both of which became, in effect, a critical reading of the film. Thus a *Variety* reviewer wrote (inaccurately) that the film offered no moral judgment of any kind on teenage sex, a *Village Voice* critic intimated that she had been in the presence of something great and innovative, and one of her younger West Coast colleagues excitedly wrote about "kiddie porn." Then, over the next several weeks, journalists speculated endlessly how Miramax, because of its affiliation with Disney, could possibly distribute the film. In short, just as one can speak about the smell of blood at the start of certain football games, the smell of money to be made now fosters an aura of "masterpiece" and "artistic breakthrough." Much as Godard points out in 2 × 50 *Years of French Cinema* that centennial celebrations of "the cinema" are in fact only celebrations of the *exploitation* of cinema, the exploitation of *Kids* has so far been indistinguishable from its critical reception, even if the responses at Cannes have been mainly quite justifiable expressions of disappointment. The film isn't bad, but the degree to which publicity has made it tower over every other American film at the festival can only distort its modest virtues and deceive its intended audience. (One American colleague who writes for a major newsweekly was instructed by his editor before the festival even started that *Kids* was the only film he could cover.)

Given the delirium of the press conference for *Smoke* at Berlin and the responses to *Pulp Fiction* at Cannes last year—both of them again Miramax films—a kind of carefully manufactured hysteria is clearly at work, and the degree to which journalists are projecting the focus of their articles and interviews for the following year, already anticipating the desires of their editors, determines the entire climate of such receptions. Any masterpiece failing to generate this kind of instant "copy" becomes by definition a bad film.

* * *

1996:[2] In his introduction to *Understanding Media*, Marshall McLuhan records the consternation of one of his editors that "seventy-five per cent of your material is new. A successful book cannot venture to be more than ten per cent new." From the vantage point of this year's Cannes Festival, a compulsion to contextualize everything new in relation to something familiar reveals a comparable problem. Indeed, the kind of movie pitch parodied at the beginning of Altman's *The Player*, in which every project becomes some version of one or two previous hits—"*The Graduate, Part 2*," "*The Manchurian Candidate* meets *Ghost*"—has by now become a kind of journalistic shorthand for the critic eager to make the film fully accessible once it's released. This necessity of establishing old references in relation to new ideas is above all an indication of how thoroughly the priorities of the film business have infiltrated film criticism.

As useful as this practice is, it often functions as a kind of nervous tic. For the writer or speaker too lazy to perform the less alluring task of description, it poses a constant temptation—a means of short-circuiting the critical process through a kind of magic or alchemy that suddenly makes the invisible visible. Being more guilty of this habit than most, and finding it especially hard to avoid during the daily pressures of Cannes, I'd like to attempt both a critique and an autocritique of this tendency, hopefully indicating when it can serve a useful critical function and when it simply interferes with critical analysis.

To begin with an example that strikes me as being especially dubious—a form of comparison that seems indistinguishable from advertising—consider the following sentence from Janet Maslin in one of her Cannes reports: "Set in Edinburgh (and already a big hit in England), Danny Boyle's *Trainspotting* is sure to prompt controversy as a

---

[2] Adapted from "Comparaisons à Cannes," translated by Jean-Luc Mengus, *Trafic* no. 19, été 1996, pp. 5–13.

hip, clever provocation that's raw enough to make *Kids* look like *Sesame Street*."

In point of fact, when Maslin calls *Trainspotting* "raw" she isn't referring to the film's style, which holds relatively little interest for her, but to her sense of the content, such as male frontal nudity and excrement: "Tauntingly decadent, *Trainspotting* lets its drug-addicted characters show off violent and grossly scatological behavior that will send some viewers racing for the exits." Stylistically, the film is actually much *less* "raw" than the pseudodocumentary manner of *Kids*; it's an imaginative stylistic exercise that for me — to play my own version of the comparison game — evokes Richard Lester in the early sixties in terms of visual play and Kubrick's *A Clockwork Orange* in terms of narrative form. In fact, these references occur to Maslin as well, but she couches them again mainly in terms of puritanical class content: "Yet this willfully outrageous film also has no trouble evoking either a grungier *Clockwork Orange* or a ruder set of Beatles." The Beatles are of course the "product" being sold in *A Hard Day's Night* and *Help!*; Lester is only the film artist involved.

One reason for focusing on Maslin is that, thanks to her position, she is the writer who has the most effect on which foreign films will open in the United States and whether or not they will succeed commercially. Yet the fact that she is clearly more interested in cinema as a business than as an art, more fascinated by Harvey Weinstein than by Kiarostami, Hou, or Godard, apparently places her in the majority — which is why the circulations of the French and American *Premiere* are higher than those of *Cahiers du Cinéma, Positif, Trafic, Sight and Sound,* and *Film Comment* combined.

On the other hand, ten years ago, *Premiere* didn't exist and Vincent Canby, Maslin's predecessor on *The New York Times,* was more interested in art than in business. Did *Premiere* and Maslin suddenly come along to "fill a need," or did they, like so many of the movies they both publicize, first manufacture the desire they now seek to exploit?

For me the principal pleasure afforded by Cannes is the opportunity to take a two-week holiday from the so-called "fun" of commercial American cinema, which tends to dominate the remainder of my year. Perhaps this "fun" would feel less oppressive if it didn't already inform the experience in the United States of news, politics, fast food, sports,

economics, education, religion, and leisure in general, making it less
an escape than the very (enforced) essence of American life. A bemus-
ing paradox: after the alleged triumph of capitalism over Communism,
we find ourselves living in a "planned" culture that evokes in some
ways the Stalinism of the fifties, with Disney now assuming the pater-
nal role of the federal government, the spirit of Uncle Walt supplant-
ing the spirit of Uncle Joe. Within such a climate, the ideological con-
formity of the press can seem no less claustrophobic, especially when
it comes to cultural references: during the last Christmas season, for
instance, I must have spent hours searching in vain for a single American review of Oliver Stone's overblown *Nixon* that failed to use the
adjective "Shakespearean." The desire to dignify (and therefore sell)
political corruption with the nobility of classical culture seemed far
more important in this transaction than any desire to understand
Stone's dramaturgy, and I would doubt that this impulse could be plau-
sibly linked to Luc Moullet's effort in *Cahiers du Cinéma* in the fifties
to link Samuel Fuller to Christopher Marlowe.

In any case, one reason why Cannes offers an alternative to my
usual work is that most of the films shown here won't open in Chicago
for another year. This is even true for certain American films if these
films are deemed "difficult" for the American public (which often
means politically threatening): last year's *Dead Man*, for instance,
which has already had commercial runs in Melbourne, Lisbon, and
Istanbul, won't reach Chicago until late June 1996. This means that I'll
have plenty of time to test and reflect on my first reactions to most films
before I write about them at any length. (Perhaps only a few months for
those like *Trainspotting* and *The Eighth Day* that already have the
smell of money and hence Maslin's interest; most likely more than a
year for films like Mohsen Makhmalbaf's *Gabbeh* and Hou Hsiao-
hsien's *Goodbye South, Goodbye* that can be safely expected to have
neither.)

By now, I've developed such an automatic reflex of finding or gen-
erating one cultural comparison per film at Cannes that I suspect it's a
habit related to seeing several films per day, a convenient filing system.
In the case of Mike Leigh's *Secrets and Lies*, the word "Ibsen" allows
me to organize certain observations I have about the film's dramaturgy
and themes. But after I come out of Hou's *Goodbye South, Goodbye*

with a certain sense of bewilderment—not knowing how to contextualize this contemporary crime film in relation to Hou's preceding trilogy about the history of twentieth-century Taiwan—I feel that one word from Marco Müller, director of the Locarno Film Festival, places me on the right track: *"Mahagonny."* Although I've never seen or read Brecht's opera, a constellation of elements in Hou's film—elements connected to the treatment of capitalism, the handling of music, the episodic narrative, and even Hou's exquisite sense of camera placement—suddenly slide into focus. This comparison, however, may be more useful to an occidental spectator like myself than to someone from Taiwan. (By the same token, when I compare Râúl Ruiz's delightful *Three Lives and Only One Death* to late Buñuel—with Pascal Bonitzer, Ruiz's cowriter and "French connection" serving as the counterpart to Jean-Claude Carrière—I conveniently ignore the fact that Ruiz himself prefers Buñuel's Mexican films.) Such a distinction may be less relevant when considering the very beautiful *Gabbeh* in relation to Paradjanov's *The Color of Pomegranates*, if only because it appears that Makhmalbaf thought of this relationship long before I did. One might argue, of course, that with these two films, the style is also shaped by the subject matter—the poet Sayat Nova in the case of Paradjanov, the nomadic tribes in southeastern Iran who specialize in weaving gabbehs in the case of Makhmalbaf. But it is still fascinating to discover that *Gabbeh* started out as a documentary and evolved into a fiction film only gradually, because that appears to have been what happened to Paradjanov's film as well—suggesting that what Makhmalbaf learned from Paradjanov was not only an attitude toward space and color, but also an attitude toward subject matter.

[1997][3] By common agreement, the fiftieth anniversary of the Cannes Film Festival, prefigured as a cause for celebration, wound up serving more often as an occasion for complaint. Disappointment in the overall quality of the films ran high, even if the arrival over the last four days of films by Abbas Kiarostami, Atom Egoyan, Youssef Chahine, and

---

[3] Adapted from "Cannes, tour de Babel critique," translated by Jean-Luc Mengus, in *Trafic* no. 23, automne 1997, pp. 5–15.

Wong Kar-wai improved the climate somewhat. But I don't mean to suggest that the shared feelings of anger and frustration demonstrated any critical unanimity. On the contrary, the overall malaise of Cannes this year forced to a state of crisis the general critical disagreement and lack of communication that has turned up repeatedly, in a variety of forms. If the pressing question after every screening at Cannes is whether a film is good or bad (or, more often, given the climate of hyperbole, wonderful or terrible) — a question that becomes much too pressing, because it short-circuits the opportunity and even the desire to reflect on a film for a day or week before reaching any final verdict about it — the widespread disagreements at the festival derived not only from different and irreconcilable definitions of "good" and "bad," but also from different and irreconcilable definitions of "film." And the ensuing Tower of Babel brought into sharp relief the competing agendas — in some cases implicit, in come cases explicit — of such an occasion.

One film that I like, for instance, unlike most of my colleagues, is Wim Wenders's *The End of Violence*, yet the very terms of my approval — that Wenders has finally succeeded in making an entertaining Hollywood film — is so much at odds with the terms of the other critics and programmers I speak with, who find the film neither entertaining nor Hollywood, and who find it "heavy" to the same degree that I find it "light," that we might as well be speaking different languages. Fifteen years ago, at the Toronto Film Festival, I experienced a similar sense of isolation after seeing and liking Wenders's *Hammett*. My conclusion then was that Wenders had belatedly fulfilled one of the central dreams of the French New Wave and its offspring (such as Bertolucci's project to adapt *Red Harvest*) — to make a European cinéphile feature employing all the resources of a Hollywood studio. But in 1980, at least, I still had the New Wave Hollywood as a reference point to employ. Today the only terms I can draw upon to describe *The End of Violence* are "Hollywood" and "art film," and both terms, I discover, are no longer categories that refer to shared realities to the same extent; more precisely, they're the ghosts of categories that continue to be used only because others haven't yet been found to replace them. So maybe one reason why what I find light, entertaining, and thoughtful others find heavy, boring, and preachy is that we're calling on different contexts and instruments of measurement. I'm thinking of all the recent stupid

American commercial films that bore and offend me, which makes *The End of Violence* look good, but others are thinking of Wenders's previous nineties films, which they (and I, for that matter) regard as relatively boring and forced, and see the film as part of the same negative pattern.

Even the usual way of identifying festival films, such as title, director, and country of origin, is sometimes inadequate or misleading. Kiarostami's *Taste of Cherry*, by all counts my favorite film at the festival, regarded by most people as purely Iranian, makes prominent use of Kurdish, Afghan, and Turkish characters, and ends with a recording of "St. James Infirmary" by Louis Armstrong. When asked in his press conference about why he used a "jazzy" trumpet at the end, Kiarostami spoke of neither the relevant images of death contained in the lyrics of "St. James Infirmary" nor of Armstrong, but of his conviction that music belonged to everyone in the world, adding that the trumpet evoked the soldiers in training that are seen in the final sequence. The fact that this final sequence was shot in video was even more troubling to some viewers than the jazz trumpet, but surely both the music and the video constitute a kind of lingua franca within both Iran and the cinema as a whole—suggesting that in an era when multicorporations may be more pertinent as defining entities than countries, the usual definitions of nationality have to be reformulated, reimagined, rethought. Like the outworn categories of film criticism, much of the current nationalistic discourse refers to the past, not to the present or the future. This isn't to say that certain references to the past don't continue to be useful.

Yousef Chahine's *Destiny* is a French-Egyptian grand spectacle and musical that recounts the life of the Andalusian philosopher Averroes. But I suspect that the most important reference point shared by Chahine and myself is actually a style of Hollywood studio filmmaking of the fifties, so that I'm reminded at various moments of films as good as *The Aventures of Hadji Baba* and as mediocre as *Kismet*—a house style that I associate mainly with M-G-M and only secondarily with various directors (e.g., Anthony Mann, Richard Thorpe, Don Weis, Vincente Minnelli, George Sidney, Mervyn LeRoy). By the same token, even though Chahine, as evidenced by his retrospective in Locarno last year, is fully recognizable as an auteur, this doesn't necessarily mean that the aspects of *Destiny* that are or should be most interesting to me are its personal traits. I'm more inclined to be fascinated by the route of a Westerner (myself) into the mysteries of Arabian and Egyptian cinema charted over distant memories of Hollywood films made over forty years ago, a process in which Chahine serves as one of many possible emissaries rather than as any particular destination. But old critical reflexes die hard, and a surprising number of films at Cannes encounter certain kinds of critical resistance precisely because the auteurist grid of director, camera, and mise en scène doesn't yield the proper results.

One case in point is the charming and lively French Canadian feature *Cosmos* shown in the Fortnight, a collection of slightly interconnected comic sketches filmed in Quebec City in black-and-white by six young writer-directors, one of them the cinematographer of the entire feature. The narrative form in which two or several stories equals one story—represented in twentieth-century literature by such works as Faulkner's *The Wild Palms*, Anderson's *Winesburg, Ohio*, and Joyce's *Dubliners*—has many interesting examples in cinema ranging from *Intolerance* to *Out 1*, from *The Little Theater of Jean Renoir* to Kieslowski's *Red*, and from Vera Chytilova's *About Something Else* to Errol Morris's *Fast, Cheap, and Out of Control*. Though less significant than these films, *Cosmos* still poses interesting methodological problems by having multiple authorship as well as multiple stories. The conventional critical approach to such a feature is to evaluate the style and mise en scène of each episode separately, but to do that in this case is nonfunctional because what these sketches have in common—a certain New Wave flavor—is much more important than what distinguishes them from one another. (This was also true of some of the early New Wave features when they first appeared, before they became recatalogued along auteurist lines.) Some of the episodes overlap via intercutting, and clearly the feature as a whole was conceived and to some extent executed collectively.

A related critical conundrum was posed by the 1995 U.S. release of the 1964 Soviet documentary *I Am Cuba*—a film that is commonly credited to its director (Mikhail Kalatozov) rather than to its cinematographer (Sergei Urusevsky) or its cowriter (Yevgeny Yevtushenko) when its eccentric style can't really be read as the expression of a single consciousness. When, in a famous early extended take, the camera on a rooftop overlooking the Havana beaches moves several stories down to tourists around a swimming pool, then follows one woman in a dress only to abandon her in favor of a bathing beauty whom it then follows into the swimming pool, even proceeding underwater with her, the usual critical procedure is to identify Kalatozov with the camera and to applaud his virtuoso mise en scène. But in fact, the shot was carried out by a relay team of three separate camera operators—a good example of collective work in action, communist filmmaking in the truest sense of the word—and in the final analysis the model of a solitary artist probably functions better here as a guide to *reading* the shot than as any reliable indication of its mode of execution.

The problem, really, is that critics are still dealing with the residue of a polemical position about mise en scène that was once necessary to win certain battles, but which has regrettably eclipsed and obscured other central creative areas—including even what the films are about. Few critics took Orson Welles at his word when he insisted that he always began with the written word, not with images, and indeed, the writer-director-performer has perhaps suffered the most from the critical emphasis on the latter two functions: how many critical studies have bothered to consider the essential importance of Charlie Chaplin and Erich von Stroheim as writers—inextricably tied to their work as actors, which their mise en scène served largely to implement?

The most striking difference for me in overall atmosphere between Cannes in the seventies and Cannes in the nineties can be seen in the press conferences, which used to resemble gladiatorial combats and are now almost completely predetermined publicity sessions, most of them controlled by compulsive politeness and relatively useless when it comes to the exchange of either ideas or information. Two characteristic questions I can recall from the seventies are (1) after the screening of *The Mother and the Whore*, addressed to Jean Eustache: "Why did you choose to make a film instead of write a novel?" and (2) after the screening of *One Hamlet Less*, addressed to Carmelo Bene, dressed in a white suit: "Do you sleep at night in pajamas or in the nude?," to which Bene replied, "Fuck you." Today, the most characteristic question is to ask a star what it was like to work with a director (or vice versa), and no less characteristic are the responses—testimonials about how wonderful he or she is.

What happened to alter this former climate of contestation, which I find this year only at the press conference for Mathieu Kassovitz's *Assassin(s)*? The latter movie is as typical of current filmmaking trends

as the title of Michael Haneke's Austrian film, *Funny Games*, the latter
functioning as both a commercial ruse and an ironic critique of a commercial ruse—making Haneke's film as divided against itself as *Assas-
sin(s)*, a lowbrow exploration of the same general theme. Even Kassovitz's flagrant borrowings from Martin Scorsese's *Taxi Driver* and
GoodFellas and Oliver Stone's *Natural Born Killers* testify to the same
puritanical duplicity that is found in these sources: the simultaneous
desire to succeed commercially in the American manner while criti-
cizing this very manner is a form of hypocrisy already found in the
Scorsese and Stone films.

The desire to see some old-style Cannes squabbling is what drove
me to Kassovitz's press conference, though alas, despite his cogent
efforts to challenge the lack of seriousness of the press, not very much
light was shed at this event—except, perhaps, for the hostility of the
press at Cannes toward any film that has an overt thesis of any kind.
(1999 postscript: Another casualty of this bias was Johnny Depp's muddled and naive but touching *The Brave*, a first feature starring Depp and
featuring Marlon Brando in a cameo—an allegory that recalled sixties
follies such as Dennis Hopper's *The Last Movie* and was received so
poorly that, like *Assassin(s)*, it has never opened in the United States.)

Clearly a lot has happened to information flow over the past twenty
years, at least within the public sector. First of all one should cite the
development of techniques designed to flatter and thereby control the
political press inaugurated in the United States by the Reagan administration. Then came the adaptation of these same techniques by Hollywood publicists, while at the same time the studios' publicity campaigns became more lavish, leading to the corrupt allegiances of
"entertainment news" in which publicists and journalists willingly join
forces against the interests of the public, leading to the mode of mutual
flattery that now predominates. Within the new system, any journalist
who asks a rude or skeptical or probing question risks losing access to
the publicists who control access to the "talent" (stars, directors, writers, etc.) and alienating his or her own editor in the process.

The cosmetic surgery performed on news in these transactions
applies to nearly all the Cannes press conferences, not merely those for
expensive commercial films. Consider, for instance, the high drama
constructed around the alleged state banning of Kiarostami's *Taste of*

Cherry because of its treatment of the theme of suicide. Certainly the question of whether the Iranian government would allow the film to be shown in Cannes was a genuine issue prior to the festival—not because of its theme, as it turned out, but because of a bureaucratic technicality—but the fact that this issue was settled before the festival began didn't stop Gilles Jacob from orchestrating its eventual arrival like a breathless cliffhanger.

Furthermore, the self-righteousness of many critics and journalists in denouncing state censorship—generally more relevant to the career of Mohsen Makhmalbaf than to that of Kiarostami—doesn't prevent them from ignoring (and thus tolerating and helping to protect, therefore supporting) the numerous instances of capitalist censorship, some of which are perhaps even more damaging to the works in question. A key example in this regard is Nick Cassavetes's *She's So Lovely*, derived from a 1980 script called *She's Delovely* by John Cassavetes that, according to Thierry Jousse, was rewritten in 1987 when Sean Penn was being considered for the leading role. For me, the primary interest of this film is the unique access it provides to the original script (presumably the 1987 version) rather than the relative skill of its author's son as a director—another case where the issue of mise en scène becomes secondary (except, here, as a relatively negative factor: what appears to be a Hollywood reading of an independently conceived script). It is, after all, a kind of companion piece to *A Woman Under the Influence* (1975), and the only (John) Cassavetes project I'm aware of that combines the working-class milieu of the earlier film with the middle-class suburban milieu of *Faces*—therefore a contribution, however partial and modest, to the Cassavetes oeuvre.

But consider all the things that interfere with that contribution, most of them separate instances of capitalist censorship. First of all the title, *She's Delovely*, which I'm told has been altered because of the financial demands of the estate of Cole Porter, the composer of the song of that title. (The song is still heard briefly in the first part of the film, and the title still figures in a key line of dialogue spoken by the central character, played by Penn, in the second part, a pure example of irrational Cassavetes wordplay: "She doesn't love you. She doesn't love me. She's delovely.") The confusing results are that the film itself still bears the original title at its festival screening, but both the press book and all the festival announcements call it *She's So Lovely*, a more awkward and less pretty title.

Secondly, there is a question of how far Nick Cassavetes has honored the original script. When I ask him about this at the press conference, he confesses that there were certain things in the script that he didn't understand (he fails to say what), and that he simply eliminated those parts. (Properly speaking, this isn't capitalist censorship, though the fact that the script hasn't been published—which would allow us to check this matter for ourselves—remains a pertinent issue.)

Thirdly and fourthly, I should mention two rumors I hear from reasonably reliable sources about the film: (1) Penn directed the last third of the shooting, when Nick Cassavetes became indisposed, and (2) Harvey Weinstein, the codirector of Miramax (which helped to produce and plans to distribute *She's So Lovely*), substantially recut the film and played an important role in overseeing the music before it was screened at Cannes, making changes that were so pronounced that Nick Cassavetes, I'm told, seriously considered removing his name from the film. Needless to say, neither of these rumors is even slightly hinted at in the press conference, where Weinstein is present along with the stars and director; all one hears about there is everyone saying how wonderful everyone else was to work with.

In short, at least four separate and successive kinds of interference prevent *She's So Lovely* from being unproblematically either "a film by Nick Cassavetes" or "a film written by John Cassavetes," although this is precisely how it is represented at the press conference and in the "preliminary press notes" distributed to journalists. So even the interesting methodological challenge of coming to terms with a Hollywood version of a John Cassavetes script—a version in which the more nonnaturalistic and irrational elements figure either as flaws or as eccentric cadenzas—becomes undermined by a process of disassociation and subterfuge whereby "Cassavetes" figures less as a description of contents than as a brand name. I'm reminded of George Hickenlooper announcing several years ago his intention to film Welles's script *The Big Brass Ring* (which he has subsequently rewritten) because he was "an auteurist at heart"—a declaration that made me wonder which auteur he could have been thinking of.

Another form of capitalist censorship—this one usually less conscious, and much more prevalent in the United States than in Europe—is a refusal to discuss capitalism itself, predicated in part on its omnipresence. (If capitalism is now the air we breathe, discussing it is presumably as superfluous as discussing the air while describing a particular landscape.) This is apparently why Neil Labute's *In the Company of Men*, in some ways the most provocative American film I see in Cannes—shown in Un Certain Régard, and already written about extensively in the states since its showing at Sundance—is almost never described as a film about capitalism and its effects, and neither is *The Sweet Hereafter*. The first describes the effects of aggressive competition via business on notions of masculinity and romance, the second evokes the effects of aggressive competition via litigation on the functioning of a community, but neither is examined too closely by critics as a commentary on the way we live. To deal with such a subject, notions of nationality, mise en scène, and authorship may be useful in taking us part of the way, but we have to travel the remaining distance without such vehicles, on our own feet—if only because the pedestrian can see things that drivers often miss, and can travel places accessible only on foot. Considering how centrally vehicles figure in three of the best films in Cannes, all of which revolve around mysteries of existence and identity—cars in *Taste of Cherry* and Manoel de Oliveira's *Voyage to the Beginning of the World*, a school bus in *The Sweet Hereafter*—it's worth considering how far the vehicles of our critical categories actually take us, and how far we might be able to travel if we learned how to walk again. (Last year's *Goodbye South, Goodbye* was also concerned with vehicles, and the film ended memorably when the last of these ran off the road and stopped.) The most beautiful shot I see in any film at Cannes, composed like a Brueghel landscape, is the bus accident in *The Sweet Hereafter*, seen from afar, and it's clearly the view of a pedestrian who stops to look, not one of a driver who speeds past.

PROBLEMS OF ACCESS: ON THE TRAIL OF SOME FESTIVAL FILMS AND FILMMAKERS[4]

"Festival film": a mainly pejorative term in the film business, especially in North America. It generally refers to a film destined to be seen by

---

[4] Adapted from "Problemes d'accès: Sur les traces de quelque films et cinéastes 'de festival,'" translated by Jean-Luc Mengus, *Trafic* no. 30, été 1999, pp. 54–70.

professionals, specialists, or cultists but not by the general public because some of these professionals decide it won't or can't be sufficiently profitable to warrant distribution. Whether these professionals are distributors, exhibitors, programmers, publicists, or critics is a secondary issue, particularly because these functions are increasingly viewed today as overlapping, and sometimes even as interchangeable.

The two types of critic one sees at festivals are those (the majority) who want to see the films that will soon be distributed in their own territories, and those who want to see the films that they'll otherwise never get to see—or in some cases films that may not arrive in their territories for a few years. The first group is apt to be guided in their choices of what to see by distributors, or else by calculated guesses of what distributors will buy. The second group, if it hopes to have any influence, will ultimately seek to persuade potential distributors as well as ordinary spectators, but whether it functions in this way or not, its spirit is generally guided by cinephilia more than by business interests. Because I belong to the second group, I generally prefer *as a filmgoer* festivals such as Rotterdam and Vienna, where business is kept to a relative minimum, to festivals like Cannes and Berlin, where business of one kind or another becomes the main focus. In recent years, sad to say, Toronto has gradually become more like Cannes and Berlin and less like Rotterdam, and this year Rotterdam was threatening to become a little more like Toronto. ("It's a different era" is the usual explanation for this gradual change, which expediently eliminates any human agency from the process; if that is the case, part of the continuing attraction of the Viennale is that, like Vienna itself, it remains happily lodged in an earlier era, and the same could be said of Sodankyla in Finland and Torino in Italy.)

Broadly speaking, "festival films" and "festival filmmakers" are like foreign visitors applying for visas in various countries and getting accepted by some, rejected by others. For one reason or another, I attended seven festivals between May 1998 and February 1999—held respectively in Cannes, Sodankyla, Locarno, Toronto, Vienna, Torino, and Rotterdam. During the same ten months, I also made visits to Providence (October), Ann Arbor (November), and Tokyo (December), tied respectively to events involving de Oliveira, Welles, and Ozu. I attended Cannes for three days in 1998 not as a critic but as a consultant who worked on the recently reconfigured version of *Touch of Evil*; I saw no films at all, and as it turned out, not even *Touch of Evil* was screened, but I heard a great deal of talk there about other films long before I saw them at subsequent festivals, so I've factored in some of this material as well.

Two filmmakers:

1. Harun Farocki (Locarno). If memory serves, the first Farocki film I ever saw was *Images of the World and the Inscription of War* at the Berlin Festival in 1989, where it was showing with English subtitles. My difficulties in seeing his films are partly a problem of not speaking German and partly a problem of living in a country that has remained triumphantly pre-Marxist since the thirties. Occasional screenings at the Rotterdam Festival, which I've attended for fifteen years, don't help because they're seldom shown there with translation in English or French, the only languages I can follow. In the United States. I could see nothing until nine films in a traveling show of eleven surfaced in Chicago in 1991; significantly, the two films omitted were both in 35-millimeter, because no cinema in Chicago and environs with 35mm projection could be found to show them.

This is shocking for a city the size of Chicago, but sadly not surprising. From *Machorka-Muff* to *Moses und Aron* (1975), every Straub-Huillet film was shown at the New York Film Festival (a pact broken for political reasons with *Fortini-Cani*); since then, only *Class Relations* and *From Today Until Tomorrow*, and many of the ten others have never shown in the United States at all. As with Farocki, the problems are (a) unavailability of 35mm projection for films of this kind ("this kind" meaning "experimental" in the case of Straub-Huillet, "experimental essays" in the case of Farocki), (b) absence of translation, and (c) absence of a European Marxist tradition: a fatal combination. So the prospect of a substantial Farocki retrospective at Locarno is exciting, especially now that an American "remake" of Farocki's 1969 *Inextinguishable Fire* (Jill Godmilow's *What Farocki Taught*) is making the rounds, a book coauthored by Farocki in English[5] is about to appear, and some of Farocki's work has

---

[5] *Speaking About Godard*, by Kaja Silverman and Harun Farocki, New York and London: New York University Press, 1998.

already come out on video in the United States. At long last, I conclude, it will become possible to catch up properly.

Unfortunately, too many other spectators at Locarno feel the same way. Programs are held each morning during the festival's final week in a small cinema at the Cinecentro Rialto, and the lines to get in are so long that the usual relation of supply to demand has become reversed: whereas many programmers are reluctant to show Farocki films out of fear that no one will come, far too many spectators turn up at the Rialto for everyone to get in. (Fortunately, the same sort of problem doesn't crop up when I belatedly catch up with the early short films of Jean-Daniel Pollet in Torino.)

It's like the dilemma of Alice in Wonderland being either too small or too large to enter a particular space. After missing one morning program as a consequence, I and a few others misbehave and contrive to remain at two consecutive programs the next day in order to avoid the risk of not getting into the second program by standing in line outside, although this ultimately entails seeing both programs without any earphone translation.

In fact, it feels as if the handful of Farocki fans scattered across the globe have suddenly converged into a crushing mob, making it impossible to navigate one's way from the line outside the cinema to the table with earphones a few paces away. Is this a Marxist or a capitalist problem? Like many things these days, it seems like a diabolical fusion: much as Oliver Stone's *Nixon* effectively recreates the monumental self-importance of Stalinist cinema, the mad rushes to see *Jean-Marie Straub und Danièle Huillet drehen einen Film nach Franz Kafkas "Amerika"* and *Peter Lorre* in Locarno replicate in miniature the premiere of a *Star Wars* sequel. I see the first of these films with translation and the second without—meaning that I can understand when Straub directs an actor by making reference to Ricky Nelson in *Rio Bravo* but can't follow the nuances of the anti-Hollywood arguments about Lorre's career.

2. Manoel de Oliveira (Toronto, New York, Chicago, Providence, Tokyo, Rotterdam). I see *Inquiètude*—for me, possibly de Oliveira's greatest film since *Doomed Love* (1978)—twice in Toronto and a third time in Providence at a Portuguese film festival held at Brown Univer-

sity; the only reason I don't see it a fourth time in Rotterdam is that it's subtitled in Dutch. Although the one-act play comprising the first episode is about old age, the theme linking all three episodes is existential identity, played out in each case by two characters—father and son, playboy and prostitute, young village woman and ancient witch— who function as parodic mirrors of one another. In its stately, dreamlike rhythms and multiple rhymes it recalls *Gertrud*, but as the Iranian filmmaker Mehrnaz Saeed-Vafa tells me after she sees it at the Chicago Festival, it also suggests *The Arabian Nights*.

On one level, I'm amazed that the New York Film Festival doesn't show the film; one of the members of the selection committee tells me that he considers it "minor" in relation to *The Convent* and *Voyage to Beginning of the World*, which the festival did show. But on another level, having served on the selection committee myself for the four previous years, I can easily perceive how the task of seeing a hundred films over two weeks in August could defeat the delicate and at times deceptive operations of a film like *Inquiètude*; in previous years, masterpieces as important as Kira Muratova's *The Asthenic Syndrome*, Edward Yang's *A Brighter Summer Day*, and Stanley Kwan's *Actress* eluded the committee for what I suspect were comparable reasons. (On the other hand, the fact that the much less selective and influential Chicago Festival shows four times as many films makes its inclusion of *Inquiètude*, however welcome, less significant.)

As with Luc Moullet and Râûl Ruiz, I owe most of my familiarity with de Oliveira's work to Rotterdam. The only living master who links the eras of silent and sound cinema, he may well represent what Buñuel calls the "last gasp" (to translate correctly the French title of his autobiography) of a twentieth-century art form if one accepts the recent death warrants of Godard (and ignores Kiarostami and Hou). That is what I find so moving and beautiful about Raymond Bellour's remarks on de Oliveira's importance in "Movie Mutations" in *Trafic* no. 24 and about Frédéric Bonnaud's essay on *Inquiètude* in *Trafic* no. 27, and why I am equally touched, at the conclusion of a symposium about Ozu in Tokyo in December, when Shigehiko Hasumi announces that it coincides with the ninetieth birthday party of de Oliveira in Porto, a gathering he regretfully had to miss in order to stage this event. And that is equally why I decide, two months earlier, to attend four days of a de Oliveira retrospective in Providence, despite the fact that this extended weekend overlaps with the beginning of the Chicago Film Festival and occurs only two days before I move with all my belongings to another apartment in Chicago: generally to resee de Oliveira films that I especially love — *Inquiètude, Benilde* (as close in a way to *Ordet* as *Inquiètude* is to *Gertrud*), *Doomed Love* — and to speak about his work at a panel discussion, specifically to see the one major work of his I've so far been unable to see, the complete seven-hour version of *The Satin Slipper.*

But unfortunately, an error in estimating the latter film's running time, combined with projection problems and a scheduling conflict, means that I and all the other out-of-town guests are obliged to leave for a banquet before the film's final hour is screened. And the next day, when the four-and-a-half-hour *Doomed Love* accidentally overlaps with the panel discussion about de Oliveira for similar reasons, the guests are again obliged to leave the film before the end in order to participate. In both cases, it's a grotesque perversion of academic film study and cinéphilia, as absurd as the difficulties in seeing Farocki's films in Locarno, though given the ambitiousness of the festival in Providence as a whole — which allows me to resee *Benilde* and *Inquiètude* in optimal conditions the two previous nights — I feel caught uneasily between frustration and gratitude. "It's another era": with the collapse of public arts funding, events of this kind become harder to organize and bring off properly with every passing year — especially when the prints come from abroad and part of the work is done by volunteers and nonprofessionals — so it's difficult to know whether to be thankful for the noble attempt or outraged at the various mishaps. Ultimately one feels both emotions, a mixture that all of de Oliveira's best features are well acquainted with.

Four films and one video:

1. *Fear and Loathing in Las Vegas* (Sodankyla). Here's a movie I admire more than like, mainly because of the unpleasantness of the material, though this is ultimately attributable to the obnoxious Hunter S. Thompson book it's based on, not to Terry Gilliam and his cowriters. What's mainly admirable is its unusual fidelity to the period it's set in

(1971) and its imaginative play in the particular zones where Las Vegas tackiness, LSD hallucinations, Gilliam beasties, and lots of vomit become difficult to separate. When I see the film a couple of weeks before it opens in Chicago in May, I judge it to be a healthy provocation for multiplexes even if I don't much enjoy it. But I find myself enjoying it more a month later when I attend a screening in the Finnish village of Sodankyla at the Festival of the Midnight Sun shortly after a lengthy public interview with Gilliam is conducted by the festival director, Peter von Bagh, in the local schoolhouse. Not really a "festival film" in the sense that the other items in this survey are, it nonetheless takes on different aspects in this informal setting.

What accounts for the difference? The capacity to view Gilliam's cinema in less conventionally auteurist terms—specifically Gilliam's account in his interview of how some of his regular coworkers often contribute and encourage the "typical Gilliam touches" that are applauded in his films while he often prefers to strike out in different directions. In other words, the corporate definitions of some studio auteurs such as Gilliam simplify their artistic personalities in order to make them more legible, so that the popular image of Gilliam as megalomaniacal visionary—matching the aggressive sense of entitlement in the hero of *Fear and Loathing*, Thompson's stand-in as played by Johnny Depp—is sharply contradicted by Gilliam himself, to all appearances a laid-back hippie. In a comparable way, having gotten to know Samuel Fuller pretty well during the last decade of his life, I find that the snappy aggression of his personality translated better into his corporate auteurist profile than his sweetness and his innocence— which was no less significant a part of his character, but which plays a much smaller role in Fuller criticism. In any case, I can't say that this clarification transforms *Fear and Loathing in Las Vegas* into a radically different film, but I can say that it pares away a certain mythology that will allow me to view his future films with fresher eyes.

2. *Touch of Evil* (Cannes, Toronto, Ann Arbor, Torino, Rotterdam). The reconfiguration of Welles's film based on forty-eight changes in sound and editing derived from a fifty-eight-page memo that he wrote to Universal studio head Edward Muhl in 1957 is scheduled to premiere in Cannes. But unfortunately this is planned to take place in the

smallest auditorium in the Palais for a few hundred VIPs, most of them American. So I'm mainly glad when the spurious claims and legal threats of Welles's daughter Beatrice persuade Gilles Jacob—who doesn't have the time while directing the festival to check the facts of the matter—to cancel this screening, which would have entailed excluding most of the world press for the sake of American vanity.

As it turns out, the cancellation gives the film more publicity than it might have had otherwise, thanks mainly to the presence in Cannes of Janet Leigh, editor Walter Murch, picture restorer Bob O'Neil, and producer Rick Schmidlin. In fact, the task of convincing the woman in charge of foreign sales at Universal to show the film abroad has been an uphill battle from the start. Initially she rejected all offers from over-seas festivals, and reportedly only after she attended Deauville and Venice did she arrive at the conclusion that people outside the United States might be interested in seeing this version—a good example of the fruits of contemporary American isolationism. (For the same rea-son, I suspect, most Hollywood studios tend to avoid Cannes premieres because they don't feel they can gauge the commercial results in advance.)

So the world premiere of the film, which I don't attend, occurs in Telluride four months later, but I'm around for its second screening shortly afterward in Toronto, along with Leigh and Schmidlin. By this time, the press coverage on the new *Touch of Evil* has mainly been accurate as well as favorable, and it continues in this vein when the film opens domestically later in September.

In Ann Arbor in October, lecturing in a class taught by Welles scholar Catherine Benamou, I explain how the persistence of Schmidlin and the participation of Murch eventually allowed us to carry out Welles's instructions without interference, discovering in the process how pertinent and consequential most of these instructions were. (For instance, the removal of a single close-up of Joseph Calleia from the Hall of Records scene, requested by Welles for cosmetic rea-sons, actually transforms the character of Menzies from a weakling to a highly principled individual in the final section of the film.) I also illustrate with a video of Murch's rough cut the two changes I made in his editing decisions—the first one a correction of a simple error (restoring the sound of Sanchez being punched in the stomach by

Quinlan during the long interrogation sequence), the second one a difference of opinion in which Schmidlin ultimately decided in my favor. (The request that Welles devoted the most space to in his memo was to cut the first scene between Leigh and Akim Tamiroff into two segments, cutting back to the scene of the explosion in between; Murch cut this scene into three segments with two cutaways to the explosion scene, and my objection, apart from the fact that Welles didn't request this, was that it played too smoothly, like the sort of mechanical cross-cutting one finds nowadays in practically every TV cop show. As Welles noted in his memo, this scene "has—and was meant to have—a curious, rather inconclusive quality," but Murch's initial fragmentation prevented it from truly functioning *as* a scene.)

With Murch and Schmidlin in Torino, and then with Schmidlin in Rotterdam, we encounter more technical problems. At the first Torino screening, two of the middle reels get scrambled and then, to the audience's frustration, the film is screened to the end. (I'm told that one Italian journalist who stayed only for the beginning, as I did, rushed off to report in his paper the next day that the screening was a resounding success.) Then, in Rotterdam, the film fails to arrive in time for the first screening—scheduled in the largest auditorium at the Pathé (the largest and perhaps best-designed multiplex in Europe), with all the tickets sold—and attracts only a fraction of the same audience when it is subsequently shown twice. But the film has already acquired a Dutch distributor, and by this time Nanni Moretti, the director of *Dear Diary* and *April*, has arranged to distribute it in Italy and other European distributors have picked it up, so such mishaps seem less serious than they might have otherwise. I'm more troubled by the fact that Rotterdam's catalogue and smaller program guide both describe it as a "director's cut," suggesting that all the efforts Schmidlin, Murch, Leigh, myself, and others have made to clarify that no such thing as a director's cut of *Touch of Evil* can ever exist haven't successfully crossed the Atlantic. Judging from the August video release of the preview version, it hadn't even crossed the Universal studio lot six months ago (I speak metaphorically, of course, because a studio's internal links nowadays are mainly by e-mail), so perhaps it's myopic to expect that a mainly accurate press coverage in the United States can be exported along with the film. But at least I can correct some of the misunderstandings when I'm interviewed by the festival's daily newspaper.

3. *Dead Cinema* (Locarno, Rotterdam). The problem, really, is the existence of ready-made labels for whoever writes ad copy or catalogue descriptions of work that eludes these categories, and the reconfigured *Touch of Evil* is far from being the only casualty of this situation. Chris Petit's exciting forty-minute experimental video *Dead Cinema*, receiving its world premiere in Rotterdam, especially piques my interest because it includes the first sound-and-image interview with critic Manny Farber ever recorded, as well as an interview with art critic Dave Hickey, another favorite of mine. But the fact that the video contains this material can't be learned from the catalogue, where it's listed under a working title, *Negative Space*[6]—which admittedly offers a clue about Farber's involvement, being the title of his only book—and is described as follows: "Latest work by the highly productive video essayist Petit, who is rapidly adding substance to the concept of digital aesthetics. A film [sic] about cultural memory, landscape and forgetting, time and television, both in the future and in today's digital world. England has good, bad and ugly things in store, as is already happening now at the present in the USA." This is mainly accurate, though it still fails to account for most of the video's interest.

4. *The Celebration* (Cannes, Toronto, Rotterdam). This is one of the four new films I hear the most about at Cannes. The other three are Lars von Trier's *The Idiots*, Todd Solondz's *Happiness*, and Gaspar Noé's *I Stand Alone* (see below). The two topics I hear the most about from American critics are the theme of incest in all these films except for *The Idiots*, and "Dogme 95," the attention-grabbing manifesto for "natural" filmmaking of von Trier and other Danish filmmakers, in relation to *The Celebration* and *The Idiots*. Both these topics are discussed as if they represented the two most important new trends in

---

[6] This became the final title a few weeks later, after Petit made a few last-minute changes to the video. See my May 12, 2000 review of this video at <www.chireader.com/movies/archives>.

world cinema. I'm highly skeptical about this—it seems grounded in the same mania for tabloid publicity and the exploitation of American puritanism that made Larry Clark's *Kids* the hit of Sundance four years ago—but I'm sufficiently curious to see *The Idiots* (which I don't much like) in Paris a few days later, and eventually I catch up with *The Celebration* and *Happiness* in Toronto.

In the early eighties, Jonas Mekas recalled to me his difficulties in 1961 in getting *The New York Times* to publish his manifesto of the New American Cinema; it was suggested that he try the *Village Voice* instead: "Then I understood, of course, that the only kind of manifesto *The New York Times* would print would be a press release, not a manifesto at all. In the same way, for an idea to get into the *Village Voice* today, it has to become not an idea but something else." Similarly, if Danish filmmakers want to get the attention of the American (and therefore the world) press today they have to write not a press release—everyone writes those now—but a manifesto. Existentially, in other words, the function of "Dogme 95" is to secure an American release for *The Celebration* and a Hollywood contract for Thomas Vinterberg. For that matter, based on the talk I hear in Cannes, I'm beginning to suspect that the theme of incest is still another way of capturing American press interest—if only because this is logically the only theme left for a press so committed to its own isolationism. (It's another era.) Even if this sentiment is culturally produced, it's disturbing that the American conviction that coming from another country can only mean aspiring to be American is matched by some of the recent filmmaking strategies of Europeans.

For me, the winning combination of *The Celebration*—making it increasingly popular as it proceeds from Cannes to Toronto to Rotterdam—is its combination of punk Ibsen (that is, Ibsen shorn of his politics and his impulse towards social reform, with some of the behavioral rudeness of Strindberg thrown in) with both the theme of incest and an exciting use of the Sony PC7, the smallest digital video camera available to Vinterberg at the time of shooting. None of these elements has much to do with the ten rules of "Dogme 95"'s alleged "Vow of Chastity"; if anything, the mistrust of high-tech filmmaking techniques reflected in that manifesto is contradicted by the exciting uses made of the Sony PC7. In fact, the film's plot and style are both based on deceptions. What appears to be the out-of-control behavior of the central character (Ulrich Thomsen) at a family gathering is in fact a series of carefully staged events, planned with the complicity of the kitchen staff. And what appears to be an out-of-control recording of this behavior is in fact a model of careful exposition—counteracting the continuity of the plot with as much discontinuity as can be managed without losing the threads of the action, executed with the full cooperation of camera crew and editing assistants. If it's a form of coquetry for Vinterberg to leave his name off the credits when he knows that we'll know it anyway, it's a similarly ironic subterfuge to use the dubious principles of "Dogme 95" to discipline his artistic choices as well as liberate them.

5. *I Stand Alone* (Cannes, Toronto, New York, Rotterdam). I have only the dimmest recollection of Gaspar Noé's *Carne* (1991) except that I didn't much like it, so when I hear widely disparate responses to his first full-length feature at Cannes this year, I'm not very interested, and I don't encounter the film until I idly ask to see it on video at the videothèque in Rotterdam almost nine months later. A particular reason why I've been in no hurry to see the film is the enthusiasm for it displayed by one of my least favorite American critics, who was one of the leading champions of *Kids,* and who subsequently describes *I Stand Alone* in print as having (I quote from memory) "the most redemptive ending of any film since Robert Bresson's *Pickpocket*"—a piece of hyperbole that conjures up the surrealist image of a redemption sweepstakes in which all potentially redemptive films since *Pickpocket* leave the starting gate at the same time and only one, in keeping with the spirit of American competition, is declared the winner. (In general, the use of the word "redemptive" is for me already a danger signal because, in a contemporary context, this usually means an extravagant bloodbath from the likes of Scorsese, Schrader, or Tarantino.) Apart from this dubious accolade, my colleagues mainly seem to agree only on how unpleasant it is, some of them taking exception to the political implications of Noé's own assertions about the film, though the film still surfaces with a certain amount of fanfare at the festivals in Toronto and New York.

"What would Sam Fuller make of this film?" is one of the questions that intrigues me the most while watching it. The timing of individual cuts to plucked strings on the sound track, then subsequently to off-screen gunshots, remind me of both the opening sequence of Fuller's *Verboten* and the linking intertitles with gunshots in Godard's *Masculin-Féminin*, though the violent changes of camera angle that often accompany these jolts are even more visceral. Following the bleak descent into rage and violence of a former butcher and convict (the same character in *Carne*, I faintly recall) who narrates his own progress with abusive, xenophobic language and murderous fantasies, the film offers images of downtrodden humanity that go beyond those of *The Honeymoon Killers* (not to mention those of Darejan Omirbaev's *Killer*), and a Monsieur Verdoux without a trace of charm or allegiance to any family, equipped with a mouth like Céline's as updated by partisans of Le Pen; the fact that the hero is the son of a Communist partisan killed by Nazis only adds to the troubling mix.

But the excitement of this film, fueled by the joint I smoked an hour earlier, is not merely a function of its odious material but its formal manner of implicating the viewer—light-years away from the glib Woody Allen attitudes of *Happiness*, the sub-Cassavetes manner (and prepolitical rebellion) of *The Idiots*, and even the more adventurous style of *The Celebration*. Overall, the film's evolution from short segments to extended scenes resembles the otherwise radically different *Rushmore* of Wes Anderson, a form of construction that builds on the solicitation of the viewer's trust and involvement so that long scenes are arrived at only after they're emotionally and dramatically earned. By the time the film arrives at its alternate endings involving incest with the protagonist's emotionally disturbed daughter, murder, and/or suicide—effectively obliging me to select which ending I prefer, "happy" or "unhappy"—I feel I'm watching a remake of *Taxi Driver* by Alain Robbe-Grillet, but crucially a remake in which none of the racist or homophobic epithets get displaced to characters other than the hero, and finally a Brechtian unpacking of fascist rage that shakes me to my core. I suspect it's fortunate that, even while I'm writing this, I've encountered none of Noé's discourse about the film, apart from the intriguing information that he originally wanted to call it *France*, and the fact that I watch (and, a few days later, resample) it alone on video, matching my own isolation with that of the hero, undoubtedly purifies my encounter with the material as well.

It's true that I'm only seeing it on video, but it's also part of the progressive shrinkage of film culture that such a fact begins to seem secondary. In the somewhat sloppy Rotterdam catalogue, as noted above, Chris Petit's video *Dead Cinema* is described as a film, and no mention is made of Farber. Calling a video a film is something most film professors in the United States habitually do as well nowadays, simply because they can't afford to book 16-millimeter prints for their courses and haven't yet read Serge Daney, most of whose writings about movies on TV have yet to be translated. And after *I Stand Alone* has a limited run in the United States later this year—given the size of its distributor, one can't expect any more—it will undoubtedly be known there mainly on video. "It's another era," my friends say, and one in which rumors about films and filmmakers often take the place of news. But the nice thing about rumors is that they're most often carried by friends rather than by publicists.

Chapter Ten
Orson Welles as Ideological Challenge

> Nothing irritates one more with middlebrow morality than the perpet-
> ual needling of great artists for not having been greater.
> — Cyril Connolly

During my almost thirty years as a professional film critic, I've developed something of a sideline—not so much by design as through a
combination of passionate interest and particular opportunities—
devoted to researching the work and career of Orson Welles. Though
I wouldn't necessarily call him my favorite filmmaker, he remains the
most fascinating for me, both due to the sheer size of his talent, and the
ideological force of his work and his working methods. These continue
to pose an awesome challenge to what I've been calling throughout this
book the media-industrial complex.

In more than one respect, these two traits are reverse sides of the
same coin. A major part of Welles's talent as a filmmaker consisted of
his refusal to repeat himself—a compulsion to keep moving creatively
that consistently worked against his credentials as a "bankable" director, if only because banks rely on known quantities rather than on
experiments. In industry parlance, a relatively bankable director—
someone like Steven Spielberg or James Cameron in the present era,
Charlie Chaplin (for most of his career, up through *The Great Dicta-
tor*) in an earlier era—is someone who knows how to "deliver the
goods," which doesn't necessarily rule out experimentation but limits
it to retooling certain tried-and-true elements. On an art-house level,
even Woody Allen remains relatively bankable because no matter how

much he experiments, most audiences still have a pretty good idea of what "a Woody Allen movie" consists of. Welles never came close to attaining this kind of public profile, and in terms of his ability to keep turning out movies that played to paying audiences, he paid dearly for this deficit. None of his pictures turned a profit on first release in this country with the sole exception of *The Stranger,* perhaps the least distinctive and adventurous item he directed—a film made in order to prove that he was bankable, and, because the commercial success even of that movie was only modest, it led to no sequels. In fact, the very notion of sequels of any kind remained anathema to Welles, and people who wonder why he couldn't or wouldn't turn out "another *Citizen Kane"*—including such unforgiving biographers as Charles Higham, Simon Callow, and David Thomson—tend to overlook not only the unique and complex set of circumstances that made his first feature possible but also the temperamental facets of his talent that made such a possibility unthinkable.

Comparing the respective film careers of Welles and Stanley Kubrick, it's interesting to consider that both started out in their early twenties, both died at the age of seventy, and both completed thirteen released features. Another significant parallel is that both wound up making all their completed films after the fifties in exile, which surely says something about the creative possibilities of American commercial filmmaking over the past four decades. But in other respects their careers proceeded in opposite directions: Welles entered the profession at the top regarding studio resources and wound up shooting all his last pictures on shoestrings and without studio backing; Kubrick began with shoestring budgets and wound up with full studio backing and apparently all the resources he needed.[1]

Even though the first of Kubrick's features, *Fear and Desire* (1952), has mainly been out of circulation for the past several years, the

---

[1] On the basis of this difference, one could argue that Kubrick succeeded in working within the system while retaining his independence on every picture except for *Spartacus* while Welles retained his independence more sporadically and imperfectly, and ultimately at the price of working outside the system. Yet the price paid by Kubrick for his own success—a sense of paranoid isolation that often seeped into his work, and finally no more completed features than Welles managed—can't be discounted either.

remainder of his work is sufficiently well known to make a recounting of his filmography unnecessary, but the same thing can't be said for all of Welles's completed features. The best known remain those released by Hollywood studios (*Citizen Kane*, *The Magnificent Ambersons*, *The Stranger*, *The Lady from Shanghai*, *Macbeth*, and *Touch of Evil*) and two independent features in the fifties that continue to circulate, *Othello* and *Mr. Arkadin*. The remaining five, thanks to their independent financing and their checkered commercial careers, tend to be less known in the United States. In chronological order, these are *The Trial* (an adaptation of the Franz Kafka novel, 1962), *Chimes at Midnight* (also known as *Falstaff*, adapting portions of all the Shakespeare plays featuring Falstaff, 1966—considered by many critics to be Welles's greatest feature), the hour-long *The Immortal Story* (an adaptation of an Isak Dinesen story, in color, made for French television, 1968), and two rather different essay films: *F for Fake* (about art forgery in general and art forger Elmyr de Hory, writer Clifford Irving, and Welles himself in particular, 1973) and *Filming Othello* (about the making of Welles's 1952 *Othello*, his first completed independent feature, 1978).

The unexpected commercial success of the reedited *Touch of Evil* in 1998, discussed in the previous chapter, seems to have made Welles relatively "bankable" again, with the result that a good many other Welles or Welles-related projects have either just surfaced (such as movies entitled *The Big Brass Ring*, *Cradle Will Rock*, and *RKO 281*) or are in the works (including possible restorations of Welles's *The Other Side of the Wind*, *The Magic Show*, *The Deep/Dead Reckoning*, and *Orson's Bag*. Yet the ideological challenge posed by Welles's career remains as real and as operative as ever, because it continues to throw into question most of the working assumptions we have about the operations of the film industry.

I'm not claiming that this challenge was always or necessarily intentional. Though part of his ambition was to confound audience expectations and to shock or surprise, some of his unorthodox work habits were arrived at over the course of his unruly career rather than conceived as deliberate provocations. In other to summarize what these habits and practices consisted of, I've drawn up the following list and tried in each case to indicate the particular received ideas about filmmaking and film culture that they challenge (in some cases, these six topics overlap):

1. Welles as an independent filmmaker. His first and second features, *Citizen Kane* and *The Magnificent Ambersons*, were studio releases, both made at and with the facilities of RKO, and this has led many recent commentators to regard Welles as an unsuccessful studio employee throughout his career rather than as an independent film-maker, successful or otherwise. Insofar as most film histories are written by industry apologists of one sort or another, this is an unexceptional conclusion, but not necessarily a correct one. To my mind, Welles always remained an independent who financed his own pictures whenever and however he could, and perhaps the only movie in his entire canon that qualifies as a Hollywood picture pure and simple, for better and for worse, is *The Stranger*. In many cases, one can easily separate his features between Hollywood productions (e.g., *The Lady from Shanghai, Macbeth*) and independent productions (e.g., *Othello, F for Fake*), but the divisions aren't always so clear-cut: the unfinished *It's All True* started out as a studio project and ended up as an independent project; according to Welles, *Arkadin* in its release form was even more seriously mangled by its producer than any of his Hollywood films; *The Trial* was largely financed by Alexander and Michael Salkind, some of whose productions (including *Superman* and *The Three Musketeers*) can be loosely labeled as "Hollywood" or "studio" releases; and even a clearly independent effort like *Don Quixote* started out as a TV project backed by Frank Sinatra.

Part of what made and continues to make *Citizen Kane* exceptional is that it was made with exceptional freedom and control *and* studio facilities, and this came about because Welles refused to sign a Hollywood contract to make pictures unless he had this control—and because he was formidable enough as a mainstream figure in the late thirties to demand it. People today tend to forget how much of an anomaly *Kane* was as a "Hollywood picture" when it was initially released in 1941; it took many decades of ideological spadework on the part of critics before it was perceived as a Hollywood classic, and para-doxically this achievement mainly came about through a demolition job—Pauline Kael's "Raising Kane"—that argued that, contrary to ear-lier claims that *Citizen Kane* was a "one-man show," made by Kael her-self as well as many other critics, it was in fact a work that mainly owed its excellence to the creative screenwriting of Herman J. Mankiewicz, who was virtually the sole author of the script. This mainstream revisionist view was subsequently complemented by Robert L. Carringer's academic book *The Making of "Citizen Kane"* (Berkeley: University of California Press, 1985). Although Carringer thoroughly demolished Kael's claims about Mankiewicz's exclusive authorship of the script, he also argued more generally that *Kane*'s greatness and singularity stemmed from its status as a collaborative venture, in which the roles played by cinematographer Gregg Toland, screenwriter Herman J. Mankiewicz, editorial supervisor John Houseman, and art director Perry Ferguson were pivotal. Left to his own devices, Carringer concluded, Welles was doomed to failure, and this accounted for *Kane*'s preeminence over Welles's other films.

This is still a popular position, and there are plenty of arguments in favor of it—although most of them are rationalizations of Hollywood's industrial methods of turning out pictures. There's a lot at stake ideologically in classifying *Kane* as a Hollywood picture, as Kael and Carringer both do, because the moment one does, one arrives at a Platonic ideal of Hollywood practice that can be used—and generally *has* been used—as a way of dismissing the remainder of Welles's career as a filmmaker. Similarly, there's just as much at stake ideologically in classifying *Kane*, as I do, as an independent feature that uses Hollywood resources—which is not to deny the importance of collaborators (including actors as well as other participants) on *Kane* and other Welles movies, but rather to insist on the bottom line of who gets the final word on any production. Since everyone is in agreement that Welles had the final word on what went into *Citizen Kane* and that he had the full resources of a Hollywood studio on that picture, there is a certain amount of scholarly agreement between Carringer and myself about what the achievement of *Kane* consisted of. (There is no such scholarly agreement between both of us and Kael regarding the film's authorship; although her facts have been conclusively disproven by Carringer and others, Kael has opted to reprint "Raising Kane" without alteration, apology, or even acknowledgment of any counterpositions in the significantly titled *For Keeps*, her latest collection.) Where we start to differ is what we take that achievement to mean. And once we combine the separate-but-overlapping arguments of Kael and Carringer—which in Kael's case also entails viewing *Kane* as the apotheosis of the Hollywood newspaper comedy—we wind up with a mainstream domestication of Welles's first feature. For roughly three decades after it was made, *Kane* remained a troubling anomaly in American film history, an unclassifiable object that was neither fish nor fowl. But once the domesticating arguments of Kael and Carringer took hold—the former in the mainstream, the latter in academia—the movie became regarded as something much safer and more familiar, a Hollywood classic to stand alongside *The Wizard of Oz*, *Casablanca*, *Bringing Up Baby*, and *It's a Wonderful Life*. (It's worth recalling that all four of the latter movies were far from being "instant" classics either: *The Wizard of Oz* "tested" so poorly that M-G-M very nearly deleted "Over the Rainbow" for making audiences too fidgety; *Casablanca* initially registered as little more than a feel-good wartime entertainment; and both *Bringing Up Baby* and *It's a Wonderful Life*, like *Kane*, were outright flops at the box office—assuming their current reputations many years later, after they were revived repeatedly on TV.)

Revisionist film historian Douglas Gomery, who specializes in economics, fundamentally agrees with my contention that Welles was an independent filmmaker throughout his career—and I hasten to add that he arrived at this conclusion on his own, without any prompting from me.[2] He argues that the simple notion that Welles was exploited by Hollywood for the purposes of Hollywood has it backward: more generally, it was Welles who exploited Hollywood for his own purposes. According to Gomery's analysis, Hollywood of the thirties and forties was dominated by four relatively strong major studios (Paramount, Fox, Metro, and Warners), four major studios that were relatively weak (RKO, Columbia, Universal, and United Artists), and a number of more marginal studios, the strongest of which was Republic Pictures. Welles wound up making films for the first three of the four weaker major studios, for Republic, and for Sam Spiegel on *The Stranger* (released by RKO); he never worked for any of the Big Four. In most cases, Gomery points out, Welles went over budget and his films wound up losing money for the studios, all of which contradicts the

---

[2] "Orson Welles and the Hollywood Industry," *Persistence of Vision* no. 7, 1989, pp. 39–43.

notion of him being exploited by Hollywood in general or by the studios in particular.

So far, so good. Where I begin to part company with Gomery, as well as with Carringer,[3] is in their uncritical acceptance of the business acumen of those studios when they decided to tamper with Welles's work. Everyone is in agreement that *Citizen Kane*, which wasn't tampered with at RKO, lost a certain amount of money, and that *The Magnificent Ambersons*, which lost even more money, was substantially tampered with by the same studio. Although neither Gomery nor Carringer conclude from this that RKO would have been commercially justified in tampering with *Kane*—assuming that RKO's contact with Welles had allowed this—they both irrationally conclude that RKO was commercially justified in tampering with *Ambersons*, despite the fact that the resulting hybrid still lost the studio an enormous amount of money.

Obviously I can't prove that Welles's own version would have made more money, but I seriously doubt that they could prove the contrary. The only evidence they can summon up to support their view is the audience responses at the film's three test-marketing previews, and, as I hope this book has already demonstrated, this is tantamount to placing one's medical faith in a team of witch doctors. Both Gomery and Carringer accept without qualm the conclusion of studio executive George Schaefer that the first preview of *Ambersons*, when a version approximating Welles's own version was shown, was a "disaster." Certainly we have many eyewitness accounts that a significant portion of that audience was unsympathetic and even hostile—just as I'm sure we have evidence that members of the early preview audiences of *The Wizard of Oz* started to squirm as soon as "Over the Rainbow" came on—but I'm not convinced that this constitutes any sort of conclusive evidence. I've seen most of the one hundred and twenty-five "comment cards" myself—fifty-three of which were positive, some of them outright raves ("a masterpiece with perfect photography, settings and acting," "the best picture I have ever seen")—and would conclude that

---

[3] "Oedipus in Indianapolis," in *The Magnificent Ambersons: A Reconstruction*, Berkeley, University of California Press, 1993.

declaring the preview a "disaster" on the basis of those cards is a highly subjective matter, very much dependent on what one is predisposed to look for. It all depends on whether the hostile responses definitively outweigh the favorable responses, and considering that the preview in question—held at the Fox Theater in Pomona, California on March 17, 1942—immediately followed a regular commercial screening of a Dorothy Lamour wartime musical, *The Fleet's In*, one might easily conclude that an audience paying to see something like that might not have been exactly primed for an unusually long and depressing feature such as Welles's version of *Ambersons*.

Theoretically a preview of *Ambersons* that followed a commercial screening of *How Green Was My Valley*, released the previous year—even though this might have made for an unusually long program—might have yielded seventy-two positive responses and fifty-three negative ones, a difference of only nineteen votes from what actually transpired. Are Gomery and Carringer absolutely convinced that a minimum of nineteen viewers at that preview couldn't have responded differently if the studio had bothered to schedule the *Ambersons* preview after something more appropriate? Or are they merely content to leave the benefit of every doubt to RKO in this matter?

2. WELLES AS AN INTELLECTUAL. Starting around 1938, when at age twenty-three Welles became a household name in the United States through the scandal of his *War of the Worlds* radio broadcast, the terms "genius" and "boy genius" became attached to his name with increasing frequency, and they clung to his public profile to varying degrees for the remainder of his life and career. On the surface, these are terms of praise, but as Robert Sklar has demonstrated at length in a brilliant essay,[4] they are just as clearly terms of abuse—especially within the anti-intellectual context of American popular culture, where Welles came into prominence in the thirties and forties. Moreover, the undertow of resentment behind these terms is not merely a matter of after-the-fact interpretation. It becomes immediately apparent if one reads the three-

---

[4] "Welles Before *Kane:* The Discourse on a 'Boy Genius,'" *Persistence of Vision* no. 7, 1989, pp. 63–72.

part profile of Welles published in the *Saturday Evening Post* in early 1940, if one listens to his radio appearances on popular comedy shows throughout the forties, or if one watches "Lucy Meets Orson Welles," an episode of *I Love Lucy* broadcast in 1956. Even the title and subtitles of the *Saturday Evening Post* profile coauthored by Alva Johnson and Fred Smith spell out part of this undercurrent of hostility: "How to Raise a Child: The Education of Orson Welles, Who Didn't Need It" (January 20), "How to Raise a Child: The Continuing Education of Orson Welles, Who Didn't Need It" (January 27), and "How to Raise a Child: The Disturbing Life — To Date — of Orson Welles" (February 3).

Interestingly enough, Welles spoke favorably about these articles to Peter Bogdanovich in 1969,[5] calling them accurate and implying that they were sympathetic. (More precisely, he noted that the authors had worked with him closely in preparing the profile, which raises the possibility that Welles's own pronounced impulses toward self-criticism and self-accusation were accurately reflected in the articles.) By the same token, judging from the many appearances of Welles on comedy shows of the forties and fifties that I've heard and/or seen, he appears to be completely complicitous and comfortable with the extremely precocious, imperious, egomaniacal, and intimidating versions of himself comically presented and ridiculed on those programs. On July 19, 1946, he even presented an extended parody of his persona — "Adam Barneycastle," played by Fletcher Markle — on the *Mercury Summer Theatre*, explaining in his introduction that after hearing Markle's half-hour *Life with Adam* on Canadian radio, he couldn't resist importing it onto his own CBS radio show.

What are we to make of this apparent masochism on Welles's part, which seems to go well beyond "being a good sport" about the threatening figure he seemed to pose to the mass media? The negative aspects of this image hounded him for the remainder of his career, and continue to crop up even posthumously in works ranging from the Oscar-nominated documentary *The Battle Over "Citizen Kane"* (1995) and Tim Robbins's *Cradle Will Rock* to Welles biographies by Charles

---

[5] *This Is Orson Welles*, by Orson Welles and Peter Bogdanovich, edited by Jonathan Rosenbaum, second edition, New York: Da Capo Press, p. 358.

Higham, Simon Callow, and David Thomson. Like most caricatures, this lampoon of Welles's personality had some basis in fact, even if it has tended to obscure other aspects of his character, often to ruinous effect. It points to fear as well as respect, intimidation as well as admiration, which was obviously part of the packaging he had to accept if he wanted to cut a figure in the mass media; and it must be admitted that Welles seemed to go along with this partial misrepresentation as a show-biz necessity. Unfortunately, this same distortion would interfere increasingly with public understanding of what he was up to as an artist, ultimately encouraging the same sort of mythology that mystifies most accounts of his more serious work today.

Welles's reputation as a "genius," which he eventually began to criticize in his late interviews, is not the same as his reputation as an intellectual, but the two images often overlap in the public imagination, especially in his case. Both are tied to his privileged upper-class background, though the usual unconscious taboos against discussions of class differences in American culture muddy the waters even further. This often leads to outright errors regarding Welles, such as David Thomson's assertion that he "always liked his revolutionaries to be sophisticated and well-heeled"—a premise that rules out, for starters, Jacaré, the central, heroic, real-life radical in the central episode of Welles's unfinished docudrama feature about Latin America, *It's All True*. But since Thomson elsewhere characterizes the footage from this episode, dealing with Jacaré and other poor Brazilian fishermen, as "picturesque but inconsequential material," one is forced to conclude that maybe it's Thomson and not Welles who likes—indeed, requires—revolutionaries to be "sophisticated and well-heeled," at least if they want to be considered consequential.[6]

The relation of culture to money is so fixed in the American popular imagination that it often becomes difficult to disentangle the two—a situation much less prevalent in Europe, where, as Jim Jarmusch once pointed out to me in an interview, street cleaners in Rome are apt to discuss Dante, Ariosto, and twentieth-century Italian poets,

---

[6] David Thomson, *Rosebud: The Story of Orson Welles*, New York: Alfred A. Knopf, 1996, pp. 77 and 237.

and "even guys who work in the street collecting garbage in Paris love nineteenth-century painting." Welles's intellectual activity often winds up imposing a lot of false assumptions about his politics, taking him to be an elitist rather than a populist—although in fact the reception of his work ran the gamut from popular (his theater and radio work in the thirties, his TV appearances) to elitist (most of his films from the forties onward, despite their populist intentions).

Welles has an interesting exchange on this issue with Bogdanovich in *This Is Orson Welles:*

PETER BOGDANOVICH: You once said that your tastes don't shock the middle-class American, they only shock the American intellectual. Do you think that's true?

ORSON WELLES: Yes.

PB: Why?

OW: Because I'm a complete maverick in the intellectual establishment. And they only like me more now because there's even less communication between me and them. I've become kind of exotic, so they start to accept me. But basically I've always been completely at odds with the true intellectual establishment. I despise it, and they suspect and despise me. I am an intellectual, but I don't belong to that particular establishment.

PB: Well, it's true that America likes its artists and its entertainers to be either artists *or* entertainers, and they can't accept the combination of the two.

OW: Or any combination. They want one clear character. And they don't want you to be two things. That irritates and bewilders them.[7]

This final formulation expresses the problem in a nutshell. Welles was too much of a vulgar entertainer to endear himself to the intellectual establishment. But he was too much of an artist and intellectual to endear himself to the general public unless he mocked and derided his artistic temperament and intellectualism, thereby proving he wasn't on a higher level than his own audience and ratifying his own populism. (Significantly, to the best of my knowledge, this wasn't a form of self-disparagement he ever practiced in Europe, where it wasn't deemed necessary to establish his equity with the public.) To a large degree, straddling this contradiction is what his art and his life were all about.

---

[7] *This Is Orson Welles,* op. cit., pp. 243–244.

3. THE TABOO AGAINST FINANCING ONE'S OWN WORK. I assume it's deemed acceptable for a low-budget experimental filmmaker to bankroll his or her own work, but for a "commercial" director to do so is anathema within the film industry, and Welles was never fully trusted or respected by that industry for doing so from the mid-forties on. This pattern started even before *Othello*, when he purchased the material he had shot for *It's All True* from RKO with the hopes of finishing the film independently, a project he never succeeded in realizing. As an overall principle, he did something similiar in the thirties when he acted in commercial radio in order to surreptitiously siphon money into some of his otherwise government-financed theater productions during the WPA period, a practice he discusses in *This Is Orson Welles*. John Cassavetes, who also acted in commercial films in order to pay for his own independent features, suffered similarly in terms of overall commercial "credibility," which helps to explain why he and Welles admired each other. (In an early stage of his work on the unrealized *The Big Brass Ring*, a late script and project, Welles thought of casting Cassavetes and his wife Gena Rowlands as presidential candidate Blake Pellarin, the hero, and his wife, Diana.)

In the case of features that were largely financed out of Welles's own pocket, such as *Don Quixote* and *The Deep/Dead Reckoning*, Welles often insisted in interviews that when or if he finished and released these features was nobody's business but his own — an attitude that often met with resentment and/or incomprehension from his fans. This raises a good many intriguing and not easily resolvable questions about the implied social contract that exists between artist and audience, and one that is undoubtedly inflected by the relative power of the industry to deliver films to theaters and the relative powerlessness of most film artists to ensure that their own films get distributed.

In Welles's case, the poor critical receptions and poor business that greeted most of his releases, at least in the United States, made him understandably hesitant to risk whatever remained of his "bankability" by releasing any of his films prematurely, or at the wrong time; he was also handicapped throughout his career by being a terrible businessman and often made wrong guesses about the commercial viability of some of his projects. I'm told that he once turned down a relatively generous offer from Joseph Levine to distribute *F for Fake* in the United

States, an offer Levine made even though he had nodded off during a screening; convinced that his film would be a big moneymaker, Welles turned him down flat, only to accept a less lucrative offer years later in order to get any American distribution at all.

When I asked him about *Don Quixote* in the early seventies, he replied that *Man of La Mancha* was currently being developed as a movie and he didn't want his own version to compete with it. This statement astonished me at the time, but after I reflected on all the abuse he received from the American press about the inferiority of his *Macbeth* to Laurence Olivier's *Hamlet,* I began to think his fears might have been justified. (When I asked him about *The Deep,* he insisted that it was the sort of melodrama that wouldn't date, and that he was more interested in releasing *The Other Side of the Wind* first—although this eventually proved to be impossible for legal and financial reasons that are documented in Barbara Leaming's Welles biography.)

4. THE UNIQUE FORMS OF SIGNIFICANT WORKS. It surely isn't accidental that we have only one completed version of *Citizen Kane* to evaluate. By contrast, we have at least two completed versions of Welles's *Macbeth,* three versions of his *Othello,* and at least four versions apiece of his *Mr. Arkadin* and *Touch of Evil,* to provide only a short list. (There's also, for example, a separate version of *The Lady from Shanghai* that has circulated in Germany containing some takes as well as shots that are different from those in the U.S. release version.)

The reasons for this confusing bounty are multiple, but all of them ultimately stem from Welles's unorthodox practices as a filmmaker. When early audiences and critics complained about the Scottish accents and the length of the first version of *Macbeth* (which is incidentally the one principally available today), Welles obligingly had the film redubbed and deleted two reels' worth of material. (Most critics assume mistakenly that the only Hollywood film on which he had final cut was *Kane*; in fact, he also had final cut on *both* versions of *Macbeth,* even if the second version was done at the behest of Republic Pictures.) *Othello,* on the other hand—Welles's first completed independent feature—was partially reedited and redubbed at Welles's own initiative, between the time of its Cannes premiere and its belated U.S. release over three years later. Although you won't find this information in any of the "authoritative" books about Welles, French film scholar François Thomas has recently discovered that Welles redubbed Desdemona — played in the film by Suzanne Clothier, who shot her sequences in 1949 and 1950 — with the voice of Gudrun Ure (later known as Ann Gaudrun), the actress who played Desdemona in his subsequent 1951 English stage production of the play, entailing a different interpretation of the same part. Over forty years later, long after Welles's death, the sound track of this second version was significantly altered — both sound effects and music were rerecorded in stereo, in the latter case without consulting composer Francesco Lavignino's written score, and the speed of the dialogue delivery was occasionally altered to improve the lip sync — in order to release the results as a so-called "restoration."[8]

Though it's theoretically possible to assign different evaluations to the separate versions of *Macbeth* and *Othello*, critics have rarely bothered to carry out this work; in fact, most of them have been unaware that these separate versions exist. The fact that both versions of *Macbeth* and the first two versions of *Othello* were all Welles's own handiwork means that we can't rank them in terms of authenticity (except to note that the second *Macbeth* wasn't instigated by him). We can't, for instance, argue that the European *Othello* is "more Wellesian" or "truer to Welles's intentions" than the initial U.S. version, and consequently it becomes impossible to speak of a "definitive" film version of Welles's *Othello*.

The same principle was carried out more publicly by Jean-Marie Straub and Danièle Huillet — a European couple who make rigorous

---

[8] In the cases of both *Mr. Arkadin* and *Touch of Evil*, Welles never had final cut on any version, so all of the existing versions represent different attempts to realize his intentions after the film slipped out of his control. (*Arkadin* was taken away from him at a relatively early stage in the editing, *Touch of Evil* at a relatively late stage.) For a more detailed critique of the third version of *Othello* — the only one readily available in the United States thanks to the pressures of Welles's youngest daughter, Beatrice, who maintains legal control of this film — see "*Othello* Goes Hollywood" in my collection *Placing Movies: The Practice of Film Criticism* (Berkeley: University of California Press, 1995, pp. 124–132) and Michael Anderegg's excellent *Orson Welles, Shakespeare, and Popular Culture* (New York: Columbia University Press, 1999, pp. 111–120).

and beautiful avant-garde films that, in recent years, have rarely been screened in the United States—when they deliberately released four separate versions of their 1986 feature *The Death of Empedocles*, each employing separate takes of each shot, to correspond to the separate languages of each version: unsubtitled German, English subtitles, French subtitles, and Italian subtitles. Straub argued that this was done in order to challenge the notion of uniqueness that we habitually assign to individual films, and he certainly had a point, but Welles made the same point more offhandedly and surreptitiously three decades earlier when he refashioned his second *Othello* without bothering to announce that he was doing so.

Why, one may ask, did Welles do this? Because he loved to work, one might surmise, and because for him all work was work-in-progress—both reasons helping to explain why he often wound up having to finance much of the work himself. To love the process of work to this degree evidently offends certain aspects of the Protestant work ethic. Judging from the jibes about Welles's obesity in his later years that often cropped up in his American obituaries—but not in most obituaries that appeared elsewhere in the world—Welles's reputation as a hedonist was often used against him to imply irrationally that all his production money went to pay for expensive meals; indeed, many people preferred to believe that the only reason he didn't make or finish or release more films was out of laziness and moral turpitude. (This is more or less the thesis of biographers Charles Higham, David Thomson, and, to a lesser extent, Simon Callow, none of whom ever met the man.)

Obviously the fact that Welles loved to make films—and often sacrificed his reputation as an actor by appearing in lots of TV commercials and bad movies in order to keep doing so—doesn't square with this hypothesis, except to imply that to some degree he wound up tarnishing part of his public profile in order to subsidize his art. The process by which a public figure became a private artist is obviously fraught with contradictions, but one should never forget that it was love of the art-making process itself that ultimately sabotaged Welles's commercial profile. And as the Chilean-French filmmaker and devoted Welles fan Râùl Ruiz once said to me, in defense of Welles's reputation as a maker of unfinished films, "All films are unfinished—except, possibly, those of Bresson." Which leads us logically to

5. INCOMPLETION AS AN AESTHETIC FACTOR. Critics confronting Franz Kafka's three novels have less of a problem with this—at least Kafka is rarely castigated as an artist to the degree that Welles is. Could this be because money is involved more centrally with making movies than with writing novels? It's also important to recognize that no two of Welles's unfinished films remain unfinished for the same reason. This is the portion of Welles's oeuvre that's most notoriously difficult to research, but on the basis of what I've been able to glean over the years, Welles wanted and made repeated efforts to finish both *It's All True* and *The Other Side of the Wind*, came close to finishing *Don Quixote* in at least one version in the late fifties (according to former Welles secretary Audrey Stainton; see her article, *"Don Quixote*: Orson Welles's Secret" in the Autumn 1988 *Sight and Sound*), and eventually abandoned *The Deep* for personal as well as commercial reasons.[9]

So much for incomplete works—which doesn't, of course, include features wrestled away from Welles's control and completed by others, such as *The Magnificent Ambersons* and *Mr. Arkadin*. But what about the incompleteness of Welles's oeuvre as a whole, an even more serious problem due to the unavailabilty of so many of his works, finished and unfinished alike? Some of these, like the films he made as integral parts of stage productions in the thirties or the portions of features (*The Magnificent Ambersons*, *The Stranger*, *The Lady from Shanghai*) deleted by studios, are almost certainly lost for good. Some films, such as his first and best TV pilot (*The Fountain of Youth*, 1956) and *Filming "Othello"* (1979), remain unavailable simply because of "business rea-

---

[9] One film commonly described as unfinished—Welles's forty-minute condensation of *The Merchant of Venice*, his only Shakespeare film in color, designed in the late sixties to serve as the climax to a CBS TV special—was in fact fully edited, scored, and mixed, though most of it was spirited away by an Italian editor after a single private screening; one hopes that eventually the full version will see the light of day. Nine minutes of this film are currently held by the Munich Film Archive. Two other completed short films—*Camille, the Naked Lady, and the Musketeers* (1956) and *Viva l'Italia!* (aka *Portrait of Gina*, circa 1958)—are unsold, half-hour TV pilots; the first of these is lost, though the second resurfaced three decades later, and was recently shown in its entirety on German TV. Needless to say, the list goes on. . . .

sons" (i.e., the indifference of the copyright holder or legal obstacles, which often amount to the same thing), with the result that most American viewers are scarcely aware of their existence. Three extended TV series made by Welles in Europe—*Orson Welles Sketch Book* (six 15-minute episodes, 1955), *Around the World with Orson Welles* (five completed half-hour episodes and one unfinished episode, 1955), and *In the Land of Don Quixote* (nine half-hour episodes, 1964)—survive but remain unavailable in the United States. And most of the unfinished work has wound up in film archives—the Fortaleza footage of *It's All True* at UCLA (although the footage that survives from that feature continues to be in peril until funds are found to preserve it), *Don Quixote* and *In the Land of Don Quixote* at the Filmoteca Española in Madrid, and, most recently, a varied collection of unfinished work (including *The Deep, Orson's Bag, The Magic Show,* and *The Dreamers*) at the Munich Film Archive, which is still seeking ways of restoring and presenting it.

Without implying that all this material is equally important or interesting—I regard most of *In the Land of Don Quixote* as amiable hackwork at best—I would argue that a significant part of it, judging from the portions that I've seen or sampled, substantially alters one's sense of Welles's oeuvre as a whole, extending its range and diversity while illuminating certain work that one already knows. This ultimately means that, fifteen years after his death, we are still years away from being able to grasp the breadth of Welles's film work, much less evaluate it.

6. A CONFOUNDING OF THE NOTION OF ART AS COMMODITY. We're finally left with the problem of how to evaluate Welles's still-ungraspable oeuvre in relation to the international film market—an issue that is currently preoccupying a good many film executives as well as archivists considering the possibility of completing and/or releasing films by Welles that haven't yet been seen. Prior to the very successful commercial release of the reconfigured *Touch of Evil*, the prospects of getting any of these films out on the world market was beginning to look rather dim. (To date, Jesus Franco's lamentable version of Welles's *Don Quixote*—hastily edited in order to premiere in a Spanish-language version at Spain's Expo 92, and subsequently completed in an English-

language version as well—has failed to find a U.S. distributor; to the best of my knowledge, it has only received a few scattered screenings in North America, most notably at New York's Museum of Modern Art.) Now that the commercial prospects are looking somewhat more favorable, numerous questions still remain—including how these "new" (or "old") works are to be represented.

"Welles's Lost Masterpiece" was the phrase used in ads for the significantly altered version of Welles's 1952 *Othello* released in 1992—although the film had never been lost at all; it had simply been out of distribution in the United States for many years. The new version, moreover, was billed as a "restoration," and this was how it was labeled by a good ninety-five-percent of the reviews in the press; in *The New York Times*, for instance, Vincent Canby called it "an expertly restored print that should help to rewrite cinema history." But as Michael Anderegg has pointed out,

> To term the project authorized by Beatrice Welles-Smith as a 'restoration' is to make nonsense of the word. One cannot restore something by altering it in such a way that its final state is something new. To restore means, if it means anything, to bring back to some originary point— itself, of course, an extremely dubious concept. . . .
>
> If you find a Greek statue with a left arm missing, you might be able to restore it if, (*a*) you can demonstrate, through internal and external evidence, that it once had a left arm and (*b*) you can discover some evidence of what the left arm looked like when it was still attached. If, however, the statue was meant to have no left arm (a statue, perhaps, of a one-armed man), or if the statue was never completed by the sculptor, or if, assuming the arm did once exist and had broken off, you have no evidence of what the missing arm had originally looked like, then adding an arm of your own design is not an act of restoration. You are, instead, making something new.[10]

According to Anderegg's subsequent analysis, the version of Welles's *Othello* described as a "restoration" alters not only Welles's original sound design and Francesco Lavignino's score, but also reloops some of the dialogue with new actors, eliminates some words "so that a lip-synch could be achieved," and reedits one sequence entirely. But of course the

---

[10] *Orson Welles, Shakespeare, and Popular Culture*, op. cit., p. 112.

use of the term "restoration" in relation to movies has become so loose and imprecise in recent years that it characteristically gets employed every time a studio decides to strike a new print, add footage without consulting the original director, or, on a few rare occasions, rework an old movie with the original director's input (as in the rereleased *Blade Runner*, which proved to be partly a restoration of Ridley Scott's original cut and partly a revision—including the insertion of a shot of a unicorn taken from Scott's *Legend*, a film made three years after *Blade Runner*). Typically, the summer before Universal Pictures released the reedited version of *Touch of Evil*, it reissued on video the preview version of the film that had already been available since the seventies and mislabeled it not only a "restoration" but the "director's cut," which was even more ridiculous—adding insult to injury insofar as Universal had never allowed Welles to complete a final cut of his own in the first place, which in fact is what occasioned his fifty-eight-page memo to Universal studio head Edward Muhl.

Significantly, in the early nineties, when I originally tried to get an American film magazine interested in publishing roughly two-thirds of this memo, a document drafted in 1957, *Premiere* and *Film Comment* both turned me down flat; if memory serves, the former considered the document far too esoteric and the editor of the latter, who wasn't even interested in reading the text, felt that *Film Comment* had lately been concentrating too much on Welles.[11] For me, the document was fascinating and revealing because it delved so deeply into Welles's artistic motivations—something that he was rarely willing to comment about elsewhere, even in his book-length interview with Peter Bogdanovich—but this consideration cut no ice with either magazine. Then, seven years later, as soon as Universal Pictures had a version of *Touch of Evil* based on following the instructions of the memo, the same text suddenly became a hot item, and *Premiere* even wound up commissioning me to write a short article about the new version of the film. (The quarterly *Grand Street* also expressed a strong interest in printing excerpts from the memo until it discovered belat-

---

[11] More recently, *Film Comment* reviewed two dubious Welles-related films, *Cradle Will Rock* and *RKO 281*, but refused to consider running any reports on restorations of unseen Welles films in Munich.

edly—not having grasped the fact earlier, through a misunderstand-
ing—that excerpts were about to appear in the second edition of *This Is
Orson Welles.*) The difference in attitudes was clear: in the early
nineties, the text had no "currency" because it wasn't tied to any currently marketable item; by the late nineties, it had suddenly taken on a
promotional value in relation to one of Universal's upcoming releases.

For more or less the same reason, a lengthy production report in
the *Los Angeles Times* in 1998 on the upcoming release of George
Hickenlooper's *The Big Brass Ring*, based on a much-revised version
of Welles's 1982 script that had been revamped by film critic F. X.
Feeney and Hickenlooper, went out of its way to disparage Welles's
original script as something that needed to be updated and reworked
in order to be relevant to a 1999 audience. The reporter gave no indication of having read the Welles script in order to test this premise; the
article was content to quote actor Nigel Hawthorne reading aloud
from David Thomson's attack on the script in *Rosebud* in order to
demonstrate that Welles's work clearly needed a polish. However ludicrous this assumption seemed to me at the time, I also realized it was
typical of entertainment journalism. The fact that Hickenlooper's
movie was shortly to become an item on the marketplace—while the
limited edition of Welles's screenplay, which had sold out its print run
of one thousand copies shortly after its publication in 1987, was no
longer an item on the marketplace—was the only thing that mattered,
and preemptive comparative evaluations of the two were relevant only
insofar as they helped to promote the Hickenlooper feature. (In fact,
Hickenlooper's film revised the original script so extensively that few
traces of the original remained.)

* * *

The half-dozen forms of ideological challenge discussed above are by
no means exhaustive when it comes to outlining the continuing provocation and interest of Welles's work. But I hope they adequately suggest
the degree to which his work and the various problems it raises throw
into relief many of the issues I've been discussing throughout this book.
For generations to come, I suspect, Welles will remain the great example of the talented filmmaker whose work and practices deconstruct

what academics, taking a cue from the late French theorist Christian Metz, are fond of calling "the cinematic apparatus." This is not necessarily because he wanted to carry out this particular project, but more precisely because his sense of being an artist as well as an entertainer was frequently tied to throwing monkey wrenches into our expectations—something that the best art and entertainment often do.

Conclusion
The Audience Is Sometimes Right

> "*What is your feeling towards your audiences—towards the public?*"
> "Which public? There are as many publics as there are personalities."
> —Gilbert Burgess, "A Talk with Mr. Oscar Wilde" (1895)

QUESTION: Aren't you laying yourself open throughout this book to the charge of sour grapes?

ANSWER: What do you mean?

Q: I mean attacking critics like Janet Maslin and David Denby because you'd so obviously like to have their jobs yourself.

A: If that's really your impression of what lies behind my arguments, then my arguments have failed. There's a hefty price tag for whatever prestige and power comes with writing for *The New York Times* and *The New Yorker,* and I consider myself fortunate that I don't have to worry about paying it. Film critics for those publications—including Vincent Canby and Pauline Kael as well as Maslin and Denby—ultimately wind up less powerful than the institutions they write for, and insofar as they're empowered by those institutions, they're disempowered as independent voices.

Q: You don't mean to suggest that they're told what to write?

A: Not at all—though they certainly don't get as much space as I do in the *Chicago Reader,* and it's questionable whether they have the same amount of freedom. Their limitations are built into the meaning and perceived function of their positions. There's a terrible feeling of resignation regarding the status quo of taste in those publications—the usual assumption that the public is a pack of idiots, which Anthony Lane treats as an occasion for jokes, for instance. And part of the resignation comes from the conviction, no doubt based on experience, that many readers want to be advised by *The New York Times* or *The New Yorker*, not by whoever happens to be writing for either outlet.

In a letter that Orson Welles once wrote to Peter Bogdanovich about the obfuscations of Kael in *The New Yorker* regarding the authorship of the *Citizen Kane* script, he compared his dilemma to that of someone with gloves on trying to clean up shit: the gloves, he noted, wind up getting shittier, but the shit doesn't get any glovier. That's a rude metaphor, and I don't mean to imply by it that those publications are the equivalent of shit. But it's also a very help-ful metaphor, because it implies—correctly, I think—that the insti-tutional power of *The New York Times* and *The New Yorker* is sub-stantially greater than that of any individual who winds up writing for either of them. No matter how bright, resourceful, or indepen-dent the writer is, the voice of the publication is ultimately stronger, and over time it winds up having the final say on matters of taste. That's what Sam Fuller meant when he told me in 1987, "If Vincent Canby got fired from the *Times* today, and he went to a bar and started talking about a movie he had just seen, nobody there would give a fuck what he thought. They'd probably just tell him to shut up." That's another rude way of putting it, but it's important to acknowledge that the exercise of power in such matters always tends to be rude, whether in the short run or over the long haul.

Certainly I have my quarrels with how Maslin and Denby, among others, have wielded their various forms of institutional power on occasion—especially because their preeminence as reviewers often seems to be gauged by the scant amount of world cinema they see or are even interested in seeing, which presumably puts them on an equal footing with their fans. But that doesn't mean that the institutional powers they enjoy are neutral factors in this process.

On June 4, 1999, an article by Sarah Kerr entitled "Janet Maslin: Why Can't the *New York Times* Movie Critic Tell Us What She Really Thinks?" was posted by the online magazine *Slate*. Kerr, who writes some of the capsule reviews of films for *The New Yorker*, was evidently moved to ask this question after reading Maslin's "overall rave" about *The Phantom Menace*, a film she finds "dull and annoying and occasionally rather offensive"; the issue of Maslin's lack of knowledge about or interest in most of the foreign films at Cannes or elsewhere, for instance, never comes up. But Kerr still concludes that Maslin "has developed a disembodied, ghostly way of writing about movies—a criticism of lowered expectations. Her main defense of the disappointing *Phantom Menace*? It's 'only a movie.' Exactly—and while we're at it, Maslin is only a critic who asks for too little." Which is another way of addressing the alienation that I've been discussing throughout this book, although it's not surprising that Kerr winds up expressing part of that alienation herself, apparently without realizing it. My definition of a critic who asks for too little is one who's sufficiently indifferent about world cinema to trust a distributor or a festival director for a comprehensive account of it; and that seems to describe Maslin and Kerr equally, judging by what they write. If, on the other hand, the index of your higher expectations is whether or not you like *The Phantom Menace*, then it isn't very high in the first place.

Kerr rightly notes that Maslin often appears to be writing not from her own point of view but from an attempt to "[gauge] in advance the public's reaction," which winds up expressing "the impression the studio hopes the film will have on an audience." Notice how the line of assumed thinking here proceeds directly, without a bump or a burp, from anticipating audience reactions to anticipating the studio's hopeful projections of these reactions—a succinct example of the kind of alienation I've been concerned with, where the audience somehow gets absent-mindedly displaced in the transaction. And I don't think it would be unfair to say that Kerr's analysis ultimately displaces the audience to the same degree as Maslin's attitude: after all, she and her editors and Maslin and *her* editors all have much more common ground than the unknown and unknowable audience, some members of which probably even like *The Phantom Menace* as much as Maslin professes to.

Q: Now you're really confusing me. Are you defending Maslin's defense of George Lucas?

A: Not necessarily. To tell the truth, I didn't bother to read that review, apart from the bits that Kerr quoted—if only because what I usually find most alienating as well as alienated about Maslin's reviewing is her efforts to anticipate other people's reactions, which often seem to matter much more to her than her own. That's partly what Kerr is writing about, and she's accurate about that charge. But Kerr's reactions to *The Phantom Menace*, as expressed in this article, don't seem much more interesting or vital to me, even if they're closer to mine. And the preempting of the audience's voice in this matter is not a problem that's going to vanish, regardless of who's writing about the film or where they write it or what they say. After all, Anthony Lane wrote one of his funniest demolition jobs for *The New Yorker* on *The Phantom Menace*, but what he had to say was no more in tune with the film's audience than what Maslin or Kerr had to say; to my mind, it was just as much an expression of alienation from the status quo of film culture as anything else I read about the movie, and I wasn't surprised when *The New Yorker* subsequently published a letter from an irate reader accusing Lane of elitism.

Q: What, then, would an unalienated review of the movie have consisted of?

A: Your guess is as good as mine. None of us reviewers has an option of that kind available nowadays because none of us has a clue about what the mass audience consists of. Maybe over time we'll get some indications. I was intrigued by the remarks of a grad student at Stanford who attended the movie's first screening there, at midnight. He suggested that many of the biggest *Star Wars* buffs were disappointed, but not in the same way that reviewers such as Lane, Kerr, and Robert Hughes were, who weren't speaking to their constituency. I'm not saying it's necessarily the job of reviewers to address constituencies—which is what Maslin and Ebert were attempting to do in their own favorable notices. But it might help for starters if reviewers realized how little they know about such matters—and how little studios know apart from what allows them to do their business (which they don't always know as well as they claim to, either).

       It's the equation of business calculations with a presumed knowledge of an audience's desire and capacities that leads to all the alienation I've been talking about—a factor that no one can escape entirely because all other gauging instruments have been factored out of the mainstream, ruled out of order. I was amazed when I watched Ebert and Kenneth Turan on Ebert's TV show the week after Cannes, when they reiterated their horror about the final prizes and spoke about some of the films they liked. At one point Turan remarked that what was great about attending Cannes was being able to spend eleven days watching movies without having to worry about the film business. I'm sure he was being sincere about this and that it didn't occur to him that a substantial part of what he wouldn't even think of seeing at Cannes would be screened out of his consciousness precisely because of the film business he claimed he wasn't thinking about.

Q: There's nothing wrong with mainstream critics speaking to the interests of mainstream viewers. Why should we try to get them interested in esoteric art movies?

A: This assumes that the line separating "mainstream" from "esoteric" is always easy to spot and difficult to refute. Sometimes it is and sometimes it isn't. Once upon a time, *Citizen Kane* was regarded as esoteric—something I touch on in the previous chapter. If this country didn't have a lot of independent art theaters when *Open City* and *Paisa* got released in the mid-forties, those movies would have been written off as esoteric as well, and I can't believe they're any more specialized than some of the Iranian and Taiwanese films being treated as "esoteric" today—films which will remain "esoteric" only as long as conservative critics and distributors ensure their unfamiliarity by treating them that way.

I also happen to believe that servicing mainstream interests, which is a more complex job than it's often cracked up to be, shouldn't rule out servicing more specialized interests, even within mainstream media; there's no reason why there can't be room enough for both. Unless the studios claim that they're not getting enough attention—which they and their mouthpieces are always claiming (cf. the complaints about the 1999 Cannes prizes)—and mainstream editors and producers insist on catering to these demands, which is unfortunately what happens. And then, in order to justify this callow behavior, the claim is made that this is all the mass audience cares about anyway. But any reviewing or journalism worth its salt is about more than catering. It should also be about cultivation and education and offering the public choices. And it should address itself to which choices are supposedly being made on behalf of the public: the kind of movies that wind up in theaters versus the kinds that don't. These considerations get elided at the outset, and when other possibilities are proposed, our equivalent to the politburo gets hysterical.

Q: I take it you're referring to the Harvey Weinstein support group again, a particular fixation of yours. What I don't understand about your objections to Weinstein is that his methods correspond in a good many particulars to those of Irving Thalberg, Louis B. Mayer, Darryl F. Zanuck, and Harry Cohn—the studio chiefs in the golden age of Hollywood who gave their own personal stamp to their products. Weinstein obviously cares about his movies in the same way, and certainly his passion is preferable to the faceless accountant mentality that characterizes most of the rest of the business.

A: Your objections remind me of those that film historian Thomas Elsaesser made to me when I showed him an earlier polemic of mine about the Weinstein brothers and Miramax.[1] In effect, Thomas told me I should get down on my knees in gratitude to someone like Weinstein because of all the vitality and excitement he was bringing to a moribund business—the same sort of argument Maslin made to me on another occasion. Maybe if Weinstein were producing the same sort of factory products as his predecessors his methods would be more defensible, but in most cases he isn't. It's also worth stressing that filmgoing habits are radically different today from what they were in the studio era. Back then, people went to the movies out of habit and as a matter of course, so the main aim of the industry was to service that taste and furnish theaters with a lot of product. Today they'll only go to a movie if something or someone guides them there—advertising, "coverage," a review, a general buzz, anything that makes the appearance of that

---

[1] "The World According to Harvey and Bob," *Movies as Politics*, Berkeley: University of California Press, 1997, pp. 159–165.

movie an event. And what I'm mainly concerned with in this book is how such events get defined and regulated—even policed.

I'll grant that Harvey Weinstein may provide the sort of paternalistic guidance and counterforce that someone like Quentin Tarantino benefits from, so it's entirely possible that *Reservoir Dogs, Pulp Fiction*, and even *Jackie Brown*—which I'm told Miramax shortened by about half an hour—are better than they might have been without his input. I'm not trying to suggest that Weinstein is wrong about everything, any more than I think that Maslin was. (I liked her enthusiastic review of *Lovers of the Arctic Circle*, for instance—which wasn't, by the way, a Miramax release. And I also happen to admire the gracefulness of Denby's prose style at the same time that I lament the narrowness and provincialism of his critical taste.) Sometimes Weinstein is simply trying to make a noncommercial movie more commercial in ways that I can appreciate, even if I don't agree with him, and plenty of other distributors behave the same way.

But the terrible irony is, the more enthusiasm that Weinstein feels about one of the movies he's distributing, the greater the odds are that he'll wind up tampering with it. The usual situation appears to be that if he likes it he thinks he can improve it, which is apparently why he wound up recutting Chen Kaige's *Temptress Moon*—a film that I liked for its hypnotic rhythms when I saw it at Cannes but found tedious after Miramax recut it and added explanatory titles. (For me, it was something like a fever dream that got depoeticized and lost much of its style once it was decided that the audience had to be able to follow the plot with greater ease.) And if Weinstein doesn't like a film enough to want to recut it, he often won't make it available to most people, despite the fact that he supposedly distributes it. In the case of Bertrand Tavernier's 1994 *Le fille d'Artagnan* [*D'Artagnan's Daughter*], this was a matter of proposing certain cuts that Tavernier didn't agree to. To his credit, Weinstein eventually released the film's original cut—but only on video, five years later, retitled *Revenge of the Musketeers*. Even this is better than the treatment he has accorded so far to Abbas Kiarostami's *Through the Olive Trees*, made the following year, which has effectively made the film all but impossible to see, even on video.

But the story gets worse. Shortly before this book went to press, a letter arrived from Joel Shepard, film and video curator at San Francisco's Yerba Buena Center for the Arts. Hoping to show Kiarostami's so-called "Earthquake trilogy" of *Where Is the Friend's House?*, *Life and Nothing More*, and *Through the Olive Trees* at his contemporary art museum, he promptly ran into a brick wall acquiring the latter film from Miramax:

When I called Miramax to book the print, I was informed that their sole surviving print had been *destroyed*. When I asked when they were going to make another print, they responded that it was "unlikely another print would ever be made." This means there are no prints of this masterpiece available in the United States. I'm going to have to get a print from Alliance in Canada for my playdate.

Just thought you might be interested in yet another piece of evidence of how Miramax is destroying so much world cinema in the United States.

To be fair, one of the sources of this gruesome behavior might have been the scheme by which Miramax was forced to buy the U.S. rights to *Through the Olive Trees* in the first place—a well-intentioned idea by a film lover that unfortunately backfired. Miramax was determined to distribute the Australian crowd-pleaser *Muriel's Wedding*, and it was offered as part of a package that also included the Kiarostami film, thereby forcing them to take it. Ironically, this is the same ploy that I'm told Miramax has used with various independent theaters: if someone wants to book a particular film from them, they sometimes have to book another film as well that they may not want to show.

No American distributor picked up Leos Carax's *Lovers on the Bridge* which when it was released in France a decade ago. There were special screenings of that movie in New York and Chicago that had to turn away crowds of people, and hardly a month went by since then that someone didn't ask me if the film was ever going to become available again. Miramax eventually responded to this interest by becoming its distributor after its price went down, and in a report put together by Pat Dowell for National Public Radio's "Morning Edition," Weinstein suggested that he did this not in order to make money but to serve the interests of film lovers. But in the same report Dowell noted that Miramax dumped the film during its Washington, D.C. engagement, so that it had no ads and no reviews, ensuring that it died a quick death. "Representatives of Miramax say this was just an error, not a lack of support," Dowell added; to me it looks like further evidence of the company's highly sporadic record. It's the sort of arbitrary exercise of power I associate with Stalinist Russia, where a certain number of important films were subsidized by the government and then banned. In those cases, the press was blocked from protesting by censorship and threats of reprisals. But when Miramax suppresses work today that's every bit as important, who in the American mainstream would even dream of mentioning the fact, much less raising an objection? Which means that neither the audience nor the work is respected—only the philistine who releases or withholds it and the money that he (not we or the film-maker) may or may not make from it.

Some of Weinstein's defenders argue that if he picks up certain films only because he doesn't want to allow his competitors to make money off them, that's perfectly OK because it's simply part of the capitalist game. But does that mean that if a distributor theoretically found a way of making more money by buying, say, a Woody Allen or a John Sayles movie and then giving it an extremely limited or unpublicized American release, that Roger Ebert would necessarily go along with this ruse and not mention the movie on his TV show? That's what happened with films by Demy, Tati, Kiarostami, and Tavernier, to cite only four examples. (It also happened to another Tati film, *Playtime*, which received its initial U.S. showing in Queens, three years after it was completed, and wound up as a tax write-off; it wasn't until much later that the film opened "normally," and by that time Tati was bankrupt and had no control over the particular versions that were playing in the states.) I know that Roger dislikes *Taste of Cherry*, the only Kiraostami film he's seen, but he's written about Tati with a great deal of reverence. What, then, are we to make of the decision of his TV show not to review the color *Jour de fête* or Demy's *The Young Girls of Rochefort* once Miramax decided to give them only limited releases? That they're less worthy of attention than all the other Miramax films that *were* reviewed? Was it because Miramax's decision to dump these films automatically made them too marginal? Or was it simply a matter of Miramax not cooperating by making clips available? I don't know the answer to these questions, but I do know that Miramax's own priorities wound up coinciding precisely with the priorities of *Siskel & Ebert,* and that these four examples are far from being the only ones I could cite.

A lot of the objections I'm raising are admittedly nothing more than objections to some of the pitfalls of capitalism, which mainstream reviewers seem to have a vested interest in either ignoring or mindlessly rubber-stamping. Why companies like Miramax should be granted infinitely more respect than the filmmakers whose work they handle continues to baffle me.

* * *

Q: I notice you've made a couple of cracks in this book about the way films are written about in *The New York Review of Books.* How would you improve the situation?

A: The only way it can ever be improved is for film criticism to be treated as a respectable discipline, at least theoretically. I realize that the lack of seriousness shown by most film reviewers toward their work makes this a dicier matter in quarters like *The New York Review,* where it must seem both reasonable and normal to assign film reviews or reviews of books about film to people like Gabriele Annan or Louis Menand when *The New Yorker* does the same thing with Anthony Lane and nobody even blinks. (Admittedly, *The New York Review* also gets more knowledgeable people on occasion—people like Joseph McBride, Michael Wood, and Geoffrey O'Brien—and nobody beats *The New York Times Book Review* for sometimes assigning film books to reviewers whose qualifications are close to zero.)

The problem is, in most of the magazines and journals, film criticism is so little respected that anyone with a name or the right connection winds up getting a crack at it, often with lamentable results. And consider the way that success is often gauged in reviewing movies for newspapers. In many cases, the more success you have, the less space you're allotted. When Dave Kehr went from the *Chicago Reader* to the *Chicago Tribune* in the mid-eighties, he lost a good half of his space; then, when he graduated from the *Tribune* to the *New York Daily News,* his space was cut roughly in half again. Almost the same thing happened when he surfaced on the Web on CitySearch, and each time his salary went up when his word count went down!

Something comparable happened when John Powers went from the *L.A. Weekly* to *Vogue.* In terms of money and power and prestige, each of these moves could be interpreted as a step up—the capacity to write less and less—and the point at which you get on television and are allotted only sound bites, you take off into the stratosphere. (As one of the *Times's* arts reviewers noted recently, off the record, "People believe that reading the *Times* makes them classy—same with *The New Yorker.* . . . Yes, they're very willing to believe that somebody is a great writer because he writes for the publication that makes them feel classy.")

How could film criticism be perceived as an honorable activity under such circumstances? By reading it. By believing that understanding movies better is desirable. But so many other interests get in the way of that belief—social, commercial, professional, recreational—that it currently operates mainly as a cult activity. And it will continue to operate that way until a few insightful editors wake from their slumbers.

I have nothing against cults, by the way. And since I survive in part as a cult writer, it's a good thing I don't. But I can't believe it's simply the taste of the public as an unalterable condition that sustains this prejudice against film criticism; that certainly isn't the message I get from my readers. It's the taste and stamina of certain editors, most of whom apparently don't know where to look.

Look at the annual collection recently launched by George Plimpton and Jason Shinder, *The Best American Movie Writing,* published by St. Martin's Griffin. There's practically no serious film criticism at all in the 1998 volume; it's mainly puff pieces and think pieces (including, incidentally, Sontag's "A Century of Cinema"), memoirs and literary pieces about film. One of the only film critics included is Powers, and significantly he's incorrectly identified on the contributors' page as the playwright of the same name. Actually, Powers was one of the better critics around until he recently gave up his job to move to Singapore, but he's obviously in foreign territory here; one suspects that if Plimpton knew he was a critic and not a playwright, he might not have been included.

Q: Sounds to me like sour grapes again.

A: Not at all—at least not because I feel personally excluded. In fact, a piece of mine just appeared in the 1999 volume, edited by Peter Bogdanovich. Yet it seems pertinent that the article of mine that he picked—and I submitted several, at his invitation—doesn't qualify as film criticism. It's a factual piece about the reconfigured *Touch of Evil.* I know Peter wanted to include something about that, so I can't really fault him for making that choice. But when I think about some of the knowledgeable, original, and highly literate film critics writing in this country—people like Janet Bergstrom, Natasa Durovičová, Tom Gunning, Miriam Hansen, J. Hoberman, Kent Jones, Dave Kehr, Bill Krohn, James Naremore, Gilberto Perez, Donald Phelps, and Lesley Stern, among many others—I can't understand why none of them is likely to turn up in any of the volumes, at least the way the series presently appears to be conceptualized. Could it be because these writers know too much about movies? If this was *The Best American Sports Writing,* I can't believe that contenders would become disqualified if they knew too much about sports, so I guess that movies have even less cultural status in the United States than sports do. I realize that slightly over half the names in my list are full-time academics, so one could surmise that it might be the language of some of them that keeps them out—*if,* that is, the editors were surveying academic film writing. But it's obvious that they aren't, because a "select directory of film magazines" published in the back of the 1999 volume of *The Best American Movie Writing,* containing eighty-four titles, manages to exclude most of the leading academic film journals, including *Cinema Journal, Film Criticism, Film History, Jump Cut, October, Quarterly Review of Film Studies, Persistence of Vision,* and *Wide Angle.* (Among nonacademic film magazines, they manage to exclude *Filmmaker, The Independent,* and *Scenario,* while including such oddities as the *San Francisco Chronicle,* but no other newspapers—just to show you how haphazard the whole thing is.) It's obvious that no film academic worth his or her salt was even consulted on this list, and I'm afraid this is absolutely typical of the lack of communication between various sectors of the film world that I discuss in Chapter Five.

To be fair to Peter, he did include one academic piece, by Elizabeth Abele, that deals with feminist film theory—a radical gesture in these quarters that should be applauded. And there's certainly much more criticism found here than in the previous volume, though nothing that deals even remotely with contemporary world cinema. To account for that absence, there's Denby's handy end-of-cinema lament, "The Moviegoers," just as one found Sontag's end-of-cinema lament in the first volume; to keep Taiwanese and Iranian cinema out of the third and fourth volumes, I guess they'll have to scrounge up a couple of more apocalyptic pieces of this kind. David Thomson, who can write about his "discovery" of Ang Lee and Taiwan without even mentioning Hou Hsiao-hsien, Edward Yang, or Tsai Ming-liang, would be the perfect candidate for writing such a piece. Like Denby, he's popular among people who don't know or care much about movies (including Janet Maslin, who gave Thomson's unresearched and misinformed book *Rosebud* a rave) precisely because he makes everything seem so tidy: Denby's implication that there are only five or ten foreign movies a year worth thinking about, all of them already high-profile items, is, ideologically speaking, almost identical to Thomson's statement that Orson Welles "always liked his revolutionaries to be sophisticated and well-heeled." The fact that both statements are completely untrue is irrelevant; what matters is that they're comforting and make you feel classy.

Q: Surely this is a matter of opinion, not fact.

A: Yes, but whose opinion? I recently got back from a four-day conference on unfinished Welles films in Munich, and I don't think it would be an exaggeration to say that well over half of the best Welles scholars in the world were present, from eight countries. As far as I could tell, no one there took Thomson's *Rosebud* even halfway seriously: the book never came up in the discussions I attended except as an example of the kind of misinformation about

Welles that continues to circulate. Yet one of the regular writers in *Film Comment* wrote that Thomson deserved a Pulitzer prize for writing it. Why? I guess the book must have made him feel classy.

* * *

Q: In Chapter Five, you argue that the cable channel Turner Classic Movies does a more responsible job of preserving our film heritage than the American Film Institute, citing what they've recently done in "restorations, revivals, documentaries about film history, and even in presenting foreign-language movies." Of course TCM has vastly more economic and material resources at its disposal than the AFI does, which suggests that big business versus state funding isn't always the enemy.

A: Yes, and I'd stand by that comparison—although I wouldn't go so far as to claim that TCM has any sort of edge over the Cinémathèque Française, especially when it comes to varied and knowledgeable programming of world cinema (which includes certain categories like experimental film that TCM completely ignores). I had to wait for years in Chicago before I could get TCM, and friends of mine in New York and Los Angeles had comparable problems. Now that we have it, it's certainly a boon to get the sort of balance between structured and unstructured programming of older films that the Cinémathèque has often specialized in. The structured programming allows you to explore certain directors, stars, and genres in depth, the unstructured programming allows you to make your own discoveries. I also applaud the sort of initiative TCM has taken in showing silent and foreign-language films, in showing everything without commercial breaks and almost everything without cuts, and in presenting letterboxed versions of widescreen films that enable you to see them in their original formats. Not that they always have a perfect record. One of the films I almost included in my list of the hundred greatest American films is Jacques Tourneur's Cinemascope western *Wichita* (1955), and the main reason why I omitted it is that I've never been able to see it in a 'Scope format—something I suspect I could have done if I was living in Paris. This morning (June 12, 1999) I thought I'd finally get a chance because TCM programmed it, but then I discovered that they were showing only a scanned version, something they also did a few days ago with Anthony Mann's 'Scope western *The Last Frontier*, made the same year. I assume you know what scanning is: a camera rescans the original image so it can fit the less rectangular TV screen, eliminating about a third of the image and also adding cuts in order to get from one side of the frame to the other. Lamentably, the 'Scope films of masters of composition like Tourneur and Mann get mangled almost every time they're seen on TV or video, which practically speaking is almost the only way you can see these films. However, Chris Fujiwara, in his definitive recent critical study *Jacques Tourneur: The Cinema of Nightfall*,[2] calls *Wichita* Tourneur's only major work in Cinemascope and devotes over a page to his compositional uses of that format.

I don't know how to account for such lapses on TCM, given their usual track record; maybe they couldn't locate the right elements that would enable them to show *Wichita* and *The Last Frontier* properly, or maybe they simply didn't bother. But they're still miles ahead of BRAVO, which recuts practically everything it shows, as well as American Movie Classics, which is much more selective about what it chooses to letterbox. It's true that Ted Turner got a bad rep when he embarked on colorizing some of the black-and-white films in his collection back in the eighties—a fad that I'm happy to say never wholly caught on, although the widespread misunderstandings of the technical and legal issues involved clouded the fact that he was already getting involved in film restoration by striking new black-and-white prints in order to carry this project out. There's a wonderfully astute and lucid essay about these contradictions and misunderstandings by Stuart Klawans, "Rose-Tinted Spectacles," that I've already quoted in this book's introduction. Let me quote a later paragraph that has particular bearing on some of the issues of this book:

Now, it is a matter as negligible as a producer's heart whether the people who were fighting against colorization had a deep understanding of clas-

---

[2] Jefferson, NC/London: McFarland & Co., 1998, pp. 227–228.

sicism. It *does* matter, though, that they got so wrought up about their hallucinations that the fantasy, having taken on a life of its own, came to dominate the debate. It did so, I would suggest, because of a fundamental trait of our society: Americans have no commonly accepted terms in which to ground their arguments about artistic endeavors and moral rights. Our society has never acknowledged the civic importance of either category; and so public discussions that touch on those issues will almost inevitably take off into the clouds.[3]

This is where the practical as well as philosophical superiority of an organization like the Cinémathèque Française comes in: although it has its own set of problems, its work derives from a public mandate about artistic endeavors and moral rights that can't be found in American society. Given that we currently have to make do with what we have, I don't think any "French solution" to our muddled film culture is feasible, but at least it offers a useful model of how another society can cope with some of the same problems.

Q: Maybe you're not proposing a "French solution," but there are certainly times in this book when it appears that you are. In fact, the encroachments of Francophilia in your arguments seem to increase as this book develops. You start off by addressing the American situation, even though you keep bringing up references to people like Jean-Luc Godard. Then in Chapter Seven you sound off about American coverage of the Cannes Film Festival, and by the time you get to Chapter Nine you're recycling stuff you've written for a French film magazine. Isn't there something snobbish and elitist about this kind of emphasis, shot through with genuflections towards an intellectual film culture that couldn't be further from American interests? I'm reminded of the complaints of Howard Hampton when he reviewed your last book in *Book Forum:* bristling at your snide definition of "homeless people" as "those without computers or TV sets," Hampton goes on to note parenthetically, "I suspect Rosenbaum's solution to the problem of the homeless and orphaned movies would be to bring them together, housing the poor in theaters holding all-night Jacques Rivette screenings."[4]

---

[3] "Rose-Tinted Spectacles," in *Seeing Through Movies,* edited by Mark Crispin Miller, New York: Pantheon Books, 1990, p. 174.

[4] Review of *Movies as Politics* in *Book Forum,* Summer 1997.

A: The snideness of my ridicule of Newt Gingrich, which I thought I'd adequately signaled by placing "homeless people" in quotes, is only connected to my support of Jacques Rivette by a loose analogy of what gets overlooked and ignored. I'd never dream of suggesting that Rivette belongs in the mainstream, and what drove me to hyperbole in that instance was the fact that Rivette's greatest and in some ways most accessible work—a thirteen-hour serial made in 1971—has still never been shown or seen in the United States. And to give you some idea of how blocked we are, when Anthology Film Archives attempted to show a complete Rivette retrospective in 1996, after the programmer tried and failed to get hold of a print of the thirteen-hour *Out 1* that had been subtitled in English for a screening in India, he refused to let me furnish my own unsubtitled video for a public screening. Yet paradoxically, the desire to see it even in unsubtitled form was still so strong that the first hour or two on video got shown anyway, unofficially, when some Rivette freak offered to screen it. A handwritten announcement of the screening was posted in Anthology's lobby, but the event had to be kept a secret from the retrospective's programmer, who was adamant about not allowing it to be shown, so of course it couldn't be advertised either. That's an extreme and somewhat comic illustration of the kind of obstacles some minority interests are up against—the fact that it's apparently easier to see *Out 1* in India than it is in this country. Why should it remain so impossible? I'm perfectly willing to let the studios do their thing on a massive scale as long as my friends and I are allowed to go off in a corner and do what we want to do as well. But this can only happen if middle management allows it to, and they prefer to proceed as if only the studios exist.

As for my Francophilia, the fact that my own self-education in film history was largely carried out in Paris when I lived there for five years (1969–74) obviously plays some role in this. But I can't deny that most of the issues discussed in this book are also matters of great concern in the French film community, where worries about "Americanization" and the overall dumbing down of film culture are equally prevalent. Sometimes the yardsticks of measurement being used are quite different, but sometimes they're more or less the same, particularly when multicorporate interests are involved. *The Economist* just reported that even though over eight million French viewers went to see *Asterix and Obelix Against César* — "a film based on a French comic strip about plucky Gauls who resist the mighty Roman empire" — during the first two months of its run, twenty-one million French viewers have seen *Titanic*. To me what's surprising is not the latter figure, but the large number of people there who went to see a strictly non-Hollywood feature.

In some ways I'm even more concerned about the overall dumbing down of a magazine like *Cahiers du Cinéma* — which was recently purchased by *Le Monde*, but which became much more market-conscious in its orientation years earlier. It still operates on a much higher level than *Film Comment* or *Film Quarterly* in terms of what it covers, but it no longer can be considered a critical trailblazer, as it used to be in the fifties and sixties — it tends to coast on its earlier reputation. As a film monthly it's roughly on a par with *Positif*, its long-term competitor, but in many ways I prefer the extensive film coverage of the Parisian weekly *Les Inrockuptibles*, which supposedly concentrates on rock but actually has lively coverage of all the arts, including literature. And the French magazine I write for most often, *Trafic* — a quarterly with no illustrations that costs about twenty bucks an issue, and currently has a circulation of about two thousand — has no parallel of any kind in the states either. It may sound about as marginal as a film magazine can get, especially because it has no American distribution apart from a few scattered subscriptions, but in fact it gets cited all the time in the French mainstream press, especially in newspapers like *Libération* and magazines like *Les Inrockuptibles*, so it has a definite cultural impact. People as diverse as Jean-Luc Godard and Gilles Jacob, the director of the Cannes Festival, read it regularly.

As for including some of my writing for *Trafic*, which is concerned with many of the same questions and issues, I thought it might be useful to broaden the scope of the discussion by factoring in the sort of material that usually gets elided from American books for market-driven as well as ethnocentric reasons. Just as the autobiographical side of my writing is often here to show where my ideas and opinions are coming from, it's useful to give English-speaking readers some notion of what sort of French readers I'm addressing on occasion.

The usual unvoiced premise is that the film cultures of this country and France are so disparate and sui generis that they might as well go on muttering to themselves rather than attempt to communicate with one another. Yet this premise is contradicted repeatedly by my own experience; what transpired at the the Cannes press conference on *She's So Lovely* is directly relevant to what I say about publicity and about Miramax elsewhere in the book, just as the technical difficulties in enabling people to see Rivette films in Manhattan, De Oliveira films in Providence, and Farocki films in Locarno are all interrelated. And one of the advantages of allowing readers to eavesdrop on discussions that usually take place outside their earshot is that it allows some recognition of a wider playing field. Maybe that's elitist, but I'd rather regard it as sharing the wealth. I've been unusually fortunate in having some access to film culture beyond American borders, and to omit any acknowledgment of that access would be condescending to American readers—like censoring what one says at a party because children are present.

Q: Let me rephrase my objections. It seems that you're seesawing back and forth in this book between journalistic reports and critical overviews. Moreover, there's a certain contradiction in claiming that the mass audience is right—which you tend to do in the critical overviews—and making particular pitches for your specialized interests, most of which couldn't possibly interest the mass audience.

A: I certainly plead guilty to the charge of mixing criticism with journalism and reviewing. I make my living as a journalist, and one of the drawbacks of that profession is writing for the moment, which makes broader and more balanced views much more difficult to arrive at. The seesawing pattern you're describing is certainly there, and it's up to the reader to decide whether this helps or hinders this book's agenda. I'd like to think that alternations between overall battle plans and particular "reports from the front" help to develop the argument by testing theory with practice and generalizations with specific cases. But it's also true that reading about films one isn't likely to see and hearing about events that have lost their journalistic immediacy can make the overall process of following an argument something of a slog. All the critical overviews in this book have been arrived at through experiences "at the front," but it's always worth considering which experiences are most instructive to read about.

As for the apparent contradiction between my defense of the audience and my defense of certain "specialized" films, I can only reiterate that the kind of film culture I'm arguing for is one that allows all sorts of interests to coexist. Every critic is limited by his or her taste, and if I don't appreciate *L.A. Confidential, Saving Private Ryan,* or *Election* as much as Denby does, that doesn't mean I don't respect the mass audience; I also happen to like *City Lights, To Have and Have Not, Rear Window, Who Framed Roger Rabbit, The Apostle, Small Soldiers,* and *Rushmore,* which are every bit as mainstream.

(By the way, I liked *The Apostle* even more before October Films decided it had to be shortened and recut—a job that was handed to Walter Murch, whom I had the good fortune of working with on *Touch of Evil.* Murch's reedit was carried out after a few reviewers wrote from festivals that the film would be better if it were shorter. I don't know if October based its decision to shorten the film on those reviews, but it's hard to believe there was no connection. Anyway, despite the fact that Murch did an excellent job, it seems horrifying that reviewers who see a film once can theoretically wind up as the final arbiters of a movie that a filmmaker—in this case Robert Duvall—has spent many years working on, and this is far from being an isolated instance of this practice. When the documentary *Waco: The Rules of Engagement* turned up in Chicago in a version that bordered on gibberish, I discovered that it was cut by half an hour after a *Variety* review from Sundance suggested it would benefit from pruning; I haven't see the longer version, but it's hard to imagine it was as difficult to follow. And I certainly have no doubts that *Taste of Cherry* suffered when it wound up being distributed throughout Italy without its final sequence—again because of well-wishers who decided that they knew more than Kiarostami did. Perhaps the most telling example that springs to mind, furnished to me by Australian film critic Adrian Martin, is the screening of *Irma Vep* without its own final sequence on Australian TV due to a lab error; when the film was subsequently revived on Australian TV with its original ending, the publicity for it boasted it was the "restored" version!)

* * *

Q: You argue that ordinary moviegoers might become more interested in subtitled movies if the industry gave them more opportunities to see them. But you seem to be avoiding the massive anti-intellectualism and xenophobia of American culture, which isn't going to disappear anytime soon.

A: Fair enough. It's a sobering thought that the *Times* just hired two young Pauline Kael fans to replace Maslin, both of them defined in part by their relative lack of interest in non-American movies, and one of them a literary critic with no background of any kind in film. So it isn't surprising that the latter thinks that *Stranger Than Paradise* was Jim Jarmusch's first feature and that the other reviewer recently referred to "Dogma 95" as a Dutch film movement. (The odds of fact-checkers spotting errors of this kind in the *Times*, judging from their former track record, are just about nil.) In fact, I think we can safely conclude by now that the *Times* is profoundly committed to the notion that anyone and everyone can be a film "expert."

But I'd also like to think that their power to determine what foreign films can get U.S. distribution may at long last be drawing to a close. I can't prove it, but there are definitely signs of an improving climate, including many more initiatives from distributors. For instance, just as this book is going to press, a Chicago colleague, Patrick McGavin, forwards me what he considers "the best news of the year, moviewise," a press release announcing that Kino International is opening Râùl Ruiz's *Time Regained*—an extremely sophisticated and imaginative 155-minute adaptation of Proust, light-years beyond anything one could expect from Merchant-Ivory—in Manhattan in June, despite the sour notice it got from Maslin at the New York Film Festival. I don't think this would have been possible a few years ago. In fact, the correspondence I get

nowadays from readers—such as a teenager in London who monitored how the Ruiz film did when it opened there earlier this year
(he says it wound up in fifth place the first week, even though it
puzzled audiences), and who e-mailed me this information
because he thought I might be interested—convinces me that
there's a growing community of people who care deeply about such
matters. And if the *Times* turns out to be one of the last places on
the planet to get this message, there's nothing new about that,
either.

I remember an anecdote from my early high school days in
Alabama; it's funny how, with every passing year, the small-town
thinking and behavior of Manhattan reminds me more and more
of what I grew up with in Florence, Alabama. A friend who was
attending Sunday school there in the fifties reported back one day
that the church he went to was just having a debate about whether
or not it was evil to learn foreign languages—at which point one of
the participants volunteered, "All I can say is, if English was good
enough for Jesus, it's good enough for me." I can't really claim that
attitudes of this kind don't exist—even if the New York spin on
these attitudes is to feel classy rather than country-smart about its
worldly wisdom. Another notable difference: whereas a high
school kid from Alabama might think that Jesus speaks English,
someone like Denby, considerably more urbane, merely thinks
that God watches Hollywood movies. (I'm recalling his review of
JFK for *New York* magazine: "Even God would be frightened by
this movie." Just the sort of insight needed at the *Times*, which, after
all, decided that Oliver Stone's showmanship—unlike all the preceding years of investigations into the Kennedy assassination—
made conspiracy theories worthy of coverage on the front page.)

Which leads me to a working assumption of this book that may
be unduly optimistic, although I hope it isn't. When I speak in
favor of Americans having more access to world cinema, my working assumption is that most Americans—or at least a substantial
number of Americans—want to be citizens of the world. I even
think that the common belief that Americans are xenophobic iso-
lationists by nature is partly the self-serving invention of Hollywood
publicists armed with millions of dollars who don't want to clutter

up their precious ad campaigns with thoughts of other tastes and cultures. But if they're right—if the public's overwhelming desire is merely to regard people outside the United States as failed Americans—then world cinema can't consist of anything but a failed attempt to make American movies.[5] And if we really *are* primitive and solipsistic enough to believe that, then I'm afraid this country deserves the limited kind of movie choices it gets. A more logical step might be to ban foreign movies entirely since these can only distract us from our national purpose.

In other words, art is a way of becoming better acquainted with the world and we have reasons for wanting to improve our knowledge on this front. But one thing that apparently differentiates this country from all others is that art is actively hated by a good many of its citizens; de Tocqueville has some sobering thoughts to offer on this subject. But at the same time, one of de Tocqueville's chapter headings could serve as one of the mottoes of this book: "The Example of the Americans Does Not Prove That a Democratic People Can Have No Aptitude and No Taste for Science, Literature, or Art."

It's interesting to reflect on how frequently these negative American attitudes are tied to class prejudices. More often than not, the moviegoer who hates the very idea of subtitled movies also hates the idea of cappuccino and brie, classical music, opera, and ballet—the whole complex of what's regarded as hoity-toity, fashionable upscale pretensions, which are commonly associated with Europe—whereas most of the foreign-language movies that exist in the world, European and otherwise, are every bit as populist and commercial in orientation as the stuff that comes out of Hollywood studios. At the same time, as Jim Jarmusch points out, members of the working class in

---

[5] To be fair, Denby's version of this formula is slightly different—that Kiarostami's work consists of a failed attempt to replicate Satyajit Ray and Vittorio De Sica, an Iranian who wants to be Indian or Italian rather than American. This ignores all of Kiarostami's formal innovations while faintly implying that filmmakers who make movies about poor dark-skinned people must be similar in other respects.

Europe don't feel obliged to regard art with contempt and suspicion the way that many of their American counterparts do.

The misperception of foreign movies is produced, of course, by the way they're packaged and sold and often discussed in the media. Back in the sixties, most Bergman films were associated with espresso in the lobby and high-class soul-searching about the meaning of life; Woody Allen still perpetrates that stereotypical notion about art movies in practically everything he says and does, which is one of the many reasons why I tend to mistrust the middle-class attitudes in his work. Even worse, he's transferred part of that class-bound ideology to his notion of the *American* art movie. Some people find *Interiors* just as objectionable as Bergman, for virtually the same reasons—I remember the reception it got at a mall theater in Florence, Alabama—but others find it less objectionable simply because it's in English. I would argue that it's the latter group that the industry has been catering to over the past few decades, reenforcing some of these biases in the process. On a larger scale, the same sort of thing happened when critics and audiences started going bananas over American genre movies dressed up in art-movie clothing—*The Godfather, The Deer Hunter,* and *Ordinary People* are three examples among many others. Then people began to conclude that if American directors could be just as "artistic" as foreign directors, there was no good reason why subtitles had to clutter up our lives.

Furthermore, one of the things that made *Last Year at Marienbad* an art-house sensation for a brief period in the sixties was the swanky settings and Delphine Seyrig's Chanel dresses, not just the formal play with narrative film conventions. The fact that Alain Resnais and to some extent Alain Robbe-Grillet, the screenwriter, were also playing with and parodying certain Hollywood tropes went over the heads of most American viewers—although Dwight Macdonald certainly got the point. (Even he apparently missed the life-size blowup of Alfred Hitchcock lurking in the hotel lobby and the shot-by-shot recreation of a sequence from *Gilda* in one of the bedroom scenes, but he caught the allusions to Marlene Dietrich and Josef von Sternberg in some of Seyrig's poses.)

The big theater chains lost a golden opportunity when they failed to show *Run Lola Run,* an edgy and highly entertaining German youth movie, in malls across the country. I can't believe that American teenagers would have refused to check out a movie they would have loved simply because it was subtitled. Other teenagers around the world didn't respond that way when it was shown subtitled in other languages, and I can't believe American teenagers are so radically different from their counterparts elsewhere. The problem is that exhibitors are locked into outmoded and self-defeating premises and no one ever thinks of challenging or even questioning them.

Such biases are the product of conditioning, and there's no reason why the Woody Allen or the Francis Ford Coppola model of the American art film have to be the only ones available. Miramax has virtually proven this point with its handling of *Life Is Beautiful,* and even if I don't happen to like that film, I can't deny their ingenuity in selling it to a wide public. As Stuart Klawans recently put it in *The Nation,* "Miramax does well with uplifting fare, such as *Life Is Beautiful* (feel good about the Holocaust!), *Shakespeare in Love* (feel good about Shakespeare!) or *Kids* (feel good that you're not one of those rotten kids!)."

The marketing of certain Hong Kong films in the United States provides another model, although in that case there's still a bit of confusion about what Hong Kong filmmaking consists of. As I suggest in Chapter Seven, John Woo's *Face/Off* is far from being the same thing as his *Bullet in the Head,* but that doesn't prevent the media-industrial complex from trying to foster the vague impression that it is.

In theory, the cappuccino notion of the art movie, a protracted hangover from the late fifties and early sixties, still holds, but in actual practice the possibilities are astronomically wider. *Lovers of the Arctic Circle,* to take a recent example, has some of the play with narrative form associated with something like *Last Year at Marienbad* yet none of the chi-chi décor and costumes, and that didn't stop it from finding an urban audience. Might it have found a suburban and small-town audience as well? Given our present setup, we have no way of knowing, because unless a distributor with the muscle of Miramax decides to give it the *Life Is Beautiful* treatment, it's not going to get into those malls. There's reason to think that *Jour de fête*, based on its commercial success in other countries, might have worked at malls even better than *Lovers of the Arctic Circle*, but it never got commercial runs in more than a couple of American cities, and even in those situations it received no fanfare at all.

Q: You've been parceling out most of the blame for this on exhibitors and distributors, but what about the critics and the media as a whole?

A: One of my basic points is that distinguishing between the priorities of distributors and exhibitors and those of the critics and the media in general is almost impossible. And rather than ascribe this to any conspiracy I'd blame it on laziness and inertia. You might say that Miramax's steamrolling has more energy and initiative behind it than any of the media responses to that steamrolling, including the responses of critics. As I put it four years ago, "The fault, dear Brutus, is not in Miramax but in ourselves, that we are their underlings."

We have to break loose from the crippling ideology that insists that movies function as a business not only first and last, but in between as well—leaving no room for the rest of us who care mainly or exclusively about the art. A case in point is *The Wind Will Carry Us*, Abbas Kiarostami's latest feature, which won the jury prize at Venice and made such a powerful and exhilarating impression on me a few days later in Toronto that I went to a second screening of it the next day and felt I was walking around inside it for the remainder of the week. More metaphorical and elliptical and closer to comedy than Kiarostami's previous feature, *Taste of Cherry*, it can't be called one of his easiest pictures, and some viewers emerge from it puzzled. (I was one of them, but it was a very happy and fruitful form of puzzlement.) Set in a remote and ancient village, where a carload of men from Tehran—apparently a documentary film crew—wait for an ailing woman who's about a century old to die, it further develops Kiarostami's notion of an interactive cinema where the spectator's imagination plays a central creative role in the proceedings; at least half of the major characters, including the old woman and most of the crew, remain off-screen. What seems relatively new to Kiarostami's work is a focus on nature and a moral questioning of media.

For me there's no greater film artist at work anywhere right now than Kiarostami, who at this point makes precisely the movies he wants to make with precisely the modest budgets and crews he requires and reaches substantial numbers of spectators across the globe who love these movies and consider them important facts in their lives. What better situation could any artist hope for? But read about the 1999 Venice Festival in *Variety* and you discover it was dull because there wasn't more wheeling and dealing. Start talking to industry specialists about *The Wind Will Carry Us*—even those who say they revere Kiarostami—and you'll encounter a lot of sorrowful head-shaking because it isn't his "breakthrough" or "crossover" movie. For me, this is like saying it's too bad Robert Bresson never got to make a film with John Travolta. What they're worried about, in other words, isn't how good or beautiful or important it is but whether or not it will allow some American suits to turn a profit.

Poor old James Joyce—condemned to be a cultural nonperson by slaving away at *Finnegans Wake* when he could have signed on as a feature writer for *Vanity Fair* or even *TV Guide* and thus gotten at least one foot in the door, leading to the possibility of . . . what? A Book of the Month Club selection, a sale to DreamWorks, a spot on Larry King? Why, for that matter, did William Faulkner waste his time with *Light in August* when he could have tried for a "crossover" triumph instead, something along the lines of John Grisham or Stephen King?

It's this ludicrous sort of reasoning that characterizes the majority of the current American press—as one can readily see by looking at the movies awarded annual prizes by most critics' organizations, in contrast to the award-winners at Cannes and Venice. But it doesn't necessarily characterize the majority of the American public, who can't be blamed for missing Kiarostami movies as they zip through town if practically everything in the media and culture insists that Kevin Costner and Kevin Smith movies are thousands of times more important, simply because they're American.

Q: So how do we set about changing things?

A: A good first step would be discovering where we are and what sort of things are being done on our behalf—the way we're being stereotyped as audience members. Then a second step might be behaving as an audience member in a way that refutes and confounds those stereotypes—although this requires more initiative than the first step, at least in conducting research about what's around and then acting on that information. It also means following your own initiatives instead of mine—although you may want to use "marginal" critics like myself and some of my colleagues as part of your research.

As for putting so much trust in estimates of box-office grosses over the opening weekend of a film's run, everyone has to stop being so gullible and trusting—and that includes a lot of journalists as well as ordinary filmgoers. In the December 20, 1999 issue of the *Los Angeles Times*, Richard Natale quotes one unidentified studio executive who admits that this is largely "a game of liar's poker." As Natale goes on to explain:

Trouble is, the preliminary figures, gathered by the studios and released on Sunday morning, are imprecise and sometimes deliberately exaggerated, yet they have supplanted the real weekend grosses as a measure of a film's initial success.

In recent weeks, the box-office grosses for such films as *The World is Not Enough* and *Pokemon* have been estimated at more than $1 million over their final opening weekend figures.

Natale goes on to cite many more creative miscalculations, and adds:

Even when the figures don't vary that much, they can be padded as part of a jockeying game for a more favorable position. On one weekend in mid-October, the Sunday estimates placed Paramount's *Double Jeopardy* in first place, Universal's *The Story of Us* in second and Fox's *The Fight Club* in third. By Monday, the final numbers revealed that *Fight Club* had been the biggest grosser, followed by *Jeopardy* and *The Story of Us*.

There's been an interesting evolution over the course of the past half-century in the press's trust in both the federal government and the entertainment industry. When I was a kid, I don't think anyone entirely believed what the movie studios said, but most people trusted the federal government implicitly. Today it's much closer to being the other way around, at least as far as the press is concerned,

and it would be interesting to try to figure out how such an aston-
ishing reversal came about.

* * *

We need to redefine film criticism. Limiting it to the evaluation
of features that turn up in multiplexes is self-defeating for reasons I
don't have to enumerate. What would our literary criticism be if it
were restricted to paperbacks carried by K-Mart? If anything, the
massive advertising campaigns of the multinationals need to be
countered, not merely supplemented, and countered by a lot more
than skeptical reviews. The working assumption of the press now —
that all interesting and important movies are uniformly available,
or else that they cease to be interesting or important the moment
they become unavailable — is that the public is too stupid and
impotent to think for itself about such matters, so that it becomes
the job of publicists and reviewers to shoulder that responsibility.
For that reason, I've argued elsewhere, in my collection *Placing
Movies* (Berkeley: University of California Press, 1995), that we'd be
much better off if we had no film critics at all. Barring that possibility, we could certainly use a few who respect the people who
read them.

Beyond that, your guess is at least as good as mine, because the
way things are going now, audiences aren't supposed to have voices,
only automatic reflexes and wallets that the media-industrial complex interprets as voices. But learning how to speak and how to be
heard is the third and most important step — if only because it puts
you on an equal footing with the filmmakers.

How can this be done? If I gave you an answer to that question I
wouldn't be respecting your own initiative very much. I'd rather
hear from you about it.

Index

ABC. *See* American Broadcasting Companies, Inc.
Abele, Elizabeth, 209
Academy Awards, 13–14, 115, 117–18, 183
Ace in the Hole, 103
Adair, Gilbert, 34–35, 147
Affaires Publiques, 110–11, 113
AFI. *See* American Film Institute
The African Queen, 101
Agee, James, 60
Aldrich, Robert, 104
All About Eve, 93n, 101, 132
All About My Mother, 132
Allen, Woody, 101, 114, 126, 175–76, 220
All Quiet on the Western Front, 64, 93n, 102
All the Vermeers in New York, 57
Almodovar, Pedro, 120, 132, 133
Altman, Robert, 97, 102, 105
Amadeus, 102
American Broadcasting Companies, Inc. (ABC), 41
American Film Institute (AFI), 16–17, 90, 91–93, 210–11
    Top One Hundred List, 100–103
American Graffiti, 102
An Affair to Remember, 103
An American in Paris, 102
Anatomy of a Murder, 103
Anderegg, Michael, 188n, 192
Andersen, Thom, 104
Annie Hall, 101
Ansen, David, 72
Anthology Film Archives, 213
Antonioni, Michelangelo, 60, 106
The Apartment, 103
Apocalypse Now, 64, 69, 91, 101
The Apostle, 216
April, 168
Archer, Eugene, 32, 33
Assassin(s), 156
Assayas, Olivier, 79

Aubier, Pascal, 146–47
Auteurism, 85–87
Avanti!, 103
Avildsen, John G., 103

Bagh, Peter von, 96, 97
The Barefoot Contessa, 103
Barenholtz, Ben, 43
Barrabas, 79
Barthes, Roland, 83
Barton Fink, 2
Basic Instinct, 138
Bazin, André, 114
Béby Inauguré, 112
Bellour, Raymond, 121, 165
Belmondo, Jean-Paul, 25
Benamou, Catherine, 167
Ben-Hur (1925), 95
Ben-Hur (1959), 102
Benning, James, 104
Bergstrom, Janet, 208
Bernays, Edward L., 15
Berry, John, 13
The Best Years of Our Lives, 93n, 101
The Big Brass Ring, 159, 177, 186, 194
The Big Carnival, 103
Bigger than Life, 103
The Big Sky, 103
The Birth of a Nation, 16–17, 79, 91, 93n, 102
Black-and-white films, 9–10
The Black Cat, 103
The Blair Witch Project, 45, 46, 109–10
Bloom, Harold, 86
Bogdanovich, Peter, 6, 183, 185, 193, 198, 208–9
Bonnie and Clyde, 93n, 101
Boorman, John, 105
Borneman, Ernest, 3–4, 3n, 5, 6, 10–11
Borzage, Frank, 105
Boyle, Danny, 149–50
Brakhage, Stan, 99, 105
The Brave, 157

Breathless, 60
Brenez, Nicole, 100, 121n
Bresson, Robert, 89, 96, 110–14, 171, 189
Bride of Frankenstein, 103
The Bridge on the River Kwai, 64, 98, 101
Bringing Up Baby, 103, 180
British Film Institute, 47, 83–84, 99, 135
Brody, Meredith, 52–53
Broken Blossoms, 103
Brook, James L., 7–8
Brooks, Albert, 7n, 56, 105, 121
Browning, Tod, 104
Bullet in the Head, 221
Bullets over Broadway, 2
Burnett, Charles, 104, 106, 145
Butch Cassidy and the Sundance Kid, 92, 102

Cagney, James, 92
Cahiers du Cinema, 81–82, 85, 113, 136, 150, 151, 214
Camper, Fred, 88
Canby, Vincent, 150, 192, 197, 198
Cannes Film Festival, 57, 117–25, 143, 145–60, 214, 215, 223
Canons, film, 84–87
Capra, Frank, 101
Carax, Leos, 204
Carne, 171
Carringer, Robert L., 179–80, 182
Casablanca, 100
Cassavetes, John, 60, 99, 104, 105, 132, 158–59, 186
Cassavetes, Nick, 158–59
Cat People, 104
The Celebration, 169–71
Censorship, 157–60
"A Century of Cinema" (Sontag), 26–27
La Cérémonie, 20, 31
Chahine, Yousef, 154
Chaouli, Michel, 84–86
Chaplin, Charlie, 16, 35, 102, 103, 105, 156, 175
Chen Kaige, 120, 203
Cheung, Maggie, 80
Chicago Film Festival, 26
Chicago Reader, 54, 58, 71, 88, 114, 121, 123n, 143, 197, 206
Chicago Sun-Times, 72, 118
Chicago Tribune, 57, 72, 92, 118, 206–7
Chinatown, 101
La Chinoise, 31, 32, 33
Chomsky, Noam, 4
Christmas in July, 104
Cimino, Michael, 103
Cinémathèque Française, 52, 83, 99, 135, 210, 212
Citizen Kane, 93n, 94, 95, 100, 178–81
City Lights, 93n, 102, 216
Clarens, Carlos, 37–38
Clark, Larry, 147–48, 169

A Clockwork Orange, 98, 102, 150
Close Encounters of the Third Kind, 102
Coen, Joel, 103
Cohn, Harry, 14
colorizing, 211–12
Confessions of an Opium Eater, 104
Cooper, Merian C., 102
Coppola, Francis, 27, 28, 100, 101
Corliss, Richard, 80
Cosmos, 155
Cozarinsky, Edgardo, 146, 147
Costner, Kevin, 102
Cronenberg, David, 98, 115, 119, 120, 124–25
Crosland, Alan, 103
The Crowd, 104
Cukor, George, 102, 103, 106
Curtiz, Michael, 100, 103

Dances with Wolves, 9, 92, 102
Daney, Serge, 57, 88, 144, 173
Dante, Joe, 63–69, 75–77
D'Arrast, Harry, 104
D'Artagnan's Daughter, 203
Dassin, Jules, 13
Davies, Terence, 120
Day of Wrath, 36
Dead Cinema, 169 173
Dead Man, 55–56, 104, 120, 151
Dear Diary, 168
The Death of Empedocles, 189
The Deer Hunter, 91, 103, 220
Demme, Jonathan, 102
Demy, Jacques, 56, 205
Denby, David, 22–23, 66, 108–9, 125–26, 197, 209, 218
    review of *Taste of Cherry*, 30–33
De Oliveira, Manoel, 119, 132, 163–65, 215
Depp, Johnny, 157, 166
Destiny (Chahine), 154
The Discreet Charm of the Bourgeoisie, 115
Disney, 10, 12, 151
Disney, Walt, 102
Docks of New York, 104
Doctor Zhivago, 98, 101
"Dogme 95," 169–71
Donen, Stanley, 101
Do the Right Thing, 104
Double Indemnity, 101
Dowell, Pat, 204–5
Dr. Strangelove, 76, 93n, 101
DreamWorks, 64
Dreyer, Carl, 35, 36–37
Duck Soup, 93n, 103, 113
Durovicová, Natasa, 208
Dymtryk, Edward, 13

Eadweard Muybridge Zoopraxographer, 104
Eastwood, Clint, 103, 136

Easy Rider, 103
Ebert, Roger, 54, 55n, 57–59, 72, 73–75, 119, 200,
    201, 205
Eco, Umberto, 83
Ed Wood, 2
11 X 14, 104
Elsaesser, Thomas, 202
Elles, 132
Emmerich, Roland, 133
Endfield, Cy, 13, 105
The End of Violence, 132, 153
Eraserhead, 43, 44, 92, 104
Esquire, 23, 59–60
E.T. the Extra-Terrestrial, 101
eXistenZ, 115, 116
Experts. *See* Film critics
Eyes Wide Shut, 55n, 125–27

Face/Off, 133, 221
Fantasia, 102
Fantomas, 79, 80
Farber, Manny, 100, 169
Far from Vietnam, 33–34
Fargo, 103
Farocki, Harun, 162–63, 215
Fear and Loathing in Las Vegas, 165–66
Fejos, Paul, 104
Ferguson, Perry, 179
Festival filmmakers, 161–62
Festivals. *See* Film festivals
Feuillade, Louis, 79–80
Film canons, 84–87
Film Comment, 7n, 150, 210
Film criticism, 206–8
    expertise in, 57–58
    need to redefine, 225
Film critics
    American, 25
    Dwight Macdonald, 59–62
    as experts, 57
    knowledge of, 61
    on state of cinema, 19–24
    types of, at film festivals, 161
Film culture
    corporate influence of, 93
    in England, 82
    European *vs.* American, 82–83
    labeling activity of, 90
Film festivals
    critics at, 143–44, 161 (*See also* specific festival)
    movies, 154, 160–62
Film industry
    jargon, 81
    MPAA and, 12
    short-term thinking of, 11
Film markets, American, control of, 46
Films
    acquiring knowledge of, 83–87

American isolationism and, 107–15
    as democratic art, 61–62
    French, 31
    as national cinema, 136
    reasons for declining quality of, 1–2
    role of business in, 40–41
    study of, on film *vs.* video, 87–89
    vs. videos, 87–90
Firstenberg, Jean, 92
Flaherty, Robert, 96, 105
Fleming, Victor, 101
Foolish Wives, 14, 104
Force of Evil, 104
Ford, John, 64, 94, 101, 102, 103, 104, 105, 136
Foreign films, 108
    misperceptions of, 220
Forman, Milos, 101, 102
Forrest Gump, 92, 102
Forsyth, Bill, 104
Frankenheimer, John, 102
Frankenstein, 103
Franklin, H. Bruce, 140
Freaks, 104
The French Connection, 102
French films, 31
Friedgen, Bud, 106
Friedkin, William, 102
From Here to Eternity, 102
Fujiwara, Chris, 211
Fuller, Samuel, 64, 70, 97, 105, 171–72, 198
Full Metal Jacket, 70–71
Funny Games, 157

Gabler, Neal, 14
The General, 104
Gene Siskel Film Center, 58–59
Gentleman Prefer Blondes, 82, 104
Gertrud, 36
Giant, 103
Gilda, 100, 104, 220
Gire, Dan, 55n
Global culture, 107–8, 120–21, 129–41
Godard, Jean-Luc, 22, 25, 28–30, 33, 147, 148,
    172, 212, 214
The Godfather, 99, 100, 220
The Godfather, Part II, 6, 99, 101
Goldberg, Whoopi, 58
The Gold Rush, 99n, 102
Gomery, Douglas, 180–81, 182
Gone with the Wind, 101
Goodbye South, Goodbye, 131, 151–52, 160
GoodFellas, 103, 157
The Graduate, 101
The Grapes of Wrath, 101
The Great Garrick, 104
Greed, 14, 96, 104
Gremlins, 64, 65, 69
Griffith, D. W., 79, 102, 103, 104

Guess Who's Coming to Dinner, 92, 97, 103
Gunning, Tom, 208

Hallelujah, I'm a Bum, 104
Hammett (Wenders), 153
Haneke, Michael, 157
Hansen, Miriam, 208
Happiness, 2n, 169
Happy Together, 131
Hartman, Phil, 72–73
Hasumi, Shigehiko, 113, 164
Hawks, Howard, 103, 104, 105, 130, 136
Haynes, Todd, 44
The Heartbreak Kid, 104
Heinlein, Robert A., 139–40
Hellman, Monte, 105
Hickenlooper, George, 194
Hickey, Dave, 169
High Noon, 101
Hill, George Roy, 102
Hitchcock, Alfred, 101, 102, 106, 220
Hoberman, J., 47, 208
Hope, Ted, 44
Hopper, Dennis, 103, 157
The Horse Thief, 113
Horwath, Alexander, 100, 120–21
Hou Hsiao-hsien, 131, 147, 151, 209
Housekeeping, 104
Houseman, John, 179
Hughes, Robert, 51, 200
Huillet, Danièle, 124, 146, 162, 163, 188–89
The Hustler, 104
Huston, John, 101

I Am Cuba, 155–56
The Idiots, 169–70
I'll Do Anything, 7–8
Independence Day, 129, 130, 132–33, 136
Independent filmmakers, defined, 39
Independent theaters, 43–46
Infotainment industry, 45, 52
Inquiètude, 119, 163–64
In the Company of Men, 136–37, 160
Intolerance, 79, 96, 104
Irma Vep, 31, 79–80, 217
I Stand Alone, 171–73
It's a Wonderful Life, 101, 180
Ivens, Joris, 33

Jacob, Gilles, 158, 214
Jacobs, Ken, 106
Jargon, film industry, 81
Jarmusch, Jim, 12, 55–56, 104, 105, 108, 120,
    138n, 184, 217, 219–20
Jaws, 102
The Jazz Singer, 100, 103
JFK, 51, 218
Johnny Guitar, 104

Jones, Kent, 100, 121n, 208
Jost, Jon, 23n, 57, 104, 110
Jour de fête, 56, 118, 205, 222
Jousse, Thierry, 158
Judex, 79
Judge Priest, 104
Junkets, movie, 49–51

Kael, Pauline, 55, 96, 178, 179–80, 197, 198, 217
Karlson, Phil, 105
Kassovitz, Mathieu, 156–57
Kazan, Elia, 13–14, 101, 102, 105
Keaton, Buster, 96, 104, 105, 112
Kehr, Dave, 59, 112, 114, 139, 206–7
Kelly, Gene, 101
Kempley, Rita, 71
Kerr, Sarah, 198–200
Kiarostami, Abbas, 30–31, 56, 118, 147, 153, 154,
    157–58, 203–4, 219n, 222–23
Kids, 169, 170, 221
Killer of Sheep, 104
The Killing, 104
The Killing of a Chinese Bookie, 104
King Kong, 93n, 102
Kiss Me Deadly, 104
Klady, Leonard, 72, 73–74
Klawans, Stuart, 10, 110, 211–12, 221
Klein, William, 33–34
Kramer, Stanley, 103
Krohn, Bill, 70, 208
Kubrick, Stanley, 64, 101, 102, 104, 126n, 134
    compared to Orson Welles, 176–77

L.A. Confidential, 24, 30, 216
Labute, Neil, 160
La Chinoise, 32, 33
The Ladies Man, 104, 177, 187
The Lady from Shanghai, 104, 177, 187
Laemmle, Carl, 14
Lane, Anthony, 11, 112, 198, 200, 206
Lang, Fritz, 29, 105, 106
Langlois, Henri, 83, 135, 147
La nouvelle mission de Judex, 79
Lap dissolve, 60–61
The Last Bolshevik, 147
Last Chants for a Slow Dance, 104
The Last Frontier, 211
The Last Movie, 157
Last Year at Marienbad, 220, 221
L'Atalante, 37
Laughter, 104
Laughton, Charles, 105
Lawrence of Arabia, 98, 101
Layton, Eric, 71
Lean, David, 101
Lee, Ang, 209
Lee, Spike, 104
Leigh, Janet, 167

Leigh, Mike, 44, 151
Lelouch, Claude, 33
Les Anges du péché, 112
Les vampires, 79–80
The Letter, 119
Letterboxing, 210–11
Letter from an Unknown Woman, 104
Lewis, Jerry, 104, 105, 114
Life Is Beautiful, 2n, 119, 221
Life Is Sweet, 44
Lim, Dennis, 72
Lloyd, Frank, 103
Loden, Barbara, 106
Loew's, 40
Lonesome, 104
Lopate, Phillip, 2
Los Angeles Times, 72, 194, 224
Losey, Joseph, 13
Love Me Tonight, 104
Lovers of the Arctic Circle, 203, 221, 222
Lovers on the Bridge, 204
Love Streams, 104
Lubitsch, Ernst, 96, 105, 106
Lucas, George, 48, 51, 86, 101, 102, 130, 136, 199
Lucky Lady, 47–48
Lumet, Sidney, 102
Lynch, David, 43–44, 92, 104

McBride, Joseph, 206
McCabe and Mrs. Miller, 105
McCarey, Leo, 103, 105
Macdonald, Dwight, 59–62, 220
Macdonald, Nick, 60
McGavin, Patrick, 59, 217
McLuhan, Marshall, 28, 149
The Magnificent Ambersons, 104, 178–82, 190
Make Way for Tomorrow, 105
Makhmalbaf, Mohsen, 151–52, 158
The Maltese Falcon, 101
Mamoulian, Rouben, 104
The Manchurian Candidate, 93n, 102
Mankiewicz, Herman J., 178–79
Mankiewicz, Jospeh L., 101, 103
Mann, Anthony, 105, 211
Man's Castle, 105
The Man Who Shot Liberty Valance, 105
Marker, Chris, 33, 147
Market research, 7
    cultural fields and, 3–4
Martin, Adrian, 100, 121n, 217
M*A*S*H, 102
Maslin, Janet, 58, 61, 72, 121–25, 149–50, 197, 198–99, 200, 202, 209, 217
Master of the House, 37
Matinee, 64, 76
May, Elaine, 104, 105
Mayer, Louis B., 14
Meet Me in St. Louis, 105

Mekas, Jonas, 105, 135, 170
Metz, Christian, 195
Midnight Cowboy, 101
Midnight movies, 43–44
Mikael, 37
Mikey and Nicky, 105
Milestone, Lewis, 102, 104
Minnelli, Vincente, 102, 105
Miramax, 12, 55–57, 117, 118, 148, 202, 203–5, 221
Modern Times, 93n, 103
Monsieur Verdoux, 105
Moretti, Nanni, 27, 168
Morgenstern, Joe, 72
Morrison, Norman, 34
Motion Picture Association of America
    (MPAA), 11–12
Movie lists
    AFI, 51, 91–94, 98, 100–103
    Rosenbaum's, 99–100, 103–6
MPAA. *See* Motion Picture Association of
    America
Mr. Smith Goes to Washington, 101
Mutiny on the Bounty (Lloyd), 103
Müller, Marco, 152
Mulligan, Robert, 97, 101
Murch, Walter, 167, 216
Murnau, F. W., 60, 61, 98, 105
Murray, Steve, 71
Music Box Theater, 56–57
My Fair Lady, 103
My Son John, 105

The Naked Spur, 105
Nanook of the North, 105
Naremore, James, 208
Natale, Richard, 224
The Nation, 107, 110, 221
National Association of Theater Owners
    (NATO), 45
National cinema, defined, 136
National Endowment of the Arts, 45
National Research Group, Inc., 6–7
Natural Born Killers, 2
Negative Space, 169
Network, 102
Newsweek, 51, 72, 110
New York, 25, 30, 66
New York Daily News, 51, 139, 207
The New Yorker, 11, 23n, 30–31, 50, 55–56, 66, 70, 108, 112, 197–200, 206–7
New York Observer, 110
The New York Review of Books, 61, 87, 206–7
The New York Times, 26–28, 32, 40, 51, 58, 61, 72, 110, 112, 118, 121–23, 150, 170, 192, 197–99, 206–7, 217–18
Nichols, Mike, 101
The Night of the Hunter, 105
Nixon, 65, 151, 163

Noé, Gaspar, 169, 171
Non-competitive negotiations, 41
North by Northwest, 93n, 101
The Nutty Professor, 105

O'Brien, Geoffrey, 206
One Flew over the Cuckoo's Nest, 6, 101
One Hundred Best American Films (AFI), 51,
    91–94, 100–103
O'Neil, Bob, 167
On the Waterfront, 101
Open City, 42–43
Ophüls, Max, 104
Ordet, 36, 165
Othello (Welles), 40, 177, 187–89, 192–93
Ozu, Yasujiro, 28, 35–36, 113, 164

Paisa, 42–43
The Palm Beach Story, 105
Panic in the Streets, 105
Paramount Pictures, 40–41, 42
Park Row, 105
The Parson's Widow, 37
Pasolini, Pier Paolo, 28, 114
The Passion of Joan of Arc, 37
Patton, 69, 103
Peckinpah, Sam, 103
Perez, Gilberto, 208
Petit, Chris, 169, 173
The Phantom Menace. See *Star Wars, Episode
    I—The Phantom Menace*
Phelps, Donald, 208
The Phenix City Story, 97, 105
The Philadelphia Story, 102
Pi, 10
A Place in the Sun, 103
Platoon, 103
Pocahontas, 10
Polanski, Roman, 101
Pollock, Sydney, 102
Polonsky, Abraham, 13, 104
Positif, 81–82, 136, 150, 214
Powers, John, 207–8
Premiere (magazine), 15, 81, 150, 193
Preminger, Otto, 103
Previews, sneak, 39
Pride, Ray, 55n
Psycho, 101
Pulp Fiction, 2, 30

Quandt, James, 111

Raging Bull, 99, 101
Raiders of the Lost Ark, 102
Rainer, Peter, 72
Rappaport, Mark, 23n, 105, 146
Ray, Nicholas, 102, 103, 104, 147
Realism, 125
Real Life, 56, 105

Rear Window, 93n, 102, 216
Rebel Without a Cause, 93n, 102
Redford, Robert, 39
Reed, Carol, 102
Red Line 7000, 130
Reminiscences of a Journey to Lithuania, 105
Renoir, Jean, 106
Resnais, Alain, 33, 60, 220
Reviewers. *See* Film critics
Rio Bravo, 105, 163
Rivette, Jacques, 138n, 212–13, 215
RKO Studios, 40
Robbe-Grillet, Alain, 220
RoboCop, 138
Robson, Mark, 105
Rocky, 103
The Rocky Horror Picture Show, 43
Rogin, Michael, 129, 130
Rolling Stone, 72–73
Romand, Françoise, 147
Rosenbaum, Jonathan, alternate one hundred
    movie list of, 103–6
Rosette, 120, 121, 123n
Rossellini, Roberto, 42–43
Rossen, Robert, 13, 104
Royal Film Archive of Belgium, 95–96
Ruiz, Râùl, 23n, 152, 164, 189, 217
The Rules of the Game, 60
Run Lola Run, 220–21
Rushmore, 172, 216

Safe, 44, 94
San Francisco Film Festival, 113
Sarris, Andrew, 32
Sátántangó, 26
Saving Private Ryan, 51, 64, 66, 71, 81, 216
Scarface, 105
The Scarlet Empress, 105
Scarlet Street, 105
Scenes from Under Childhood, 105
The Scenic Route, 105
Schaefer, George, 181
Schafner, Franklin, 103
Schein, Barry, 45
Schell, Jonathan, 107, 116
Schindler's List, 9, 51, 66, 101
Schlesinger, John, 101
Schmidlin, Rick, 167–68
Schoedsack, Ernest, 102
Schrader, Paul, 27, 28, 112–13
Scorsese, Martin, 101, 102, 103
The Searchers, 93n, 103
The Second Civil War, 69, 76–77
The Seventh Victim, 100, 105
Shadows, 60, 105
Shakespeare in Love, 221
Shane, 92, 102
Shepard, Joel, 204
Sheridan, Michael J., 106

Sherlock Jr., 105
She's So Lovely, 158, 215
The Shooting, 105
The Shop Around the Corner, 105
Showgirls, 138
Sight and Sound, 81–82, 150, 190
The Silence of the Lambs, 102
Singin' in the Rain, 93n, 101
Sirk, Douglas, 85, 106, 147
Siskel, Gene, 57–59, 62, 72, 73
Sklar, Robert, 182
Slate, 198–99
Small Soldiers, 63–69, 216
   reviews of, 71–77
   story of, 67–68
Smith, Kevin, 40, 108, 223
Sneak previews, 39
Snow, Michael, 98
Snow White and the Seven Dwarfs, 99, 102
Soho News, 50
Sokurov, Aleksandr, 23n, 27, 120
Solondz, Todd, 169
Some Like It Hot, 101
The Son of Gascogne, 146–47
Sontag, Susan, 22, 23, 26–27, 207, 209
The Sound of Fury, 105
The Sound of Music, 102
Spielberg, Steven, 14, 64, 70, 98, 101, 102, 175
Splitting, 41
Stagecoach, 93n, 102
Starship Troopers, 130, 132–33, 136, 137–40
Stars in My Crown, 105
Star Wars, 86, 101, 130, 132–33
Star Wars, Episode I — The Phantom Menace,
   46–47, 51–52, 81, 117, 136, 138, 199–200
The Steel Helmet, 105
Stern, Lesley, 208
Sternberg, Joseph von, 61, 96, 98, 105, 106
Stevens, George, 102, 103
Stone, Oliver, 52, 103, 151, 157, 163, 218
Stranger than Paradise, 105, 217
Straub, Jean-Marie, 124, 146, 162, 163, 188–89
The Strawberry Blonde, 105
A Streetcar Named Desire, 93n, 102
Stroheim, Erich von, 14, 104, 156
Sturges, Preston, 96, 104, 105
Subtitles, 9, 11, 132
Sundance Film Festival, 39–40, 117, 143–44, 148
Sunrise, 60, 61, 62, 96, 105
Sunset Boulevard, 93n, 101
The Sweet Hereafter, 160
Sylvia Scarlett, 106

Talbot, Dan, 44
Tarantino, Quentin, 12, 40, 103, 202
Tarkovsky, Andrei, 27
The Tarnished Angels, 106
Tarr, Béla, 23n, 26, 27
Tashlin, Franklin, 75, 77, 106

Taste of Cherry, 30, 31, 124, 153, 154, 157–58, 160,
   216, 222–23
Tati, Jacques, 56, 205
Tavernier, Bertrand, 203
Taxi Driver, 91, 99, 102, 157, 172
Téchiné, André, 55
Teles, Galvao, 132
Telluride Film Festival, 143–44
Temptress Moon, 203
Tesser, Neil, 58
Test marketing, 2–9
That's Entertainment! III, 106
There's Something About Mary, 2n, 65
Thieves, 55
The Thing (Carpenter), 50–51
The Thing Called Love, 6
The Third Man, 93n, 98, 102
The Thirteenth Floor, 115–16
This Land Is Mine, 106
Thomas, François, 188
Thomson, David, 22–24, 61, 176, 184, 194, 209
Through the Olive Trees, 27, 56–57, 118, 203–4
Thunderbolt, 106
Tih Minh, 79
Time, 51–52, 81, 110
Time Regained, 217–18
Times Literary Supplement, 61, 84–85
To Kill a Mockingbird, 97, 101
Toland, Gregg, 179
Tom, Tom, the Piper's Son, 106
Tootsie, 102
Toronto Film Festival, 26
To Sleep with Anger, 106
Total Recall, 138
Touch of Evil, 94–95, 161–62, 166–69, 177, 187,
   188n, 191, 193, 206
Touchstone Pictures, 12
Tourneur, Jacques, 104, 105, 210, 211
Toy Story, 64, 71, 72, 73
Track of the Cat, 106
Trafic, 144–173, 214–15
Trainspotting, 149–50, 151
Travers, Peter, 72, 73
The Treasure of the Sierra Madre, 101
The Tree of Wooden Clogs, 114
Tregenza, Rob, 12
Trier, Lars von, 169–70
Trouble in Paradise, 106
The Truman Show, 24
Try and Get Me!, 105
Tsai, Ming-liang, 209
Turan, Kenneth, 72, 201
Turner Classic Movies, 92, 93, 210–11
20th Century–Fox, 40
2001: A Space Odyssey, 93n, 101

Ulmer, Edgar G., 103
Unforgiven, 103
U-Turn, 52

Vachon, Christine, 44
Valenti, Jack, 97
Les vampires, 79–80
Vampyr, 37
Vanity Fair, 24
Varda, Agnes, 33
Variety, 48, 72, 81, 118, 121, 125, 148, 216, 223
Verhoeven, Paul, 130, 133–34, 137–39
Vertigo, 102
Videos, *vs.* films, 87–90
Vidor, Charles, 104
Vidor, King, 104
Vigo, Jean, 35, 37
Village Voice, 25, 47, 72, 148, 170
Vinyl, 106
Virtual-reality thrillers, 115–17
Von Trier, Lars, 133, 169
Voyage to the Beginning of the World, 132

Waco: The Rules of Engagement, 216
Wadleigh, Michael, 106
Wall Street Journal, 6–7, 72
Walsh, Raoul, 105
Wanda, 106
Warhol, Andy, 106
Warner Brothers, 40, 41–42
Water Bearer Video, 79
Weinstein, Bob, 145
Weinstein, Harvey, 12, 117–18, 121–25, 145, 159, 202–3, 204–5
Welles, Orson, 3–4n, 33n, 60, 83, 94–95, 100, 104, 105, 156, 175–95, 198
    compared to Stanley Kubrick, 176–77
    as independent filmmaker, 178–82
    as intellectual, 182–85
    about Pauline Kael, 198
    self-financing of work and, 186–87
    unique forms of significant works, 187–89
Wellman, William, 106

Wenders, Wim, 132, 153
Western, 132
West Side Story, 102
Whale, James, 103, 104
While the City Sleeps, 106
Wichita, 210–12
The Wild Bunch, 93n, 103
Wilder, Billy, 101, 103
Will Success Spoil Rock Hunter?, 106
Wilmington, Michael, 55n, 59, 72, 92
The Wind Will Carry Us, 222–23
The Wings of the Dove, 56
Wise, Robert, 102
Witt, Michael, 28, 29
The Wizard of Oz, 101, 180, 181
Wolcott, James, 24–25, 30
A Woman Under the Influence, 158
Wong Kar-wai, 131, 147
Woo, John, 133, 221
Wood, Michael, 206
Woodstock, 106
The Wrong Man, 106
Wuthering Heights, 102
Wyler, William, 101, 102

Yakir, Dan, 25
Yang, Edward, 147, 164, 209
Yankee Doodle Dandy, 92, 103
Yeelen, 113
The Young Girls of Rochefort, 56, 118, 205

Zabriskie Point, 106
Zanuck, Darryl F., 13
Zemeckis, Robert, 102
Zéro for Conduct, 37, 113
Zinnemann, Fred, 101, 102
Zugsmith, Albert, 104
Zukor, Adolph, 14